SELECTED SPIRITUAL WRITINGS OF ANNE DUTTON

EIGHTEENTH-CENTURY, BRITISH-BAPTIST, WOMAN THEOLOGIAN

Baptists
History, Literature, Theology, Hymns

General editor: *Walter B. Shurden* is Callaway Professor of Christianity in the Roberts Department of Christianity and executive director of the Center for Baptist Studies, Mercer University.

John Taylor. *Baptists on the American Frontier: A History of Ten Baptist Churches*. Edited by Chester Young (1985).

Thomas Helwys. *A Short Declaration of the Mystery of Iniquity (1611/1612)*. Edited by Richard Groves (1998).

Roger Williams. *The Bloody Tenant of Persecution for Cause of Conscience*. Historical introduction by Edwin Gaustad. Edited by Richard Groves (2001).

James A. Rogers. *Richard Furman: Life and Legacy* (1985; reprint with new forewords, 2002).

Lottie Moon. *Send the Light: Lottie Moon's Letters and Other Writings*. Edited by Keith Harper (2002).

James P. Byrd, Jr. *The Challenges of Roger Williams: Religious Liberty, Violent Persecution, and the Bible* (2002).

Anne Dutton. *Selected Spiritual Writings of Anne Dutton, Eighteenth-Century, British-Baptist, Woman Theologian*. Volume 1. *Letters*. Edited by JoAnn Ford Watson (fall 2003).

David T. Morgan. *Southern Baptist Sisters: In Search of Status, 1845–2000* (fall 2003).

William E. Ellis. *"A Man of Books and a Man of the People": E. Y. Mullins and the Crisis of Moderate Southern Baptist Leadership* (1985; reprint, fall 2003).

Jarrett Burch. *Adiel Sherwood: Baptist Antebellum Pioneer in Georgia* (winter 2003).

Anthony Chute. *A Piety above the Common Standard: Jesse Mercer and the Defense of Evangelistic Calvinism* (spring 2004).

William H. Brackney. *A Genetic History of Baptist Thought* (September 2004).

Henlee Hulix Barnette. *A Pilgrimage of Faith: My Story* (November 2004).

SELECTED SPIRITUAL WRITINGS OF ANNE DUTTON

EIGHTEENTH-CENTURY, BRITISH-BAPTIST, WOMAN THEOLOGIAN

Volume 2
DISCOURSES, POETRY, HYMNS, MEMOIR

compiled and with an introduction by
JOANN FORD WATSON

MERCER UNIVERSITY PRESS
MACON, GEORGIA USA
OCTOBER 2004

ISBN 0-86554-795-5   MUP/H602

Selected Spiritual Writings of Anne Dutton.
Eighteenth-Century, British-Baptist, Woman Theologian.
Volume 2. *Discourses, Poetry, Hymns, Memoir.*
Copyright ©2004
Mercer University Press
Printed in the United States of America

Library of Congress Cataloging-in-Publication Data

Dutton, Anne, 1692–1765.
    [Selections. 2003]
    Selected spiritual writings of Anne Dutton :
eighteenth-century, British-Baptist, woman theologian /
compiled and with an introduction by JoAnn Ford Watson.
    p. cm.
Includes bibliographical references and index.
    ISBN 0-86554-794-7 (alk. paper) [vol. 1]
    ISBN 0-86554-795-5 (alk. paper) [vol. 2]
1. Christian life—Baptist authors. I. Watson, JoAnn Ford. II. Title.

BV4501.3.D882 2003
230' .61—dc21

                                        2003010713

CONTENTS

Volume 2. DISCOURSES, POETRY, HYMN, MEMOIR

Portrait of Anne Dutton   vi

Preface   vii

Introduction by JoAnn Ford Watson   xi

Bibliography   xv

A Discourse upon Walking with God:
  in a Letter to a Friend   1-74

A Narration of the Wonders of Grace, etc.   75-241

  Editor's Preface   77-78
  A Memoir of Mrs. Anne Dutton   79-109
  Preface by Anne Dutton   110-114
  A Narration of the Wonders of Grace, in Six Parts   115-150
  A Poem on the Special Work of the Spirit   151-174
  Sixty-one Hymns Composed on Various Subjects   175-241

Index   243-245

ANN DUTTON.
From the frontispiece to
Selections from Letters on Spiritual Subjects /etc./ (1884).

PREFACE

Permissions were granted from, and acknowledgments are due to, the following.

Mr. Bennett Lovett-Graff, managing editor, Gale Group, 12 Lunar Drive, Woodbridge, Conn 06525, for A. D. [Anne Dutton], *A Discourse upon Walking with God: In a Letter to a Friend. Together with Some Hints upon Joseph's Blessing, Deut. 33.13, &c. As Also a Brief Account How the Author Was Brought into Gospel-Liberty.* London: Printed by the Author and sold by E. Gardner, 1735. Primary source, microfilm, an imprint of the Gale Group, Microfilm Collection (The Eighteenth Century) Unit ESTC t 53689 (unit 272, reel 9486). Mr. Roger L. Loyd, director, Divinity School Library, Duke University, Durham, North Carolina, and Ms. Linda McCurdy, director of Research Services, Rare Book, Manuscript, and Special Collections Library, Duke University, for providing a photocopy from the Frank Baker Collection of Wesleyana material of pages 78–79, missing from the copy used from the Gale Group.

Mr. James Pakala, Buswell Library director, Covenant Theological Seminary, 12330 Conway Road, St. Louis, Missouri 63141-8697 for providing a photocopy of and granting permission to publish, Anne Dutton, *A Narration of the Wonders of Grace, in Six Parts. I. Of Christ the Mediator, as Set Up from Everlasting in All the Glory of Headship. II. Of God's Election and Covenant—Transactions Concerning a Remnant in His Son. III. Of Christ's Incarnation and Redemption. IV. Of the Work of the Spirit, Respecting the Church in General, throughout the New Testament Dispensation, from Christ's Ascension to His Second Coming. V. Of Christ's Glorious Appearing and Kingdom. VI. Of Gog and Magog; Together with the Last Judgment. To Which Is Added, A Poem on the Special Work of the Spirit in the Hearts of the Elect, Also, Sixty-One Hymns Composed on Several Subjects.* Edited and revised by J. A. Jones. London: John Bennett, 1833.

The portrait of Anne Dutton (page vi) is from Thomas Gibbons, George Jerment, and Samuel Burder, *Memoirs of Eminently Pious Women*, 3 vols., a new edition, revised and enlarged by Samuel Burder (repr.: three volumes in one, Philadelphia: J. J. Woodward, 1834). It was obtained from Denison University, Doane Library Archives and Special Collections. The picture is from the leaf imprint lithograph of Anne

Dutton between pages 380 and 381. Permission to publish a photograph of the lithograph was granted by Ms. Lynn Scott Cochrane, director of Libraries, Denison University, Granville, Ohio. Preparation of the photo for publication is courtesy of Otto's Studio, Mansfield, Ohio.

The works of Anne Dutton in this compilation are reproduced generally in the format and style of the original editions. This includes, in general, the retention of archaic, variant, and British terms and spellings, for example, "relict" for "widow," "Whitfield" for "Whitefield," "Charlestown" for "Charleston," "honour" for "honor," and so forth. There is some modernization of fonts and punctuation: the Old and Middle English *f* routinely becomes "s" and the former printer's convention of beginning *every line* of a running quotation (at line breaks and thus in the middle of the quotation) with opening quotation marks is ignored. Page references to Anne Dutton's works pertain to the original editions, not as reprinted in this present version.

These volumes required years to research, locate, retype, and compile. This work would have been impossible without the assistance of the Ashland Theological Seminary librarians: Dr. Russell Morton, research librarian; Rev. Brad Weidenhamer, retired head librarian; and Ms. Sylvia Locher, current head librarian. The work would not have been completed without the most valuable contribution of my graduate assistant, Ms. Kathleen Slusser, Ashland Theological Seminary. I am very grateful to her for the preparation of the manuscript. I thank Dawn Morton for assistance in compiling the index. I thank my husband, Dr. Duane F. Watson, for his careful editorial skills and kind assistance. I thank my daughter, Christina, for her wonderful love and encouragement. I dedicate this work to my parents for a lifetime of support.

JoAnn Ford Watson

INTRODUCTION[1]

A Discourse upon Walking with God

In 1735 Dutton published *A Discourse upon Walking with God*.[2] This work had a wide circulation.[3] As mentioned above, Wesley recorded in his diary on 4 December 1740 that he had "read Mrs. Dutton's book"; this probably is the book he read.[4] As also mentioned above, Whitefield read it and wrote to her about it that "Your book on *walking with God* has been blessed to one Mr. B___, and others in South Carolina."[5]

A Discourse was written by Anne Dutton with her initials "A.D.", as a "Letter to a Friend," a "Dear and Honour'd Brother," who had written a letter to her out of his work among the poor.[6] In this work, Dutton shows herself to be a beautiful expositor of the truths of Scripture. She offers spiritual insights for practical daily living of the soul's walk with God. She uses Scripture to describe Christ's presence dwelling in her. She writes of the spiritual life that she "Took up my Abode in thee, as an Indweller to abide with thee for ever."[7] She weaves Scripture throughout *A Discourse* to tie spiritual truths related to her devotional theme of

---

[1]A general introduction to the life and work of Anne Dutton appears in vol. 1, pp. xi-xliv.

[2]Full title: *A Discourse upon Walking with God: in a Letter to a Friend. together with Some Hints upon Joseph's Blessing, Deut. 33.13, &c. as also A brief Account how the Author was brought into Gospel-Liberty* (London: Printed for the author: and Sold by E. Gardner, in Bartholomew-Close, near West-Smithfield, 1735).

[3]See Arthur Wallington, "Wesley and Anne Dutton," *Proceedings of the Wesley Historical Society* 11/2 (June 1917): 45.

[4]*The Works of John Wesley*, vol. 19, *Journal and Diaries II (1738–1743)*, ed. W. Reginald Ward and Richard P. Heitzenrater (Nashville: Abingdon Press, 1990) 443.

[5]*The Works of the Reverend George Whitefield*, 6 vols. (London: Edward and Charles Dilley, 1771–1772) 1:250; Whitefield's letter 267.

[6]*Discourse upon Walking with God*, 1, 3, 4.

[7]*Discourse upon Walking with God*, 95.

walking with God. She uses both the Old and New Testaments to teach her doctrine of "Gospel-Holiness."[8]

In response to her addressee's request that she give him "a few hints from Joseph's blessing," Dutton focuses particularly on Joseph's blessing and Christ's work on the cross.[9] She develops the parallel between Joseph and Christ's kingdom, the church. She states, "I look upon Joseph to be a Type of the Church."[10] Also noteworthy is her use of love language and her mystical imagery of the soul's relationship with Christ.[11]

Dutton concludes *A Discourse* with an answer to the "Brother's" request to offer her own conversion account. Of her conversion she writes: "But such was the superabundant Grace of my God, to me a sinful Worm, That *after* I had *believ'd*, I was *Seal'd with the Holy Spirit of Promise, Eph.* 1.13. Which was done by the Holy Ghost as a *Comforter.* . . . "[12] Dutton concludes her discourse with "In him I rest, with dear Christian Love, your unworthy Sister, A.D."[13]

The Poet and Hymn Writer

In addition to her many letters and her essays or discourses, Anne Dutton also wrote poetry and hymns. The most prominent and well-known of her works in her own day was *A Narration of the Wonders of Grace. . . . To which is Added, A Poem on the Special Work of the Spirit on the Hearts of the Elect. Also, Sixty One Hymns Composed on Several Subjects.* Whitebrook calls it "Her chief literary production."[14] It was first published in London in 1734. There were six "editions": 1734, 1734, 1735, 1818, 1831, and 1833, the last "new edition" (1833) with a preface by the editor, John Andrews Jones, and "A Memoir of Mrs. Anne Dutton."[15] John Andrews Jones, minister of the gospel, Mitchell Street, London, was a biographer of Dutton. He wrote this memoir of her life

---

[8]See *Discourse upon Walking with God*, 50.

[9]*Discourse upon Walking with God*, 133.

[10]*Discourse upon Walking with God*, 153, 156.

[11]*Discourse upon Walking with God*, 117-18.

[12]*Discourse upon Walking with God*, 161.

[13]*Discourse upon Walking with God*, 170.

[14]John Cudworth Whitebrook, *Ann Dutton: A Life and Bibliography* (London: A. W. Cannon and Co., 1921) 8.

[15]See Whitebrook, *Ann Dutton*, 15.

that includes her childhood, marriages, ministry, correspondence, death, and burial. The memoir is affixed to the 1833 edition of *A Narration of the Wonders of Grace* (London: John Bennett).[16]

Stein notes that in 1743 Dutton wrote *A Discourse concerning the New-Birth: To Which are Added Sixty-Four Hymns; Compos'd on Several Subjects; With an Epistle Recommendatory, by the Reverend Mr. Jacob Rogers, B.A.*[17] These sixty-four hymns appear to be the previous sixty-one hymns with three more added. As evidence, Julian quotes the first verse of hymn 42 in the sixty-one-hymn collection and it is the same as hymn 42 as in the sixty-four-hymn collection.[18]

In the preface to the first part of her autobiography Dutton told the reader "that thou hadst never had the following Narrative, if the Lord himself had not encourag'd me to attempt this Work."[19] The *Narration* consists of 1,504 lines arranged in six parts, namely:

I. Of Christ the Mediator, as Set Up from Everlasting in All Glory of Headship
II. Of God's Election and Covenant—Transactions concerning a Remnant in His Son
III. Of Christ's Incarnation and Redemption
IV. Of the Work of the Spirit, Respecting the Church in General, throughout the New Testament Dispensation, from Christ's Ascension to His Second Coming
V. Of Christ's Glorious Appearing and Kingdom

---

[16]I have used excerpts of the memoir in the introduction to volume 1 (xii-xix). This memoir appears in part in other editions of Dutton's works. It appears in the 1769 edition of *Letters on Spiritual Subjects, and Divers Occasions; Sent to Relations and Friends . . . To Which are Prefixed, Memoirs of the Dealings of God with Her, in her Last Sickness* (London: G. Keith, 1769). It is found in the Yale University Beinecke Rare Books and Manuscript Library.

[17](London: J. Hart, 1743). Stephen Stein, "A Note on Anne Dutton, Eighteenth-Century Evangelical," *Church History* 44 (1975): 487n.15.

[18]*A Dictionary of Hymnology*, ed. John Julian (New York: Scribners, 1892) 316; see also Wallington, "Wesley and Anne Dutton," 48.

[19]See Stein, "A Note on Anne Dutton," 489. Dutton, *A Brief Account of the Gracious Dealings of God, with a Poor, Sinful, Unworthy Creature, in Three Parts . . . With an Appendix. And a Letter Prefixed, on the Lawfulness of a Woman's Appearing in Print* (London: John Hart, 1750) pt. 1, p. 3.

VI. Of Gog and Magog; together with the Last Judgment

From the standpoint of supralapsarian Calvinism, in the *Narration* Dutton reviews the whole course of redemption, from the eternal purposes of God to the final glorification of the elect. Heavily indebted to Scripture, biblical references are in the margins throughout the *Narration.*

Dutton's abilities in narration and poetry are highly praised. Her language is beautiful and flowing. Whitebrook notes the "favorable" versification of her *A Narration of the Wonders of Grace.* As "a favorable sample of the versification," Whitebrook points to twelve lines near the end of part 6:

Oh! bliss indeed to see God's face,
And feast on the riches of his Grace
Which are in Christ laid up, to be
Unfolded to Eternity!

Hope then shall to fruition come,
And faith, as in its perfect bloom,
Shall into vision changed be,
When we Jehovah's glory see.

But love, unto eternity,
Will join our souls to One in Three;
When we shall see, and shall adore,
Our God in Christ, for evermore.[20]

Whitebrook also praises "A Poem on the Special Work of the Spirit in the Hearts of the Elect" in its 948 lines of "heroic couplets."[21] He offers the first twelve lines of the "opening section to serve for a taste of its quality."

When God, the mighty Spirit, doth begin
To save us influentially from sin,
He comes, as sent from th' Father and the Son,
To do the Work design'd e're time begun.

---

[20]Dutton, *A Narration of the Wonders of Grace, in Six Parts* . . . (London: John Bennett, 1833) pt. 6, pp. 32-33, ll. 1469-80—stanza (quatrain) breaks added; and as referred to by Whitebrook, in his *Ann Dutton,* 8.

[21]See Whitebrook, *Ann Dutton,* 8.

The Spirit keeps election in his eye,
And knows exactly for whom Christ did die;
And what the counsels were in Heav'n above
When he engag'd in offices of love.

And thus he seeks, and finds the chosen sheep
The Father gave the Shepherd Christ to keep;
And though among the fallen world they lie;
He comes resolv'd that there they shall not die.[22]

Dutton is given a paragraph in Julian's *Dictionary of Hymnology.* Julian notes that Dutton's sixty-four *Hymns Composed on Several Subjects* was published in London in 1743.[23] A line of her poetry may have inspired B. Beddome's hymn, "Faith Is a Precious Grace."[24] Wallington notes Dutton's contribution as a hymn writer, yet is not very complimentary. Wallington describes Dutton's hymn 42 as "a fair average verse," that "does not impress us with her talents in this direction."[25]

John A. Jones, Anne Dutton's biographer, writes that Dutton's poetry is unharmonious and her hymns are plain and for use by country Baptist folk. "Good versification," Jones suggests, "is not here. If it may be termed *poetry* at all; it is indeed *rugged* poetry," that is, it was written for "plain and homely folk" in the "*midland* countries" of England where Great Gransden was located.[26] Jones goes on to say that he hopes the reader,

having "tasted that the Lord *is* gracious," will not *reject* Anne Dutton *because* of the inharmoniousness of her verse; but, blessing God for "those bright beams of gospel light" shining in every page; will kindly listen to her *own* voice; for though long since fallen asleep in Jesus, she "yet speaketh."[27]

---

[22]"A Poem on the Special Work of the Spirit in the Hearts of the Elect," ll. 1-12, in *A Narration of the Wonders of Grace,* 34—stanza (quatrain or double couplet) breaks added; see Whitebrook, *Ann Dutton,* 9-10.

[23]*Dictionary of Hymnology,* 316, 319.

[24]*Dictionary of Hymnology,* 316.

[25]Wallington, "Wesley and Anne Dutton," 48.

[26]"Editor's Preface," in *Narration of the Wonders of Grace,* iv.

[27]"Editor's Preface," in *Narration of the Wonders of Grace,* v.

Whitebrook offers three verses (stanzas 1, 2, and 5) from hymn 49 to illustrate that Dutton's hymnody is only fairly average.

Our God in Christ, his dwelling place,
    A strength is to his poor,
And needy ones, in their distress,
    What can we wish for more?

Whate're *Jehovah* is, or has,
    He not only decreed,
But gave in th' covenant of grace,
    To Christ, and all his seed. . . .

And since God's power keeps the Saints,
    As in a fortress strong;
And richly doth supply our wants;
    Let's make the Lord our song.[28]

Although her hymn-writing ability was only average, Dutton nevertheless made a significant and lasting contribution to Evangelical Protestant hymnody in getting her hymns published and reviewed.

---

[28]*Narration of the Wonders of Grace*, 102-103. And see Whitebrook, *Ann Dutton*, 9.

BIBLIOGRAPHY

Primary Sources: Anne Dutton[29]

A Brief Account of the Gracious Dealings of God, with a Poor, Sinful, Unworthy Creature, in Three Parts . . . With an Appendix. And a Letter Prefixed, on the Lawfulness of a Woman's Appearing in Print. London: John Hart, 1750. This autobiography was published in three parts over a period of years. Part 1 and part 2 were originally published together with separate titles as *A Brief Account of the Gracious Dealings of God, with a Poor, Sinful, Unworthy Creature, Relating to the Work of Divine Grace on the Heart, in a Saving Conversion to Christ, and to Some Establishment in Him* and *A Brief Account of the Gracious Dealings of God, with a Poor, Sinful, Unworthy Creature, Relating to a Train of Special Providences Attending Life, by which the Work of Faith was Carried on with Power.* London: John Hart, 1743. Part 3 and the "Letter" were included with the 1750 publication (see above). Part 3 is entitled *A Brief Account of the Gracious Dealings of God, with a Poor, Sinful, Unworthy Creature, Relating to Some Particular Experiences of the Lord's Goodness, in Bringing Out Several Little Tracts, to the Furtherance and Joy of Faith.*
The publications referred to in the title ("Several Little Tracts") are pamphlets published by John Hart before 1750.
(Parts 1 and 2 [1743] are available in the United States at Harvard University and Baylor University. The complete work [1750] is in the British Library, London.)

Brief Hints Concerning Baptism. London, 1746. May be identical to *Letters on the Ordinance of Baptism* (1746). (Whitebrook, 18 no. 25.)

Brief Hints on God's Fatherly Chastisements, Showing Their Nature, Necessity and Usefulness, and the Saints' Duty to Wait upon God for Deliverance When under His Fatherly Corrections. 1743. (Whitebrook, 17 no. 14.)

A Caution against Error When It Springs Up together with the Truth, in a Letter to a Friend. 1746. (Whitebrook, 17 no. 24.)

---

[29]"Whitebrook" refers to the bibliography of John Cudworth Whitebrook, in his *Ann Dutton: A Life and Bibliography*, 15-20, as offprinted from "The Life and Works of Mrs. Ann Dutton," in *Transactions of the Baptist Historical Society* 7:129-46.

A Discourse Concerning God's Act of Adoption. To Which is Added a Discourse upon the Inheritance of the Adopted Sons of God. London: E. Gardner, 1737. (British Library, London.)

A Discourse Concerning the New-Birth: To Which Are Added Sixty-Four Hymns; Compos'd on Several Subjects; with an Epistle Recommendatory, by the Reverend Mr. Jacob Rogers, B.A. London: John Hart, 1743. (Yale University Beinecke Rare Books Library.)

A Discourse Concerning the New-Birth: To Which Are Added Two Poems: The One on Salvation in Christ, by Free-Grace, for the Chief of Sinners: The Other on a Believer's Safety and Duty: with an Epistle Recommendatory, by the Reverend Mr. Jacob Rogers, B.A. London: John Oswald and Ebenezer Gardner, 1740. (British Library, London.)

A Discourse upon Justification: Shewing the Matter, Manner, Time and Effects of it. To Which are Added Three Poems: I. On the Special Work of the Spirit in the Hearts of the Elect. . . . III. On a Believer's Safety and Duty. London: printed by John Hart and sold by J. Lewis and E. Gardner, 1740, 1743. (The 1743 edition is at Harvard University Libraries.)

A Discourse upon Walking with God: In a Letter to a Friend. Together with Some Hints upon Joseph's Blessing, Deut. 33.13, &c. As Also a Brief Account How the Author Was Brought into Gospel-Liberty. London: printed for the author and sold by E. Gardner, 1735. (Gale Group.)

Divine, Moral, and Historical Miscellanies in Prose and Verse. Edited by A. Dutton. 1761. (British Library.)

Five Letters to a Newly Married Pair. 1759. (Whitebrook, 18 no. 33.)

Hints of the Glory of Christ: As the Friend and Bridgroom of the Church: From the Seven Last Verses of the Fifth Chaper of Solomon's Song: In a Letter to a Friend. London: printed by John Hart and sold by J. Lewis, 1748. (British Library, London.)
Originally published as Meditations and Observations upon the Eleventh and Twelfth Verses of the Sixth Chapter of Solomon's Song. 1743. (Whitebrook, 16 no. 13; 18 no. 27.)

The Hurt that Sin Doth to Believers, etc. 1733. Second edition, 1749. (Whitebrook, 18 no. 30.)

A Letter from Mrs. Anne Dutton to the Reverend Mr. G. Whitefield. Philadelphia: printed and sold by William Bradford, 1743. (Library Company of Philadelphia.)

A Letter on the Application of the Holy Scriptures. Poppings Court: printed by John Hart and sold by J. Lewis, 1754. (Whitebrook, 18 no. 31.)

A Letter on the Divine Eternal Sonship of Jesus Christ: . . . Occasioned by the Perusal of Mr. Romaine's Sermon . . . Entitled, A Discourse Upon the Self-Existence of Jesus Christ. With Three Letters on Assurance of Interest in

*Christ: . . . Written as the Author's Thoughts, on Part of Mr. Marshal's . . .
The Gospel-Mystery of Sanctification. And Two Letters on the Gift of the
Holy Spirit to Believers . . . By One Who Has Tasted that the Lord is
Gracious.* London: printed by John Hart and sold by G. Keith, 1757.
(Oxford University Bodleian Library.)

*A Letter on the Duty and Privilege of a Believer to Live by Faith, and to
Improve His Faith unto Holiness.* 1745. (Whitebrook, 17 n. 21.)

A Letter on Perseverance, against Mr. Wesley. 1747. (Whitebrook, 18 no. 38.)

A Letter to All Men on the General Duty of Love among Christians. 1742.
(Whitebrook, 16 no. 7.)

*A Letter to all the Saints on the General Duty of Love: Humbly Presented, by
One That is Less Than the Least of Them All, and Unworthy to be of Their
Happy Number.* London: printed by John Hart and sold by Samuel Mason,
1742; printed by John Hart and sold by J. Lewis and E. Gardner, 1743.
Philadelphia: Joseph Crukshank, 1774. (Harvard University Andover;
Harvard Theological Library has the 1743 edition.)

*A Letter to All Those That Love Christ in Philadelphia. To Excite Them to
Adhere to, and Appear for, the Truths of the Gospel.* 1743(?). (Whitebrook,
17 no. 19.)

A Letter to the Believing Negroes, lately Converted to Christ in America. 1742.
(Whitebrook, 16 no. 9.)

A Letter to Christians at the Tabernacle. 1744(?). (Whitebrook, 18 no. 37.)

*A Letter to Mr. William Cudworth, In Vindication of the Truth from his
Misrepresentations: With Respect to the Work of the Spirit in Faith,
Holiness, The New Birth &c. Being a Reply to his Answer to the Postscript
of a Letter Lately Published, &c.* 1747. (Whitebrook, 18 no. 26.)

*A Letter to the Reverend Mr. John Wesley. In Vindication of the Doctrines of
Absolute, Unconditional Election, Particular Redemption, Special Vocation,
and Final Perseverance. Occasioned Chiefly by Some Things in His
Dialogue between a Predestinarian and His Friend; and In His Hymns on
God's Everlasting Love.* London: printed by John Hart and sold by Samuel
Mason, 1742. (Pitts Theology Library, Emory University.)

*A Letter to Such of the Servants of Christ Who May Have Any Scruple about the
Lawfulness of Printing Anything Written by a Woman.* 1743. (Whitebrook,
17 no. 18.)

Letters against Sanddemanianism and with a Letter on Reconciliation. (Whitebrook, 18 no. 36.)

Letters on the Being and Working of Sin in a Justified Man. 1745. (Whitebrook,
17 no. 20.)

Letters on the Ordinance of Baptism. 1746. May be identical to *Brief Hints
Concerning Baptism.* London, 1746. (Whitebrook, 18 no. 25.)

Letters to the Reverend Mr. John Westley [sic] *against Perfection as Not Attainable in This Life*. London: John Hart, 1743. (Pitts Theological Library, Emory University; John Rylands Library, University of Manchester.)

Letters on Spiritual and Divers Occasions. London: G. Keith, 1749. (Whitebrook, 18 no. 29.)

Letters on Spiritual Subjects, and Divers Occasions, Sent to Relatives and Friends. London: printed and sold by John Oswald and Ebenenzer Gardner, 1740. London: printed by John Hart and sold by J. Lewis, 1748.

Letters on Spiritual Subjects and Divers Occasions, Sent to the Reverend Mr. George Whitefield And others of his Friends and Acquaintance. To Which is Added, A Letter on the Being and Working of Sin, in the Soul of justify'd Man, as Consistent with His State of Justification in Christ, and Sanctification Through Him: With the Nature of His Obedience, and of His Comfort, Consider'd: As the One is from God, and the other to Him; notwithstanding his Corruptions may be great, and His Graces Small in His Own Sight. As Also, A Letter on the Duty and Privilege of a Believer, To Live by Faith, and to Improve his Faith unto Holiness. By One Who Has Tasted that the Lord is Gracious. London: John Hart, 1745. (Pitts Theology Library, Emory University. Incomplete copy.)

Letters on Spiritual Subjects Sent to Relations and Friends. Two parts. Second revised edition. Edited by Christopher Goulding. London: T. Bensley, 1823–1824. (Duke University Library.)

Letters Sent to an Honourable Gentleman, for the Encouragement of Faith. By One Who Has Tasted that the Lord is Gracious. London: printed by John Hart and sold by J. Lewis and E. Gardner, 1743. (Boston Athenaeum.)

Meditations and Observations upon the Eleventh and Twelfth Verses of the Sixth Chapter of Solomon's Song. 1743. Published later as a pamphlet entitled *Hints of the Glory of Christ as the Friend and Bridegroom of the Church: From the Seven Last Verses of the Fifth Chapter of Solomon's Song, &c.* 1748. (Whitebrook, 16 no. 13; 18 no. 27.)

Mr. Sanddeman Refuted by an Old Woman: or Thoughts on His Letters to the Author of Theron and Aspasio. In a Letter from a Friend in the Country to a Friend in Town. London: John Hart, 1761. (Brown University Library.)

A Narration of the Wonders of Grace, in Six Parts. I. Of Christ the Mediator, as Set Up from Everlasting in All the Glory of Headship. II. Of God's Election and Covenant—Transactions Concerning a Remnant in His Son. III. Of Christ's Incarnation and Redemption. IV. Of the Work of the Spirit, Respecting the Church in General, throughout the New Testament Dispensation, from Christ's Ascension to His Second Coming. V. Of Christ's Glorious Appearing and Kingdom. VI. Of Gog and Magog; Together with the Last Judgment. To Which Is Added, A Poem on the Special Work of the Spirit in the Hearts of the Elect, also, Sixty One Hymns Composed on Several Subjects. A new edition. Revised, with a preface and collected memoir of the author, by John Andrews Jones. London: John Bennett, 1833. Pages xxxii + 115. (Covenant Theological Seminary, St. Louis.)

Second edition. "Corrected by the author, with additions." London: printed for the author and sold by John Oswald, 1734. Pages viii + [9-]143.

First edition. London: printed for and sold by the author, 1734. Pages viii + 139.

Occasional Letters on Spiritual Subjects. Seven volumes. Popping's Court: John Hart and Bartholomew Close: J. Lewis, 1740–1749.

A Postcript to a Letter Lately Published, on the Duty and Privilege of a Believer to Live by Faith, &c . . . Directed to the Society at the Tabernacle in London. . . . As Also, Some of the Mistakes of the Moravian Brethren. . . . By One Who Has Tasted that the Lord is Gracious. London: printed by John Hart and sold by J. Lewis and E. Gardner, 1746. (Union Theological Seminary, New York.)

Selections from [Occasional] Letters on Spiritual Subjects: Addressed to Relatives and Friends. Compiled by James Knight. London: John Gadsby, 1884. (Turpin Library, Dallas Theological Seminary.)

A Sight of Christ Necessary for All True Christians and Gospel Ministers. 1743. (Whitebrook, 16 no. 11.)

Thoughts on the Lord's Supper. London, 1748. (Whitebrook, 18 no. 28.)

Three Letters on I. The Marks of a Child of God. II. The Soul-Diseases of God's Children; . . . III. God's Prohibition of His Peoples Unbelieving Fear: . . . By One Who Has Tasted that the Lord is Gracious. London: printed by John Hart and sold by G. Keith and J. Fuller, 1761. (Oxford University Bodleian Library.)

A Treatise on Justification: Showing the Matter, Manner, Time, and Effects of It. Third edition. Glasgow: printed by William Smith for Archibald Coubrough, 1778. The author is listed as "the Rev. Mr. Thomas Dutton," presumably one of Anne Dutton's pseudonymns. (British Library, London.)

Primary Sources: Dutton's Contemporaries

B. D. [Benjamin Dutton]. *The Superaboundings of the Exceeding Riches of God's Free Grace, towards the Chief of the Chief of Sinners, &c.* No publisher, no date.

Baker, Frank, ed. *The Works of John Wesley.* Volume 26. *Letters II (1740–1755).* Oxford: Clarendon Press, 1982.

Bunyan, John. *The Holy War.* London: printed for Dorman Newman and Benjamin Alsop, 1682.

_____. *Pilgrim's Progress*. 1678. Repr.: Ulrichsville OH: Barbour Publishing, 1985.

_____. *The Works of John Bunyan: With an Introduction to Each Treatise, Notes, and a Sketch of His Life, Times, and Contemporaries*. Three volumes. Edited by George Offor. Repr.: Edinburgh and Carlisle PA: Banner of Truth Trust, 1991. Original: Glasgow: W. G. Blackie and Son, 1854.

Cudworth, William, *Truth Defended and Cleared from Mistakes and Misrepresentations*. See Arthur Wallington, "Wesley and Ann Dutton," 48.

Middleton, Erasmus. *A Letter from the Reverend Mr. [Erasmus Middleton] to A[nne] D[utton]*. 1735. (British Library, London.)

Wesley, John. *A Dialogue Between a Predestinarian and His Friend*. London: W. Stratan, 1741.

_____. *Wesley's Standard Sermons*. Two volumes. Edited by Edward H. Sugden. Fifth edition. London: Epworth, 1961.

_____. *The Works of John Wesley*. Fourteen volumes. Third edition. Edited by Thomas Jackson et al. London: Wesleyan Conference Office, 1873–1893. Repr.: Grand Rapids: Zondervan, 1958-1959.

_____. *The Works of John Wesley*. Volume 19. *Journal and Diaries II (1738–1743)*. Edited by W. Reginald Ward and Richard P. Heitzenrater. Nashville: Abingdon Press, 1990.

Wesley, John and Charles. *Hymns of God's Everlasting Love*. Bristol: S. and F. Farley, 1741.

_____. *The Poetical Works of John and Charles Wesley*. Thirteen volumes. Edited by George Osborn. London: Wesleyan-Methodist Conference Office, 1868–1872.

Whitefield, George. "A Letter to the Rev. Mr. John Wesley in Answer to His Sermon Entitled 'Free Grace' " (24 December 1740). In [Whitefield's] *Journals*, 571-88. London: Banner of Truth Trust, 1960.

_____. *The Works of the Reverend George Whitefield*. Six volumes. London: Edward and Charles Dilley, 1771–1772.

Secondary Sources

Austin, Roland. "The Weekly History." *Proceedings of the Wesley Historical Society* 11/2 (June 1917): 239-43.

Burder, Samuel. See under Thomas Gibbons.

Dana, Daniel. See under Thomas Gibbons.

A Dictionary of Hymnology. Edited by John Julian. New York: Scribner's, 1892.

Gibbons, Thomas. *Memoirs of Eminently Pious Women, Who Were Ornaments to Their Sex, Blessings to Their Families, and Edifying Examples to the Church and World*. Two volumes. London: printed for J. Buckland, 1777.

(2) Dana's abridged edition: "Abridged from the large work of Dr. Gibbons, London, by Daniel Dana." Women and the Church in America 9. Newburyport MA: printed for the subscribers by Angier March, 1803.

(3) Jerment's expanded edition: "Republished [with some omissions] in 1804, with an additional volume by George Jerment." Two volumes. (Volume 1 contained all of Gibbons's material, originally in two volumes; volume 2 contained additional material by Jerment.) London: printed by W. Nicholson for R. Ogles, 1804.

(4) Burder's new and further expanded edition: "A new edition, embellished with eighteen portraits, corrected and enlarged by Samuel Burder." Three volumes. (Volume 1 comprises the original material of Gibbons; volume 2 is Jerment's 1804 addition; volume 3 adds Burder's new material.) London: Ogles, Duncan, and Cochran, 1815.

(Gibbons's *Memoirs* is most readily available today in the following Burder edition. Consequently, *Memoirs* is routinely cited in the literature under "Burder" as author.)

(5) Reprint of the Burder expanded edition: "From a late London edition, in three volumes; now complete in one volume." One volume. Philadelphia: J. J. Woodward, 1834ff. (This is the edition routinely cited herein, and that in its 1836 reprinting.)

Green, Richard. *Anti-Methodist Publications: Issued during the Eighteenth Century: A Chronologically Arranged and Annotated Bibliography of All Known Books and Pamphlets Written in Opposition to the Methodist Revival during the Life of Wesley; Together with an Account of Replies to Them, and of Some Other Publications. A Contribution to Methodist History.* London: C. H. Kelly, 1902. Repr.: New York: Burt Franklin, 1973.

Haykin, Michael. "The Celebrated Mrs. Anne Dutton." *Evangelical Times* (April 2001). (The third in an extended series of articles under the general title "A Cloud of Witnesses.")

Heitzenrater, Richard P. *Wesley and the People Called Methodists.* Nashville: Abingdon, 1995.

Herbert, George. *The English Poems of George Herbert.* Edited by C. A. Patrides. London: S. M. Dent and Sons, 1991.

Jerment, George. See under Thomas Gibbons.

Johnson, Dale A. *Women and Religion in Britain and Ireland: An Annotated Bibliography from The Reformation to 1993.* ATLA Bibliography Series 39. Lanham MD: Scarecrow Press, 1995.

MacHaffie, Barbara J. *Her Story: Women in Christian Tradition.* Philadelphia: Fortress, 1986.

The Oxford Dictionary of the Christian Church. Second edition. Edited by F. L. Cross and E. A. Livingstone. Oxford: Oxford University Press, 1974. Third edition. 1997.

Robinson, H. Wheeler. *The Life and Faith of the Baptists.* Revised edition. London: Kingsgate Press, 1946; first edition, 1927; repr.: Wake Forest NC: Chanticleer, 1985. The section on Anne Dutton appears on pp. 50-56: "Studies in Baptist Personality: (6) A Baptist Writer (Ann Dutton)."

Starr, Edward, editor. *A Baptist Bibliography.* Rochester NY: American Baptist Historical Society, 1959. (Section D, 201-204, lists about seventy works by Anne Dutton.)

Stein, Stephen. "A Note on Anne Dutton, Eighteenth-Century Evangelical." *Church History* 44 (1975): 485-91.

Wallington, Arthur. "Wesley and Anne Dutton." *Proceedings of the Wesley Historical Society* 11/2 (June 1917): 43-48.

Watson, JoAnn Ford, "Anne Dutton: An 18th Century British Evangelical Woman." *Ashland Theological Journal* 30 (1998): 51-56.

Whitebrook, John Cudworth. *Ann Dutton: A Life and Bibliography.* London: A. W. Cannon and Co., 1921. Also appears as "The Life and Works of Mrs. Ann Dutton," *Transactions of the Baptist Historical Society* 7 (1920–1921): 129-46. (*Transactions*, 1908–1921, became the *Baptist Quarterly*, 1922 to date.)

Whitley, William Thomas. *A Baptist Bibliography: Being a Register of the Chief Materials for Baptist History, Whether in Manuscript or in Print, Preserved in Great Britain, Ireland, and the Colonies.* Two volumes. London: Kingsgate Press, 1916, 1922. Repr.: Two volumes in one: Hildesheim: Georg Olms, 1984.

A

DISCOURSE

UPON

WALKING with G O D :

IN A

LETTER to a FRIEND.

TOGETHER WITH

Some Hints upon J O S E P H ' s Blessing, DEUT. 33. 13, &c.

AS ALSO

A brief A C C O U N T how the Author was brought into Gospel-Liberty.

By *A. D.*

L O N D O N :
Printed for the A U T H O R : And Sold by
E. Gardner, in Bartholomew-Close, near
West-Smithfield, 1735.
Price bound 1 s. 6 d.

A

DISCOURSE

UPON

WALKING with GOD.

In a LETTER to a FRIEND.

Dear and Honour'd Brother,

GRACE and Peace be multiplied unto you thro' the Knowledge of God, and Jesus our Lord. Yours I received, in which I perceived the vast Desires wrought in your Soul by the Holy ghost, after Communion with God, and Conformity to him; and I rejoyce, that there's enough in Christ to fill you. It is an unspeakable Blessedness to be made to *hunger and thirst after Righteousness;* what your Enjoyment as such will be, you may read in that blessed Promise dropt from the Mouth of him, who is *the faithful and true Witness, Mat. 5. 6. They shall be fill'd.*

They were blest in Christ before Time, *with all spiritual Blessings,* in the everlasting Covenant Settlements, as antecedent to, and the Foundation of all their Hungering and Thirsting. They are blest thro' Christ in Time, with the initial Communication of those Blessings, under the Creation-Work of the Holy Ghost, forming a new Nature in them, and drawing it out into vast Desires and sweet Foretastes, as a Principle suited to the Enjoyment of all their comprehensive Blessedness: But the full Completion thereof is reserv'd for the Time of their being fill'd; when made fit Vessels to hold all that vast Glory which is prepar'd for 'em in Christ's Kingdom here, and in the Ultimate State of an endless Eternity beyond it; and then we shall be Fill'd indeed, and no more pain'd with Desire for want of Enjoyment of the most full and compleat Happiness. Mean while, let us not think, That there are any spiritual Desires wrought in us in vain; No, They are drawn out on purpose to be Fill'd. For the Holy Spirit who *searcheth the deep Things of God,* and knows all that vast Glory which is prepared for Us, by the Father, and the Son, in Electing and Redeeming Love; He works proportionably in us, to prepare us for it; that so our longing Appetites might be every way suited to the rich Dainties of the Feast. And the Glory reserv'd for us being inexpressible in itself; therefore it is that he works such inexpressible Desires in us, which nothing but the Enjoyment of it can Fill. And blessed be God, that will be enough to fill us brim-full for ever; for our God will be our *Glory* and *All in All* to Eternity, *Isa.* 60. 19. I *Cor.* 15. 28.

I am glad to hear that the Lord has brought you among his poor People at *N____n*; and hope he designs to make you an useful Instrument for the Good of his dear Children there; sending forth a *plentiful Rain* upon you, and by you, to the Refreshment of his *weary Inheritance, Ps.* 68. 9. Be not discouraged from abiding with them because of their low Estate; remembering that the Lord Jesus is with you, even among *the Myrtle-Trees in the Bottom, Zech.* 1. 8. And when God doth *arise* to *have Mercy upon Zion,* he usually makes his *Servants take Pleasure in her Stones,* and *favour* her *Dust, Ps.* 102. 13, 14. Christ puts the feeding of his Sheep and Lambs upon your Love to him, *John* 21. 15, 16. (especially now they have no Shepherd) and if you can do any Service to the dear *Flock* he has *purchased* by his *Blood, Acts* 20. 28. he'll take it as *done to himself, Matt.* 25. 40. And as it will be Matter of your Joy here, so of your abundant Honour in the Day of Christ.

As to the main Request of your Letter, *I said, Days should speak, and Multitude of Years should teach* that *Wisdom, Job* 32.7. At least those *that are of full Age, and have their Senses exercis'd, Heb.* 5. 14. And not such a Babe as I, who have need that one to teach me what be *the first Principles* of the Mystery of Walking with God, *Ver.* 12. Tho' for the Time indeed, I might have attained a far greater Proficiency of Knowledge therein: But alas! *I am a Child that cannot speak, Jer.* 1. 6. Look up to Christ therefore as your Prophet, his Spirit will teach you, and give you Fellowship with the Mystery. I doubt not, my dear Brother, but you know far more what it is to Walk with God, than unworthy I. I am ashamed and confounded, and 'tis my daily Burden that I can walk no more with him: I find such sad Interruptions of Communion. Indeed I see a ravishing Glory in it, which at times, draws out my Soul into earnest Longings after it; and I call them unspeakably happy that are blest with a steady Course of Walking with God; but *I count not my self to have attained, Phil.* 3. 12. You have much mistaken Thoughts of Me, for I am *less than the least of all Saints, Eph.* 3. 8. and not worthy to be counted among the happy Number that are honour'd to Walk with God. But yet, through Grace, I have been so favour'd, as to know something of what it means. And tho' I fear I shall *darken Counsel by Words without Knowledge, Job* 38. 2. yet since you have desired me to tell you in some Particulars what it is to Walk with God, take it (as he shall open a Babe's Mouth) in the following Hints. And,

First, To Walk with God, doth necessarily suppose an Agreement between God and the Soul.

Secondly, A way in which both walk.

Thirdly, A continued Course or Series of Steps, taken in that way.

Fourthly, Free Communion, or mutual Fellowship. And,

Fifthly, A Sameness of Intention, Design, or End. To each of these a little.

First then, To Walk with God, doth necessarily suppose an Agreement between God and the Soul. For *how can two walk together except they be agreed? Amos* 3. 3. All Men, since the Fall, are not only Strangers to God, but Haters of him; that *say unto God, Depart from us, we desire not the Knowledge of thy Ways, Eph.* 2. 12. *Rom.* 5. 10. and 1. 30. *Job* 21. 14. And God, on the other hand, as a righteous revenging Judge for the Breach of his holy Law, appears against the Sinner in the condemning Sentence thereof, array'd in all the Terrors of his Wrath, *Rom.* 3. 5. *Gal.* 3. 10. *Nah.* 1. 2. So that it is impossible that there should be any Friendship or Communion with each other as such.

There was indeed, once, a perfect Amity and mutual Friendship between God and Man; when in his original Estate, he came out of his Maker's Hand a pure piece of Workmanship, exalted to the Heights of Nature-perfection; every way fitted for, and fill'd with the Enjoyment of Communion with God, as the God of Nature, displaying his Glory in the Face of the Creatures in this lower World.

But soon, alas! the Honour of this Walking with God was over. Satan envies God the Glory, and Man the Happiness of this blissful State; assaults him with his Temptations, and soon prevails; Sin enters, and *Death by Sin, Gen.* 3. 1, &c. *Rom.* 5. 12. Man turns Traitor against his rightful Sovereign, breaks his Law, and takes up Arms against him, under Satan that Arch-rebel, the Prince of Darkness. And God as a terrible Judge, for the just Vindication of his own Honour, appears against Man in the awful Sentence of a broken Law; *In Dying thou shalt die, Gen.* 2.

17. And what could he expect from God as a Judge of his own Law, but a *certain fearful Judgement* and *fiery Indignation,* which should *devour the Adversary? Heb.* 10. 27. Thus there was a War commenc'd between God and Man. Guilty, filthy, Man, resolv'd to go on in a Course of obstinate Rebellion against God; and a righteous God resolv'd that he would abate nothing of the exact Demands and just Threatnings of his holy Law. And who could ever have thought that now there was a Possibility of Peace between them again? Man was too *filthy* and *abominable* for infinite Holiness to delight in, *Job* 15. 16. God was of *purer Eyes than to behold Iniquity, Hab.* 1. 13. Man was guilty of despising boundless Goodness; of rebelling against Divine Sovereignty; and of injuring infinite Honour: And hence the Justice of God became engag'd to do his Being right, by resenting the Injury, requiring full Satisfaction, and inflicting answerable Punishment upon the Transgressor; who, alas, was but a finite Being, and as such could never, no, not by an Eternity of Torment, make infinite Reparation for the infinite Wrong he had done. And God was just, not only to the Honour of his own Being, but also to the Truth of his Law. The irrevocable Threatning was gone out of the Lips of Truth itself, *dying thou shalt die.* And God being unchangeable in all his infinite Perfections, Holiness could not bear with Sin; Justice must have Satisfaction; and Truth could not lie; Hence infinite Power became engag'd, in a way of Almighty Wrath, to execute Vengeance on every Transgressor; while *every Transgression receives a just Recompence of Reward, Rom.* 2. 9. *Heb.* 2. 2.

Thus poor Man, by Sin, had *destroy'd* himself, *Hos.* 13. 9. And had God call'd the whole Creation into Counsel, to find out a way how all his Perfections might be glorify'd, and the Sinner sav'd, it would for ever have nonplust the Wisdom of all intelligent Beings. It was a Secret *hid* in the Three-One God, Father, Son, and Spirit, *Eph.* 3. 9. who sat in Counsel about it for a Remnant in Christ before Time was: In the Contrivance of which, there is the most glorious Display of *the manifold Wisdom of God, Eph.* 3. 10, 11.

It was the good Pleasure of Jehovah, to chuse a Remnant in Christ unto eternal Life; and absolutely to bless them therein, in the irreversible Grant of it, in the *Promise* made *before the World began, Eph.* 1. 3, 4. *Tit.* 1. 2. And for the more abundant Glory of all the divine Perfections, they were ordain'd to be put into a first *Adam;* and in him suffer'd to fall into the Heights of Provocation, the Depths of unspeakable Misery, the

Breadths of over-spreading Ruine, and the Desert of the Length of Eternal Punishment; That so the exceeding Heights, Depths, Breadths and Lengths of Grace and boundless Mercy, might be the more illustriously display'd, in raising them up thro' a crucify'd Jesus, to the ultimate Heights of that Glory which were at first design'd for 'em, thro' all the intermediate Changes infinite Wisdom had ordain'd. So that here was Provision made for us before our Need came on; a healing Remedy provided before the Wound was given: But this Project of eternal Wisdom was reserv'd to be reveal'd in its appointed Season.

Poor Man was utterly undone; and there was no Help for him, either in himself or any Creature. And as for God, he look'd upon him to be his worst Enemy: And in this dreadful Plight, he not only became a Terror to himself, but the Triumph of Devils; who now thought they had him safe enough involv'd in eternal Ruine; having had an Experience themselves of the Almighty Power of Divine Wrath, tho' provok'd but by one Sin, to the hurling Myriads of once glorious Spirits, from their high Seats in Heaven, into the bottomless Pit of remediless Torment; reserving them *in Chains of Darkness, to the Judgment of the great Day, Jude 6.* And Oh the Terrors of *Adam's* guilty Heart, when he fought in vain to hide himself from Omniscient Eyes! Under dreadful Apprehensions of avenging Wrath, he flees from his terrible Judge, *Gen. 3. 8.* God pursues him, *Adam, where art thou? ver. 9.* And what now could he expect but *Death, the Wages of Sin? Rom. 6. 23.* But oh, behold! the Love-Wonder opens with a Ray of glorious Light, in the first Promise, *Gen. 3. 15. The Seed of the Woman shall break the Serpent's Head.* Here Light, the Light of Life for a Sinner, thro' a dying Saviour, breaks forth with an amazing Glory, from amidst that Death and Darkness which preceded it, to the Astonishment of glorious Angels, the Confusion of malicious Devils, and the joyful Wonder of the saved Sinner; who, hereupon, calls his Wife's Name *Eve, The Mother of all Living. Adam* expected nothing but Wrath and Death. God proclaims Peace and Life, works Faith in his Soul, opening the Treasures of his Love to him, that had his Heart fill'd with Hatred; and by the omnipotent Power of reigning Grace, not only subdues the Rebellion of his Will, but sweetly attracts it into the strongest Motion after himself, as his only complacent Rest.

And now the Man's new-made, and comes forth, as in a new Edition, The *Workmanship* of the Holy Ghost, *created* anew *in Christ Jesus,* bearing a more transcendent Image, than in his first Creation: And being fitted for, he was favour'd with, a more transcendent Communion, and an higher Walk with God, as the God of all Grace, displaying his Glory in *the Face of Jesus,* than in his Paradisaical State he was capable of. Oh the Superaboundings of reigning Grace!

And as the First Man, under the Guilt of a broken Law, hated God, and fled from him; so doth every Son of *Adam* to this Day. But God *knows his own* that he has *loved with as everlasting Love, 2 Tim. 2. 19. Jer. 31. 3.* And ordain'd to the highest Union and Communion with himself in Christ, *Acts* 13. 48. *John* 17. 23. And when the appointed Moment of Calling-Love comes on, he sends *the Spirit* down *into* their *Hearts* in the virtue of Christ's Redeeming Blood, *Gal. 4. 6.* To *Quicken* 'em when *dead in Sins, Eph. 2. 1.* to *create* 'em anew *in Christ, ver. 10.* every way conformable to the *Image of his Son,* the glorious Pattern in his Eye, *Rom.* 8. 29. That so they might be capable of the highest Communion, and sweetest Intercourse with God. And when thus made alive, the Holy spirit sets before the Eye of the new-Creature, the Misery of a natural State, *Rom.* 7. 9. and also reveals the glorious Remedy, *Gal.* 1. 16. *preaching Peace by Jesus Christ, Acts* 10. 36. And as the Enmity was fundamentally *slain* by Christ's Death *on the Cross, Eph.* 2. 16. so now, by the Power of the Holy Ghost, it's actually slain, in the virtue of his Death brought into the Soul. For now God, as the God of Love and Peace, opens his heart unto the Soul, and shews it how he has *loved* it before Time, *Jer.* 31. 3. yea loved it when *dead in Sins. Eph.* 2. 4, 5. And from that great Love did *give* Christ To it, and For it, *John* 3. 16. To stand in its Room, wounding him for its Transgressions; that *by his Stripes* it might *be healed, Isa.* 53. 5. And that now Justice being fully satisfy'd, he *abundantly pardons* all its Iniquity, *Isa.* 42. 21. and 55. 7. And while God thus manifests his everlasting Love to the Soul, Oh! how it's *drawn with Loving-Kindness,* to love him again! I *John* 4. 19. Now it *looks* on him it has *pierc'd* and *mourns, Zech.* 12. 10. Loves what God loves, and hates what he hates. God hath nothing against the Soul, but *rests in his Love,* and *rejoyceth over it with singing, Zeph.* 3. 17. The Soul hath nothing against God (so far as reconcil'd) but delightfully cleaves to him, as its *All in all, Ps.* 73. 25, 26. The Spirit reveals God's Love as a Father, Christ's as an Husband, and his own Love as an In-dweller and Comforter; and sweetly calls it into the freest Intercourse. And the Soul *drawn* by these *Love-Cords, Hos.* 11. 4. delightfully obeys; forsaking all other Lovers, *Isa.* 26. 13. *Hos.* 14. 8. And is fill'd with astonishing Wonder at infinite Condescension, that such an Hell-deserving Wretch, that might have been a Companion of Devils and damned Spirits, should be admitted into the high Privilege of Fellowship with God, in his Three glorious Persons, thro' the Man Christ Jesus. Aye high indeed, higher than what innocent *Adam* was acquainted with; yea in some sense higher and more glorious, than is conferr'd on the Angels in Heaven; For in Christ Jesus We stand in a nearer Relation to God than Angels. And God communicates of himself to every Creature answerable to the Relation it stands in to him. Oh adorable Grace! *Lord, what is Man,* filthy abominable Man, *that thou shouldst be mindful of him? and the Son of Man that thou settest thine Heart upon him? Ps.* 8. 4. *Job* 15. 16. and 7. 17. Thus God and Man are agreed, and meet together in the sweetest Amity in his crucify'd Son. And without this it would be impossible for 'em to Walk together. But

Secondly, To Walk with God, doth necessarily suppose a way, in which both God and the Soul walk. Which may be consider'd either comprehensively or distributively.

First, Comprehensively. And so Christ is *the Way, John* 14. 6. God's Way to us, and Our Way to God; and also the Way in which all our mutual Fellowship is maintain'd. I before consider'd Christ as the great Meeting-place, where God and the Soul are agreed. And now I would hint something of his being the great Walking-place, where every Step of their delightful Solace in and with each other is taken. And he is so

First, in his Person, as Mediator. It was the Pleasure of the Great Jehovah, to advance the Man Christ Jesus, into the Dignity of Personal Union with God the Eternal Son, the Second Person in the Sacred Trinity. Hence his Name is call'd Emmanuel, [God with Us] *Matt.* 1. 23. And the same Person who is call'd a *Child born,* is likewise styled the [*mighty God*] *Isa.* 9. 6. with many other Places of the like Import. And *in him dwells all the Fulness of the Godhead bodily,* (or substantially) *Col.* 2. 9. All the infinite Perfections, and Persons, of the Divine Being dwell in him. The Father, Son, and Spirit dwell in Christ, and not only dwell in him, but also Walk in him, in all the Paths of Grace towards the Chosen of God. Thus the Apostle, *John* 1. 7. *If we walk in the Light, as he is in the Light, we have Fellowship one with another.* By *Light,* or Holiness in this Text (as I conceive) we are first, to understand Christ himself, *the true Light,* as he elsewhere calls him, *John* 1. 9. God, says he, is in Christ, dwells in him, Walks in him, and if we walk where he walks, we have Fellowship one with another. Secondly, we may take Light derivatively, for all that Holiness the Saints receive out of Christ's Fullness. But both comes much to one for my purpose. For none can walk in true Holiness, but such as walk in Christ. And in *Eph.* 1. 3. we are said to be *bless'd [in] him, according as* we were *chosen in him, ver. 4.* and to be *made accepted in the beloved, ver.* 6. in the [Person] of the beloved, antecedent to our being made accepted in the [Righteousness] of the beloved, which follows, *ver.* 7.

And Oh how gloriously is infinite Wisdom display'd in the Constitution of the Person of Christ! Well may he be call'd [Wisdom] *Prov.* 8. 12. And his Name [Wonderful] *Isa.* 9. 6. Because his Person is a [Wonder]. *Without Controversy great is* this *Mystery of Godliness, God manifest in the Flesh,* I *Tim.* 3. 16.

Here now in Christ the Way, as *the Man God's Fellow, Zech.* 13. 7. the *high and lofty One that inhabits Eternity, Isa.* 57. 15. God can maintain the freest Converse with that low Thing, Man, a Creature *of Yesterday, Job* 8. 9. the Work of his Hands, without debasing his infinite Majesty; yea, to the Honour of all his divine Perfections; for in Christ, *All the Promises of God are Yea and Amen, to the Glory of God by us,* 2 *Cor.* 1. 20. And this Promise among the rest, of his *dwelling in us,* and *walking in us,* 2 *Cor.* 6. 16. And when the *Psalmist* would meditate on all God's wondrous Works and talk of his Doings, he takes a View of him as marching on with his People in this Way. *Thy Way* (says he) *o God, is in the Sanctuary:* that is in Christ typ'd out by it) *Ps.* 77. 13. And that this is to the Glory of his Divine Being, is manifest by the following Words, *Who is so great a God as our God?* As if he should say, Thou hast by this thy Walk with us in Christ, glorify'd thyself as God, according to thine infinite Greatness. And when the Lord promis'd to *place* his *Tabernacle* among his People of old, *Lev.* 26. 11. his next Words are, *And my soul shall not abhor you, but I will Walk among you, and will be your God, and ye shall be my People.* God walk'd among his People of old, by the visible Tokens of his Presence in the Tabernacle, as a Type of his walking with us in New-Testament times in his Son: The Body of whose Flesh is *a greater and more perfect Tabernacle,* which all *the Train* of the Godhead's Glory fills, *Heb.* 9. 11. *Isa.* 6. 1. And as the Person of Christ, as Mediator, is the Way in which God walks with us, to the Glory of all his divine Perfections; so also his Person, as such, is the Way in which we Walk with God, to the *full* and *unspeakable Joy* of our Souls, I *Joh.* 1. 4. I *Pet.* 1. 8.

Were we to approach an absolute God, we should be but like *dry Stubble,* to *consuming Fire, Job* 13. 25. *Heb.* 12. ult. But Oh! here it is, in Christ this *Days-Man,* that God's *Terror* don't make us *afraid, Job* 31. 7. We converse with infinite Majesty dwelling in our Clay; clothed with our Flesh; and so the Displays of its Glory are delightful, and not destructive to us. Thus *John* 1. 14. *The Word was made Flesh, and dwelt among us, (and we beheld his Glory, the Glory as of the only-begotten of the Father) full of Grace and Truth.* It was his Glory, who was *the Brightness* of his Father's; *The express Character of his Person, Heb.* 1. 3. and the undivided Glory of the Essence, being equally the same in all the Three Persons in God: Hence it is that our Lord says, *He that hath seen me, hath seen the Father, John* 14. 9. Because in the Person of Christ, we behold the same essential Glory that is in the Person of the Father; (and also in the Person of the Holy Ghost; he being God equal with both) and not only do we behold the essential, but also the personal Glory of all the Three, radiantly display'd in *the Face of Jesus. As 2 Cor. 4. 6. For God who commanded the Light to shine out of Darkness, hath shined in our Hearts, to give the Light of the Knowledge of the Glory of God in the Face of Jesus Christ.* Which is so far from destroying us, that it becomes the Ministration of Life; *While we all with open Face, beholding as in a Glass the Glory of the Lord, are chang'd into the same Image, from Glory to Glory;* as in the preceding Chapter. Oh amazing! that *the Bush* should be *on Fire,* and yet not *consum'd, Exod.* 3. 2. That the Godhead should dwell in the Man Christ [Personally] in all its flaming Glories; and yet the Nature not be consum'd, but preserv'd; And thro' him in all his [Relatively] and yet their Persons not be consum'd, but preserv'd thereby, even amidst a thousand consuming Trials! Well might *Moses* say, *I'll now turn aside and see this great Sight!* Thus Christ is the Way in his Person, as Mediator; The great Medium of Converse between God and Creatures. But

Secondly, He is also the Way, as our Kinsman-Redeemer, that has *obtain'd eternal Redemption for us, Heb.* 9. 12. And as such he is the great Medium of Converse between God and Sinners. In which is compriz'd, both his Suretiship Undertakings in the everlasting Covenant; and also his Suretiship Performances in the Fulness of Time—He not only voluntarily undertook to pay the vast Sums we ow'd; from whence it became a righteous Thing with God, to demand Satisfaction at his Hands; But he also in the Fulness of Time, (according to his Engagement from everlasting) assum'd our Nature, *Heb.* 2. 16. Sustain'd our Persons, *Col.* 1. 18. Fulfill'd the Law for us, *Matt.* 5. 17. with *Rom.* 5. 18. Bare our Sins, I Pet. 2. 24. Was made a Curse, *Gal.* 3. 13. Conflicted with the Powers of Darkness, *Luke* 22. 53. Endur'd his Father's Wrath, *Matt.* 27. 46. And at last dy'd in our Room, *Rom.* 5. 6. Descended into the Grave, *Eph.* 4. 9. And rose again for our Justification, *Rom.* 4. 25. And having finish'd his Work below, he ascended to Glory, in the Triumphs of his Conquest, *Eph.* 4. 10. Attended with the *Chariots of God,* and the Shout of Thousands of Angels; as *the Lord strong and mighty, the Lord mighty in Battle, Ps.* 68. 17, 18. with 47. 5. and 24. 8. And as our great Representing-Head, he enter'd into the Holiest of all, and sat down at the right Hand of the Majesty on high, *Heb.* 9. 24. and 1. 3. And by this Discharge of his Suretiship Engagements, he has answer'd all the Laws Demands, *Rom.* 10. 4. Satisfy'd Justice, *Isa.* 42. 21. Made an End of Sin, *Dan.* 9. 24. Spoiled Principalities and Powers, *Col.* 2. 15. Establish'd a lasting Peace between God and us, *Col.* 1. 20. made *Reconciliation for Iniquity, and brought in an everlasting Righteousness;* yea, had brought us in it, is his own Person, into the Presence of his and our Father, *John* 20. 17. presenting us *in the Body of his Flesh, thro' Death holy and unblameable, and unreproveable in his Sight,* Col. 1. 22. Thus Christ is the Way in what he is To us, and has done For us, in which God walks with his poor sinful Children.

Here all the divine Perfections harmonize. *Mercy and Truth meet together, Righteousness and Peace kiss each other, Ps.* 85. 10. Here it is that God can be *just, and yet the Justifier of him that believes in Jesus, Rom.* 3. 26. Just to *Forgive us our sins, and to cleanse us from all Unrighteousness, I John* 1. 9. Just in abundant Pardon, *multiplying to pardon* the multiply'd Sins of our daily Provocations, *Isa.* 55. 7. And it was the glorious Display of this Grace, in his Walk with us in Christ, made the Prophet break forth, as being fill'd with astonishing Wonder, *Mic.* 7. 18. *Who is a God like unto thee, that pardoneth Iniquity, and passeth by the Transgression of the Remnant of his Heritage? He retaineth not his Anger for ever, because he delighteth in Mercy.*

Here's Room for God to Walk with us in his everlasting Kindness, *Isa.* 54. 8. Covenant-Faithfulness, *Ps.* 80. 33. Abundant Goodness, *Jer.* 31. 14. Infinite Wisdom, ordering all Things for our Good, *Eph.* 1. 8.

Rom. 8. 28. And in his almighty Power sustaining us under our Weakness, defending us from our Enemies, by which we *are kept* as in a Garrison, *thro' Faith unto Salvation, I Pet.* 1. 5.

Again, here's Room also for us to walk with God in all Relations, with suitable Dispositions. With God, as a Father, *Eph.* 5. 1. Christ, as an Husband, Brother, Friend, *Ps.* 45. 11. *Heb.* 2. 11. *Job.* 15. 14. With the Holy Ghost, as an Indweller, Sanctifier and Comforter, *Eph.* 4. 30. *For the Blood of Jesus cleanseth us from all Sin, I John* 1. 7. And gives us *Boldness* in the Presence of God, *Heb.* 10. 19. His Righteousness cloaths us, *Isa.* 61. 10. His Fulness supplies us, *Joh.* 1. 16. His Merits present us and all our Services acceptable to God, I *Pet.* 2. 5.

But O! how doth infinite Wisdom shine in the Contrivance of this living Way; and infinite Grace also in the Provision of it for us? Ay, for us while thousands perish in their own Ways! That this Way of Holiness should be for us, and that we as *the Redeemed of the Lord* should *walk* here, when *the unclean shall not pass over it, Isa.* 35. 8, 9. (That were not set apart in electing Love, *Jude* 1. Wash'd in Redeeming Blood, *Rev.* 1. 5. nor sanctify'd by the Holy Ghost's Work in Regeneration, I *Cor.* 6. 11.) and that this *Path which the Vulture's Eye hath not seen, Job* 28. 7. should not only be provided for us, but also *reveal'd* in us, *Gal.* 1. 16. And made so *plain,* that such *Fools* as we should not *err therein,* while in our Way-faring State passing from Earth to Heaven, is distinguishing Grace to a Wonder: We were as blind as others by Nature; and not only ignorant of it, but opposite to it; and yet *the Redeemed of the Lord shall walk* here. Aye [shall] notwithstanding their natural Averseness, great Unworthiness, heinous Provocations, and repeated Backslidings. For it is a [shall] not only of Free, Absolute, but also of reigning, omnipotent Grace, that secures our Walking here, notwithstanding all the Opposition of Hell against it; by strongly subduing our Rebellion, and sweetly alluring us, into the most complacent Willingness *in the Day of Power, Ps.* 110. 3. The *everlasting Salvation* we have in this way, *Isa.* 45. 17. make us *sing* of eternal *Mercy* now, *Ps.* 89. 7. But O! when we shall see it in all its full Glories, with what rais'd Notes shall we shout forth *Hallelujahs,* in the Presence *of God, and the Lamb for ever, Rev.* 7. 9, 10. and 19. 1. Thus much as to the Way, in which both God and the Soul walk, as taken comprehensively. But

Secondly, The Way may also be consider'd distributively. And thus all the lesser Paths, comprehended in Christ the great Way may be so styled. And the Way in this Respect may be reduc'd to four general Heads: *First,* the Way of Faith. *Secondly,* the Way of instituted Worship. *Thirdly,* The Way of Divine Providence, And, *Fourthly,* The Way of Conversation-Holiness.

First, The Way of Faith. By which I intend the Doctrine of Faith, or the Way of Divine Revelation, call'd *the Way of God, Acts* 18. 26. in which God walks with his own in peculiar Grace; revealing to these *Babes* the Mysteries of the Gospel, while they are *hid from the wise and prudent* World, *Matt.* 11. 25. I *Cor.* 2. 10. The divine Revelation, is alike made to all in the written Word; but God makes it a Way in which he manifests himself unto us, so as he *doth not unto the World, John* 14. 22. Our Eyes have the Blessedness to see, *Matt.* 13. 16. While they *seeing see not, ver.* 13. O the Sovereignty of Grace! *I'll make all my Mountains a Way* (saith the Lord) *and my high Ways shall be exalted, Isa.* 49. 11. I'll make all my [Mountains] all the high Acts of my Grace in Christ, which are firm as Mountains, a [Way] where I'll delightfully walk with my People: *And my high Ways shall be* [exalted] i.e. Lifted up in the glorious Doctrines of the Gospel, and, by my Spirit, in the Hearts of my People, as so many high Ways for them to walk in. And as in this way of Faith doctrinally, divine Revelation, God walks with his, in the Sovereignty of his Grace; so they also, herein walk with him in *the Obedience of Faith* practically, *Rom.* 16. 26. The Grace of *Faith,* as a *Fruit of the Spirit,* in the Souls of Believers, *Gal.* 5. 22. is a Principle suited to the Doctrine of Faith. As an Eye, it looks to Faith's Object, *Heb.* 12. 2. As an Hand it lays hold thereon, *Heb.* 6. 18. And as a Foot it Walks therein, *Col.* 2. 6. While all the glorious Doctrines of Faith, shining in Christ *the Path of the Just, Prov.* 4. 18. by the Holy Ghost's Light, become as so many high Places, on which the Soul delightfully Walks with God, *Hab.* 3. 19. In this Way of Faith, all the famous Worthies mention'd in the Eleventh of the *Hebrews,* walked with God; Yea, all the Saints that ever were, are, or shall be, have, do, and shall walk here.

And further, God calls all his Children (tho' some in a more eminent manner than others) to walk with him in this way of Faith, even when they want the Light of spiritual Sense. God always Walks with his in Christ, according to the Revelation of his Mind to 'em, tho' not always apparently. And they answerably walk with him in Faith, receiving his divine Testimony, setting to their *Seal that he is true, John* 3. 33. Judging him both able and faithful who hath promised, *Rom.* 4. 21. *Heb.* 11. 11. And as such trusting in him even when he seems to *slay* 'em, *Job* 13. 15. When dark Dispensations cover 'em, and they have no Light of Sense to walk by, yet even then can they *trust in the Lord*, and *stay themselves upon their God, Isa.* 50. 10. *Altho' the Fig-tree should not blossom, nor Fruit be in the Vines, the Labour of the Olive fail, the Field yield no Meat, the Flock be cut off from the Fold, and no Herd in the Stalls;* yet they go on in Faith rejoycing *in the Lord,* and joying *in the God of their Salvation;* while by his *Strength* their *Feet* are made *like Hinds feet,* to *walk* upon their *high Places, Hab.* 3. 17, 18, 19, And in this way of Faith God is glorify'd exceedingly, by his [displaying] and his Peoples [ascribing] the Glory of his unchangeable Grace, *Mal.* 3. 6. Eternal Mercy, Covenant-Faithfulness, *Psal.* 89. 1. and Almighty Power, *Exod.* 15. 6. in performing the Truth to Jacob, the Mercy promis'd from the Days of old, *Mic.* 7. 20. Fulfilling with his Hand whatsoever his Mouth hath spoken, I *Kings* 8. 24.

Secondly, Instituted Worship is another Way in which God and his People walk with each other. The moral Obligation whereto we have in the First Command, *Thou shalt have no other God but me, Exod.* 20. 3. *Thou shalt worship the Lord thy God, and him only shalt thou serve, Matt.* 4. 10. The particular Direction whereof is contain'd in the Scriptures of the Old and New Testament, 2 *Tim.* 3. 16, 17. God in Old-Testament times made Revelation of his Mind herein to his People by his holy Prophets, and eminently by that great Prophet *Moses.* But in these *last Days* of New-Testament times, he hath *spoken unto us by his Son, Heb.* 1. 2. According as *Moses* had long ago foretold, *A Prophet shall the Lord your God raise up unto you like unto me; unto him shall ye hearken, Deut.* 18. 15. Christ as the great Prophet of the Church, the *Son over his own House, Heb.* 3. 6. hath made a compleat Revelation of the divine Will relating to Gospel-Worship, which the Faith of New-Testament Saints delightfully submits to; owning Christ as Prophet, and also as King in Sion. As Prophet, he made the divine Revelation; as King, he cloath'd it with the Authority of his divine Command. thus *Matt.* 28. 19, 20. *Go ye therefore, teach all Nations, baptizing them in the Name of the Father, and of the Son, and of the Holy Ghost: teaching them to observe all Things whatsoever I have commanded you: and lo, I am with you always to the end of the World, Amen.* God has *chosen Sion for his Habitation, Psal.* 132. 13, 14. And *set his King upon his holy*

Hill, Ps. 2. 6. And here he will *dwell for ever,* for he hath *desired it.* And as God's *Dwelling-place is in Sion, Psal.* 76. 2. so his peoples also, *Ps.* 69.35. For God will *save Zion, and build the Cities of Judah, that they may dwell there.*

Further, as the Churches are *builded together, for an Habitation of God thro' the Spirit, Eph.* 2. 22. so he also Walks there: *I will Walk in 'em,* says God, 2 *Cor.* 6. 16. which is true of particular Believers, is much more so of the Churches. Christ *Walks* amidst *the Seven golden Candlesticks, Rev.* 2. 1. And *loves the gates of Sion more than all the Dwellings of Jacob, Psal.* 87. 2. 'Tis here his People *see his goings, Psal.* 68. 24. And Gospel-Worship, whether publick or private, is a glorious Way wherein God and his People Walk together.

First, Publick: *The Law goes forth out of Zion, and the Word of the Lord from Jerusalem;* his People, taught in his Ways, *Walk in his Paths, Isa.* 2. 3. He *cloaths* her *Priests with Salvation;* her *Saints shout for Joy;* Abundantly *blesseth her Provision;* her *Poor* are *satisfy'd with Bread, Psal.* 132. 15, 16. God *inhabits the Praises of Israel, Psal.* 22. 3. and *Praise waiteth for him in Sion, Psal.* 65. 1. 'Tis here he walks with his People, as a God hearing Prayer, *ver.* 2 and they with him by *the Spirit of Supplications, Zech.* 12. 10. pouring out their Hearts before him, *Psal.* 62. 8. while his Ear is open to their Cry, *Psal.* 34. 15. and sometimes Answers are very immediate, *while they are yet speaking he hears, Isa.* 65. 24. An Instance whereof we have, *Acts* 4. 29, 30, 31. *And now, Lord, behold their Threatnings; and grant unto thy Servants, that with all Boldness they may speak thy Word,* &c. *And when they had prayed, the Place was shaken where they were assembled together; and they were all filled with the Holy Ghost, and spake the Word of God with Boldness.* And as publick Worship is a Way in which God and his People walk together, so

Secondly, Private Worship both in the Family and Closet. Thus *Abraham* our Father Walk'd with God. And how doth the Lord as it were boast of his holy Walk before him? *Gen.* 17. 19. *For I know him* (says God) *that he will command his Children, and his Houshold after him, and they shall keep the Way of the Lord.* And as *Abraham,* so all his spiritual Seed, bless'd with the same Faith, admitted into the same Privilege of Walking with God, pass on in the same Steps of the Faith of their Father *Abraham, Gal.* 3. 29. *Rom.* 4. 12, 16. They meditate in Jehovah's Law, *Psal.* 1. 2. and on all his wondrous Works, *Psal.* 143. 5.

He makes it sweet to them, *Psal.* 104. 34. and acceptable in his Sight, *Ps.* 19. 14. They cry unto the Lord in their Trouble, He hears their Cry, and fulfils their Desire, *Psal.* 3. 4. and 145. 19. They give Thanks to his Name, and he accepts their Praises, *Ps.* 30. 12. and 50. 23. I *Pet.* 2. 5. accounting them only *the true Worshippers,* that *worship in Truth,* as to the Matter, *in Spirit,* as to the Manner of their Worship, *John* 4. 23.

Oh infinite Condescension! *Will God indeed dwell with Men on Earth! 2 Chron.* 6. 18. Will *the High and Lofty One,* the Great [I AM] *Isa.* 57. 15. *Exod.* 3. 14. familiarly Walk with Worms, that are *less than nothing, and Vanity! Isa.* 40. 17. Will He that is far above all Blessing and Praise, *Neh.* 9. 5. that humbleth himself to behold the Worship of Heaven, *Psal.* 113. 6. yet bow down a gracious Ear to the chattering Prayers and Praises of mortal, sinful Men, whose Foundation is in the Dust! *Psal.* 31. 2. *Isa.* 38. 14. *Job* 4. 19. 'Tis well for us that this Path of divine Worship is comprehended in Christ: else God and we could never Walk together in it. But

Thirdly, Divine Providence is also a Way, in which God and his People walk together. Which may be divided into two Parts, Prosperous and afflictive.

First, Prosperous; The Saints are indeed for the most part *a poor and an afflicted people, Zeph.* 3. 12. But yet some Prosperity, more or less, our dear Father is pleas'd to afford to all his Children. They are *Heirs of promise, Heb.* 6. 17. and *Godliness hath the promise of the Life that now is,* as well as that *which is to come,* I *Tim.* 4. 8. *All Things* are theirs, and *the World* among the rest, I *Cor. 3. 21, 22.* They are *Heirs* of it, *Rom.* 4. 13. *The Meek shall inherit the Earth, Matt.* 5. 5. And they are enter'd upon the Possession of it now by Faith, in that Measure of it infinite Wisdom has alotted for every Child. They are call'd to *inherit a Blessing,* I *Pet.* 3. 9. And *all the Promises of God are Yea, and Amen* in Christ Jesus, 2*Cor.* 1. 20. Even those, *Deut.* 28. 11, 12, 13. *And the Lord shall make thee plenteous in goods, in the fruit of thy body, and in the fruit of thy cattle, and in the fruit of thy ground, in the land which the Lord sware unto thy fathers to give thee. The Lord shall open unto thee his good treasure, the Heaven to give rain unto thy land in its season, and to bless all the work of thine hand: and thou shalt lend to many Nations, and shalt not borrow: and the Lord shall make thee the Head, and not the Tail,* &c. The Lord is, indeed, *good to all, and his tender Mercies* (in the Bounties of his Providence) *are over all his Works, Ps,* 145. 9. And the Wicked, generally speaking, have the greatest Share of outward good things, their *portion* being *in this Life, Ps.* 17. 14. But God walks with his own in a very distinguishing Manner from the World, in the way of providential Bounty. They are bless'd in their Basket and Store, in their coming in, and going out, and in all they set their Hand unto, *Deut.* 28. 5, 6, &c. Aye, bless'd indeed, for *in blessing* they are *blest, Gen.* 22. 17. They have the Inside of the Blessing, (God's Heart in every Favour they enjoy) while others have only the outside; may, their very *Blessings* are *curs'd* to 'em, *Mal.* 2. 2. And the *prosperity of fools destroys* 'em, *Prov.* 1. 32. Hence it is, *A little that a righteous Man hath is better than the Riches of many wicked, Ps.* 37. 16. The Saints see the Fountain whence all their Blessings flow, I *Chron.* 29. 14. while others *boast of their Wealth,* as if gotten by their own Hand, *Ps.* 49. 6. They possess *all things* as their own in Christ. *2 Cor.* 6. 10. while the wicked, alas! have no spiritual Right to the least Bit or Drop, *Prov.* 16. 8. They see the Face of God in every Smile of Providence, *Gen.* 33. 10. But *if favour be shewed to the Wicked,* they behold not *the Majesty of the Lord, Isa.* 26. 10. God's People *taste and see that the Lord is good* in every Mercy, *Ps.* 34. 8. They not only taste and see the Goodness of the Mercy, but of God in the Mercy; while the Wicked in their full Prosperity are utter Strangers to God, and Enemies both to him and his, *Ps.* 73. 3, &c. The Wicked have no Assurance of a Day's Favour; they are *set in slippery places, ver.* 18. But the Saints Mercies are Covenant Mercies, *Ps.* 111. 5. *The sure mercies of David, Isa.* 55. 3. So that they may sing with him, *Surely Goodness and mercy shall follow me all the Days of my Life, Ps.* 23. 6.

And Oh the Glory of God's Walk with his, in his Wonder-working Providence! *Ps.* 107. 8. *The young Lions do lack and suffer Hunger, but they that seek the Lord shall not want any good thing, Ps.* 34. 10. He'll *keep* them *alive in Famine, Ps.* 33. 19. Aye, and that by a miraculous Power, if ordinary Means fail. The Ravens must feed *Elijah,* rather than he shall die for Want, I *Kings* 17. 6. And *the Barrel of Meal* shall not waste, nor *the Cruse of Oil* fail, that he may be sustained, *ver.* 14, 15. The Mount of their Extremity of God's Opportunity, *Gen.* 22. 14. He not only helps 'em, but *that right early, Ps.* 46. 5. And as God walks with his, in the Bounties of his Providence, as their own God and Father, *Ps.* 67. 6. 103. 13. Supplying all their Need, *Phil.* 4. 9. So they also herein Walk with him as his *dear Children, Eph.* 5. 1. not trusting in *uncertain Riches but in the Living God,* who *gives* them *all Things richly to enjoy,*

I *Tim.* 6. 17. honouring the Lord with their *Substance, Prov.* 3. 9. And *in every thing* giving Thanks to the Glory of his great Name, I *Thess.* 5. 18. I *Cor.* 10. 30, 31. And as Prosperous, so

Secondly, Afflictive Providence, is a Way in which God and his People walk together. *Man is born unto Trouble as the Sparks fly upward, Job* 5. 7. Afflictions are the natural Fruits of Sin, and to the Wicked the Fruits of the Curse, *Deut.* 28. 20, &c. God as a righteous Judge inflicts 'em as vindictive Punishments, and every Drop thereof is a sure earnest of the approaching Storm of avenging Wrath, *Nahum* 1. 2. But yet when God's *Hand is lifted up, they will not see, Isa. 26. 11.* They *cry not* when he *binds* 'em, *Job* 36. 13. But quarrel with divine Sovereignty, *Isa.* 45. 9. And *after their Hardness and impenitent Heart treasure up to themselves Wrath against the Day of Wrath, Rom. 2. 5.* Till being *often reprov'd, and hardning* their *Neck,* they are *suddenly destroy'd, and that without Remedy, Prov. 29. 1.* But God hath his Way in which he walks in Mercy with his own, even in Affliction-storms, *Nah.* 1. 3. with *Ps.* 25. 10. Thro' much *Tribulation* they *must enter the Kingdom, Acts* 14. 22. They are *predestinated* to be conformable unto Christ in Sufferings as well as in Glory, *Rom.* 8. 29. *ver.* 17. But himself having born their *Sorrows,* and carried their *Griefs, Isa. 53. 4.* the Curse is taken out of 'em; and it's *given* unto them *on the Behalf of Christ, not only to believe, but also to suffer for his Sake, Phil.* 1. 29. They *fill up* but *what is behind of the Afflictions of Christ in* their *Flesh, Col.* 1. 24. And when they *pass thro' the Waters,* the Lord being with 'em, *the Rivers* do'n't *overflow them;* and *thro' the Fires,* the *Flame* doth not *kindle upon 'em, Isa. 43. 2.* In this Way of afflictive Providence, God walks with his People in Covenant-Faithfulness, *Ps.* 89. 30, &c. 119. 75. As a Wife, Tender, Gracious Father, *Rom.* 11. 33. *Ps.* 103. 13. Working *all Things after the Counsel of his own Will,* for *the good* of his Children, *Eph.* 1. 11. *Rom.* 8. 28. and *the glory* of his own Name, *John* 11. 4. He *rebukes* 'em in *Love, Rev.* 3. 19. *Chastens* 'em *for their profit,* that they might be *partakers of his Holiness, Heb.* 12. 10. Blesseth his chastening Hand, and *teacheth* them *out of his Law, Ps.* 94. 12. Opening their Ear, and sealing their Instruction, *Job* 33. 16. By these he *purgeth* out their Corruptions, *Isa.* 27. 9. Trieth their Graces, I *Pet.* 1. 6, 7. *Rom.* 5. 3, 4. And prepares 'em for an *eternal Weight of Glory,* 2 *Cor.* 4. 17. God's People also Walk with him herein, (so far as his Love is shed abroad in their Hearts) by submitting to his divine Sovereignty, *Ps.* 39. 9. Putting their Mouths in the Dust, *Lam.* 3. 29. Justifying him in all his Proceedings, *Matt.* 11. 19. Acknowledging his infinite Goodness, *Ezra* 9. 13. And glorifying him in the Fire, *Isa.* 24. 15. Here they learned to keep God's Commandments, *Psal. 119. 67.* Humble themselves under his mighty Hand, *Jam.* 4. 10. Are patient in Tribulation, *Rom.* 12. 12. Yea rejoyce, and glory in it also, *2 Cor.* 7. 4. *Rom.* 5. 3. Knowing that when in *the Furnace of Affliction, Isa.* 43. 10. the Lord sits by as a *Refiner, Mal.* 3. 3. and that when he has try'd them they shall come forth as Gold, *Job* 23. 10. Aye, not only doth the Lord sit by when they are in fiery Trials, but is with them there; which will make them walk at Liberty, in the midst of a burning fiery Furnace, *Dan.* 3. 25.

Here *Abraham* Walk'd with God, when he offer'd up *Isaac, Gen.* 22. Here *Aaron* Walk'd, and held his Peace when his two Sons were slain, *Lev.* 10. 3. Here *Eli* Walk'd, when the Lord sent him that dreadful Message, that he would cut off his House, *It is the Lord,* saith he, *let him do what seemeth him good,* I *Sam.* 3. 18. Here *David* Walk'd, when fleeing for his Life before rebellious *Absalom,* and the Priests had brought the Ark of God along with him, *Go,* saith he, *carry it back unto its place; if I shall find favour in the Eyes of the Lord, he will bring me back, and shew me both it and his Habitation. But if he say, I have no Delight in thee, Behold, here am I, let him do unto me as seemeth good unto him,* 2 *Sam.* 15. 25, 26. Here also *Hezekiah* Walk'd, when the Lord threatened him with the *Babylonish* Captivity, and that his *Sons* should be *Eunuchs in the palace of the King of Babylon. Good* (saith he) *is the Word of the Lord which thou hast spoken,* 2 *Kings* 20. 19. And what an eminent Instance hereof was holy *Job?* The Lord sends one Affliction upon the Neck of another, takes away his Substance, bereaves him of his Children, strips him quite naked. But how doth *Job* take this, will he flee off now, and Walk no more with God? No, no. He can give God leave to do what he will, with him or his, and not be angry. He falls down and worships, acknowledgeth infinite Goodness, adores divine Sovereignty, and blesseth the Name of Jehovah, for taking as well as giving, *Job* 1. 20, 21. *Then Job arose and rent his Mantle, and shaved his Head, and fell down upon the ground and worshipped. Naked came I out of my Mother's Womb, and naked shall I return thither: the Lord gave, and the Lord hath taken away, and blessed be the Name of the Lord.* But *the Time would fail me* to multiply instances, recorded in God's Book. Thus all the Prophets and Old Testament Saints Walked with God in Afflictions. And here the

Apostles and New-Testament Saints Walked also, in a glorious Advance of Gospel-Light and Liberty. Aye, here they walk with God, not only in Afflictions, but in Afflictions unto Death, if God calls 'em to it. They *count* not their *Lives dear,* that they *may finish* their *Course with Joy, Acts* 20. 24. but pass on triumphing thro' all Difficulties, Tribulation, Distress, Persecution, Famine, Nakedness, Peril or Sword, as *more than Conquerors thro' him that hath loved* them, *Rom.* 8. 35, 37. Oh this Walking with God in Tribulation! It's a *Joy the Stranger intermeddles not with, Prov.* 14. 10. But thus all the Saints, according to their several Degrees of Faith and Light, do, more or less, walk with God, in this way of afflictive Providence. And as God Walks with his herein, to sympathize with 'em in all their Sorrows, *Isa.* 63. 9. to sustain 'em under all their Burdens, *Ps.* 55. 22. and to do 'em good by every Stroke, *Ps.* 119. 71. So also in his own time completely and gloriously to deliver them, *Ps.* 34. 19. which they by Faith trust the Lord for, *Ps.* 22. 8. nor doth he disappoint their Expectation, *Ps.* 9. 18.

The Lord will not *contend for ever, Isa.* 57. 16. His Fatherly *Anger,* in providential Frowns *endureth but for a Moment; Weeping* may *endure* while *the Night* of Affliction lasteth; but *Joy cometh in Morning* of Deliverance; For *in his Favour* there *is Life, Ps.* 30.5. *He doth not willingly afflict* his Children, *Lam.* 3. 33. 'Tis but *if need be* they *are in Heaviness,* I *Pet.* 1. 6. And when he *speaks against* 'em, and they are in the midst of Distresses, he *earnestly remembers* 'em *still,* and his *Bowels are troubled for them, Jer.* 31. 20. But to *exercise Loving-kindness,* he therein *delighteth, Jer.* 9. 24. *Judgment is his Strange Act, Isa.* 28. 21. but to walk with his People in the pure unmixed Display of his Goodness, is his native Delight: When he thus does 'em good, it's with his *whole Heart,* and his *whole Soul, Jer.* 32. 41. And as God walks with his People in all his providential *Ways,* which *are Mercy and Truth, Ps.* 25. 10. whether prosperous or afflictive, so they answerably walk with him herein, in Duty and Thankfulness. And O happy Souls, that are honour'd to Walk with God, in all the providential Changes that pass over them! *Moses,* the Man of God, sets forth their Happiness as incomparably great, *Deut.* 33. 20. *Happy art thou O Israel: who is like unto thee, O People saved by the Lord,* &c.

Fourthly, Conversation-Holiness is another Way in which God and his People walk together, call'd *the Way of God's Commandments;* which the *Psalmist* said he would *run* when God should *enlarge* his *Heart, Ps.*

119. 32. Herein the Saints are commanded to walk, I *Pet.* 1. 15. *But as he that hath called you is holy, so be ye holy in all manner of Conversation.* And it may be distinguish'd from Heart-Holiness, or the new Nature, in the Souls of the Saints, communicated out of Christ's Fullness by the Holy Spirit; this being the Principle from whence it proceeds. All holy Actions must have an holy Principle from whence they flow; and holy Rule to which they are conform'd, and an holy End to which they are directed. Love to God is the Principle, his Word the Rule, and his Glory the End. Conversation-Holiness extends itself to Thoughts, Words, and Actions. Holy Thoughts, are the Walk of an holy Soul with God immediately; holy Words and Actions, so far as before Men, its Walk with him remotely.

And that God and the Soul sweetly walk together in this Way of Holiness, is plain, I *John* 1. 5, 7. *God is Light, and in him is no Darkness at all. If we walk in the Light, as he is in the Light, we have Fellowship one with another.* God is *Light;* Light here, as I conceive, is put for Holiness. And we may read it thus, God is *Holiness,* and in him is no *Darkness,* no Sin, or Contrariety hereto: And if we walk in Holiness, or in the Holy Jesus, (for here only can we walk with God, who was typ'd out by the Holy of Holies, the Place of his immediate Presence) deriving all our Holiness out of Christ's Fullness; conforming all our Actions to the Rule of his Word, and directing the End to the Glory of God in him. If we thus walk in Holiness as he is in Holiness, *we have fellowship one with another.* The Holy God is in the Holy Jesus only to be beheld, and enjoy'd in a saving Soul-transforming manner: God is in Christ only to be obey'd; and in him only doth he accept our Services. 'Tis the Holiness of this Temple, sanctifies all our Performances. And if we thus Walk in the Light, as he is in the Light, we have Fellowship one with another. God with us, and we with God; we familiarly walk together in the sweetest Friendship. (Aye, notwithstanding all the Vileness of our Hearts, and Pollution of our Services; *for the Blood of Jesus Christ his Son cleanseth us from all Sin.)* So *Isa.* 64. 5. *Thou meetest him that rejoyceth, and worketh Righteousness, those that remember thee in thy ways. Thy ways,* not only because thou hast appointed 'em for thy People to walk in, but also because that there thou wilt familiarly walk with them. And generally speaking, those that walk most holily, are most favour'd with God's sensible Presence. In this way of Conversation-Holiness God walks with his People,

First, By Teaching them his Statutes; which the *Psalmist* so often prays for, *Ps.* 119.

Secondly, By Heart-attracting, Soul-transforming Discoveries of the Glory of his Holiness, and the Excellency of all his righteous Precepts. And,

Thirdly, By free and full Acceptation of all their holy Performances.

In the first, He walks with us as the Lord our God, *that teacheth us to profit,* leading us in the Way where we should go, *Isa.* 48. 17.

In the second, He sets his own Holiness before us as a Pattern, and gives us to see the Excellency of all his holy ways, to raise and ennoble our Spirits: *Be ye holy, for I am holy,* I *Pet.* 1. 16. *Perfect, as your Father is perfect, Matt.* 5. 48. And

In the Third, He walks with us as a tender, gracious Father, pitying all our Weakness, pardoning all our Sinfulness, and continually accepting all our Services, with the highest Complacency and Well-pleasedness, I *Pet.* 2. 5. And the Saints answerably Walk with God herein.

First, in that, From his efficacious Teaching, they wait for, and receive Direction to walk in his Ways, *Psal.* 123. 2. Turning their Feet to his Testimonies, *Ps.* 119. 105. *ver.* 5. 9.

Secondly, Under shining Discoveries of the Glory of his Holiness, and of all his righteous Precepts, they *purify* themselves *even as he is pure,* I *Joh.* 3. 3. and love his Law exceedingly, *Ps.* 119. 97. esteeming *all his Precepts concerning all things to be right,* and hating *every false Way, ver.* 128. And

Thirdly, in that, while God opens his free and full Acceptance of all their Performances, their Hearts are thereby *enlarged* to *run the way* of his *Commandments;* always *abounding* in his *Work* and Service, I *Cor.* 15. 58. And

Further, This Conversation-Holiness, extends itself unto a Walking with God, in every Place, Station, Relation, and Circumstance of Life; whether Spiritual, Natural, or Civil; in the Church, Family, or Commonwealth. Hence every Man is exhorted, *in* that *Calling wherein* he is *called,* therein to *abide* with God, I *Cor.* 7. 24. And *servants* in particular, to *obey* their *Masters in Singleness of Heart, as to the Lord; knowing* that therein they *serve the Lord Christ, Col.* 3. 22, 23, 24. which holds true in all other Relations whatsoever. And O! with what unspeakable Pleasure doth an holy Soul walk with God in all relative Duties; rejoycing that the Lord hath commanded them, that so it may perform 'em under that very Notion of Obedience, *Ps.* 119. 111. There's not a common Action of Life, but it would interest God in, I *Cor.* 10. 31. Oh how *easy* is Christ's *Yoke,* and how *light* his *Burden,* to the Saints, walking with God under the sweet Constraints of his Love, *Matt.* 11. 30. *2 Cor.* 5. 14. Wisdom's *Ways* are to them *pleasantness,* and all her *paths* are *peace, Prov.* 3. 17. They're not their *own,* I *Cor.* 6. 19. And whether they *live,* they *live unto the Lord;* and whether they *die,* they *die unto the Lord.* Living and Dying, they are the Lord's, *Rom.* 14. 8. They count all that part of their Life lost, in which they do not live unto God: All their Time lost, that is not spent for his Glory. Yea, there is such an holy Eagerness in their Souls after Walking with God, that makes 'em count all their former Walk with him not worth the Name. There is still set before 'em such an intensive, extensive, and perpetual way of Walking with God in Holiness, which their Feet have yet never trac'd, that makes 'em forget the things that are behind, and reach forth after those which are before: and the more Holiness any Soul attains, the more eager it is in its Pursuit after it. Thus the great Apostle *Paul,* (who is thought by some to have had the greatest Measure of Holiness, next unto the Man Christ) *counts* not himself *to have attained;* but still presseth forward, that if it were possible, he *might attain to the* very *Resurrection of the Dead.* (To be as holy, as if he was rais'd from the Dead) *Phil.* 3. 11, 12. This *path of the just,* shines forth with an attracting Glory, at the Soul's first Entrance into the Way of Holiness; but the further it advanceth therein, the more the Path shines, *Prov.* 4. 18. So that it passeth on *from Glory to Glory, perfecting Holiness in the Fear of the Lord,* 2 *Cor.* 3. 18.

Again, This Gospel-Holiness, in which the Saints Walk with God, is of a far higher kind, than was to be found in perfect *Adam's* Heart. It flows from an higher Fountain, is influenced by higher Motives, and is directed to an higher End: *Adam's* Holiness, flow'd from Christ's Nature Fullness, This, from his Grace-Fulness; His was influenced by the common goodness of God, This, by his special and supernatural Goodness; That was directed to the Glory of God, as a bountiful Creator, This, to his Glory as a new Covenant Father. Not Love to God only, as the God of Nature, but as the God of Grace in Christ, is the Fountain whence this flows, I *John* 4. 9, 19. Not common Bounties only, but distinguishing Grace and Mercy, display'd in a crucify'd Jesus, are the influencing Motives of this, *Eph.* 2. 4, 5. *Gal.* 2. 19, 20. Not the Glory of God as the God of Nature only, but as *the God of all Grace* and

Mercy, and *Father of Glory,* is the End to which this is directed, I *Pet.*
5. 10 *Eph.* 1. 17. I *Cor.* 6. 20.

O what a noble thing is Gospel-Holiness! Not to obtain Life do the
Saints walk herein; but to glorify God for the eternal Gift of it to 'em, I
John 5. 11. With what high and heavenly Freedom do they here Walk
with God under the sheddings abroad of his *Love* in their Hearts, *which*
casteth out Bondage-*fear,* I *John* 4. 18. They obey now, no more as
Servants that work for Wages but as thankful Children blest with the
Inheritance, *Gal.* 4. 7. that shall *abide in the House for ever, John* 8. 35.
Oh happy Souls, who being deliver'd out of the Hand of all their
Enemies, thus *serve* God *in Holiness, without Fear, Luke* 1. 74, 75.

Thus much for the Way in which God and his People Walk together,
taken both comprehensively and distributively: or the lesser Paths,
comprehended in Christ the Great Way. I proceed to take a little Notice,
That for a Soul to walk with God, doth not only suppose a mutual
Agreement, and also a Way in which both Walk. But,

Thirdly, A continued Course, or Series of Steps taken therein. God
not only begins to Walk with us in Christ, but he goes on with us in him
as our everlasting Friend. *The Gifts and Calling of God are without*
Repentance, Rom. 11. 29. God never repents that he has call'd Christ to
the Office of interposing and atoning Mediator, *Prov.* 8. 22. *Ps.* 110. 4.
that so he might have an everlasting Way, wherein he might walk with
us, to the Honour of all his divine Perfections; nor doth he repent that he
hath given Christ to us, as our everlasting Way to walk with him in.
God's Heart was so full of Love towards us from everlasting, that he held
a Counsel within himself, how he might honourably walk with us;
maintaining an everlasting Friendship. And in the Triumphs of boundless
Love he breaks forth, exulting in this Project of infinite Wisdom; *I have*
found David my servant; with my holy Oyl have I anointed him, Ps. 89.
20. And he is the *Lord* Jehovah, *that changeth not, Mal.* 3. 6. Time
makes no Alteration in his Heart; no, nor his Peoples Sins neither. Not
all our Lowness, Baseness, vileness, and daily Provocations can wean his
Heart from us. He has chosen such foolish, base, vile, provoking Worms
as we, to be his everlasting Companions, I *Cor.* 1. 27, 28. *Job* 40. 4. *Isa.*
62. 5. He hath desir'd to Walk with us, *Ps.* 132. 13. [Us] not our
[Vileness] yet it's Us, [notwithstanding] our Vileness. O amazing Grace!
and because he hath thus lov'd us, he goes on to purify us more and
more, *Isa.* 1. 25. to make us meet for Fellowship with him, who is a God

of purer Eyes than to behold Iniquity, Hab. 1. 13. He well knew all the Perverseness, Obstinacy, and Rebellion of our Nature, *Isa.* 48. 4, 8. and that we should be no better than those whom his Soul hates, *Mal.* 1. 2. 3. And yet in everlasting Kindness he resolv'd to walk with us, *Isa.* 54. 8. God, not only was well pleased to walk with us in Christ at first, but in him he is still well pleased; yea, and will abide everlastingly well pleased, *Matt.* 3. 17. *Isa.* 54. 10. O this prepared Way! Christ is (if I may so say) a Way cast up, where all Difficulties and Obstacles are remov'd. Here God can walk with us according to his own Heart, in infinite Love and Grace, Goodness and Mercy, Power and Patience, Wisdom and Faithfulness; and accordingly he doth: *For Israel hath not been forsaken, nor Judah of his God; tho' their Land was fill'd with Sin against the Holy One of Israel, Jer.* 51. 5.

God Walk'd with his People of old, when he brought them forth out of *Egypt* thro' the Red Sea, and all along thro' that great and terrible Wilderness. Which was typical of our spiritual Deliverance from all our Enemies, by the Blood of Jesus; and our Passage thro' a World of Trials, to the heavenly Rest. When the Time drew near for *Israel's* Deliverance out of *Egypt, I will go out,* says God, *Exod.* 11. 8. 'Twas he *led forth* their *Armies.* And when they pass'd thro' the Red Sea, 'twas he *marched* before 'em, *Hab.* 3. 15. *That led 'em forth by the right hand of Moses, with his glorious Arm, dividing the water before 'em, to make himself an everlasting Name, Isa.* 63. 19. And how did God Walk with his People quite thro' the Wilderness, in *a pillar of Cloud by day,* and in *a pillar of Fire by night? Num.* 14. 14. And this notwithstanding all their Provocations, *Neh.* 9. 19. And as God, in this Pillar of Cloud and Fire, continued to Walk with his People of old, in a typical and external manner, visible to their corporeal Sight; so much more doth he walk with his People now, in a real, spiritual and transcendent Glory, visible only to Faith: and the very Term of [Walking] doth imply a continued Course. 'Tis not two or three Steps taken in any way, is sufficient to denominate it Walking therein. In this Mystery then, of God's Walking with us, and we with him, we are to observe a continued Course. God not only begins to walk with us at first, in the Person of Christ, as the alone Mediator; and in him also as the great Redeemer; but he continues to go on with us in this great Way, according to his unchangeable Heart-Love, *Jer.* 31. 3. *Mal.* 3. 6. the unchangeable Dignity of the Mediator's Person, *Rom.* 9. 5. *Heb.* 13. 8. and the eternal Efficacy of the Redeemer's Merits, *Heb.* 9. 12. and

10. 14. Christ as our great High-Priest, not only made Peace for us on the Cross, but he also maintains it for us on the Throne: He was once *Dead,* but is *Alive,* and *lives for evermore, Rev.* 1. 18. to maintain an everlasting Friendship between God and us.

We are poor sinful, sinning Creatures; and Satan our grand Enemy, is always accusing us Day and Night before God, *Rev.* 12. 10. But Christ always appears in the Presence of God for us. *Heb.* 9. 24. as our righteous Advocate to plead our Cause, I *John* 2. 1. If Satan accuse us, Christ pleads what he is to us, and has done for us, to the full Satisfaction of Law and Justice; and so he brings us off clear in a way of Righteousness, with Honour in open Court. If Satan improve the Charges he brings against us, to shew how unworthy we are, that God should continue to Walk with us; Christ pleads his own Worthiness, and the Interest he hath in his Father's Heart, as also the inseparable Relation and Union Grace has taken us into; which always prevails with the Father for continued Communion. How doth he found his Pleas for us in that *Seventeenth* of *John,* (a Pattern of his Intercession now in Heaven) upon his personal Relation to, and Interest in his Father? *ver.* 24. *For thou loveth* [Me] Father, *before the Foundation of the World.* And how doth he plead our Union with him? *ver.* 16. *They are not of the World, even as I am not of the World.* As if he should say, Father, They are [One] with Me; a distinct Company from the World; and must therefore share in the same Privileges I enjoy. Again, how doth he plead our Relation both to him and his Father? *ver.* 9. 10. *I pray not for the World, but for them that thou hast given me, for they are [Thine.]* Thy Heart is set upon 'em, thou hast loved 'em into a supernatural and eternal Relation to thyself; and so thou canst not deny my Request for 'em, because in praying for them I pray for thy own:) *and all thine are [Mine] also.* And as thou hast loved the Head, thou canst not but love the Members; thy Love to them being but an Overflow of thy Love to me; and in loving them, thou dost but love me, as they are my *Fulness, Eph.* 1. 23. O how prevalent must these Pleas be with Christ's, and our Father! especially if we consider, that the Father himself loveth us! *John* 16. 27. Christ as our Advocate defends us from all Charges; As our Intercessor pleads for the Communication and Continuation of all Favours. And if the Father always heard him when below, *John* 11. 42. much more now he hath exalted him at his own right hand, far above all Principalities and Powers, and bid him Ask, and he will Give him, *Eph.* 1. 20, 21. *Ps.* 2. 8. And since Christ always carried it for us in Heaven, we have the highest Assurance of God's continual Walk with us; notwithstanding all the Opposition of the united Powers of Darkness.

The Apostle *John* brings in the Advocateship of Jesus Christ, to this very Purpose, to strengthen the Faith of the Saints he wrote to, about God's continual Walking with 'em. *That which we have seen and heard, declare we unto you, that you may have Fellowship with us: and truly our Fellowship is with the Father, and with his Son Jesus Christ,* I *John* 1. 3. But the Saints might reply, How must this Fellowship be maintain'd? We are poor weak sinning Creatures; alas, we shall be always provoking our Father to depart from us; will he continue to walk with us notwithstanding all our Provocations? To this he answers by way of Anticipation, chap. 2. 1. *My little Children, these things write I unto you that you sin not.* (It becomes you to be holy, since you are call'd to Walk with an holy God; and if you do'n't walk holily, you'll dishonour your high Calling, and the holy Companions you are call'd to walk with: You'll grieve the Holy Spirit, dishonour your holy Head, and lose the sensible Presence of your holy Father; and therefore *I write unto you that you sin not. But) If any Man sin,* (Let him not sink under it, and be discouraged, as if the God of all Grace would break Friendship, and walk no more with him; For) *we have an Advocate with the Father, Jesus Christ the Righteous;* that lives in Heaven on purpose to maintain Fellowship between God and us: And *because* he *lives,* we shall *live also, John* 14. 19. Thus the *Apostle* to the *Romans, If when we were Enemies, we were reconcil'd to God by the Death of his Son: much more being reconciled, we shall be saved by his Life, Rom.* 5. 10. And to assure the Saints about God's continual Walking with 'em, are all those Apostolical Benedictions and Prayers used in their Epistles: *Grace and Peace be multiply'd unto you, from God our Father, and the Lord Jesus Christ,* &c. It was not enough that Grace and Peace were multiply'd to 'em at first, when God and they began to Walk together; but they must be multiply'd continually, in order to their continual Walking together.

And Oh blessed be God, Grace is a boundless Ocean, that all the multiply'd Streams can never draw dry. It has been streaming forth continually, in all its various Channels, to all the Saints, in all the Ages of Time; and yet there is never the less in it. The God of all Grace has as much Grace in his Heart, to walk with Us now, in these latter Ages of the World, as he had when he first began to walk with *Adam, Enoch,*

Noah, &c. Yea, let me say, That Grace is not only multiply'd, to continue his Walk with us, but in it also.

God began to Walk with his People at first in great Grace: And therefore it's said of one he walk'd with, even so early as before the Flood, That, *Noah found Grace in the Eyes of the Lord,* Gen. 6. 8. And as God went on with his People throughout the Old Testament times, how did the Discoveries of Grace rise? *The Waters* were *risen* in *Exekiel's* Time, chap. 47. 5. But the Grace in which God walks with New-Testament Saints, was a Reserve of Favour which in other Ages was not made known, *Eph.* 3. 5. And as God walks with the Church in general, so with every Believer in particular. Every Step he takes with us is a Rising Discovery of his Grace. And the further he leads us on the higher still 'twill rise; from the Ancles to the Knees; from the Knees to the Loins; until he leads us into the infinite Ocean of Grace, where we shall delightfully swim for ever.

But mean while, God goes on with us now in Christ, as Jehovah; Jehovah, the strong God, Merciful, Gracious, Long-suffering, abundant in Goodness and Truth, *Exod.* 34. 6. And as in Christ the great Way, so in all the lesser Paths comprehended in him.

In the Way of Faith or Divine Revelation, enlightening our Minds in the Knowledge of his Will, *Eph.* 1. 17, 18, 19.

In the Way of instituted Worship, as Sion's God, blessing her Provision, hearing her Prayers, and accepting her Praises, *Ps.* 132. 15. 65. 2. 50. 23.

In the Way of Divine Providence, whether Prosperous or Afflictive, working all things together for our Good, *Rom.* 8. 28. and

In the Way of Conversation-Holiness, ordering our Steps in his Word, and graciously accepting our Walk unto all pleasing, *Psal.* 119. 133. *Rom.* 14. 18. *Col.* 1. 10. Thus our God Walks with us continually according to his Covenant Promises. *I will bring the Blind* (saith he) *by a Way they knew not: I will lead them in Paths they have not known: I will make Darkness Light before them, and crooked Things straight. These things will I do, and not forsake them,* Isa. 42. 16.

But then we must observe, That the Lord always walks with us Really, for our Advantage, yet not always sensibly to our Perception. Christ walked with the Disciples going to *Emmaus,* and they felt glorious Effects of his Presence; but yet their Eyes were holden that they knew him not, *Luke* 24. 13, 14, 15, 16, 32. And thus it is oft-times with God's dear Children: for tho' *as the Mountains are round about Jerusalem, so the Lord is round about his People from henceforth and for ever, Ps.* 125. 2. Yet they, poor Hearts, oft think he is far from them. As the Church, *Lam.* 1. 16. *Mine Eye runneth down with Water, because the Comforter which should relieve my Soul is far from me.* And yet the Comforter ever abides with us, *John* 14. 16. tho' his comforting Influences are at times suspended, *Psal.* 51. 12. And thus our God continually walks with us; tho' at times he covers himself with such *thick Darkness* that vails the Glory of his Face from our Sight, *Ps.* 97. 2. Faith, indeed, can pierce the Cloud; and see him continually with us, holding us by his right Hand, that we shall not be moved. *Ps.* 73. 23. But alas! it's oft impenetrable to spiritual Sense. And then *Zion* says, *The Lord hath forsaken her. Isa.* 49. 14. Till he reproves her unbelieving Words, with a *Why sayest then oh* Jacob? and *why speakest thou oh* Israel? *Hast thou not known? hast thou not heard? that the everlasting God, the Lord, the Creator of the Ends of the Earth, fainteth not, neither is weary?* (of walking with thee, nor of supplying thy Strength to walk with him) *For he giveth Power to the Faint, and to them that have no Might, he encreaseth Strength. Isa.* 40. 21, 28, 29.

But, Oh how a fresh Discovery of this Grace, makes a weary Child of God, just ready to faint under Absence, and want of sensible Influences, to *renew* its *Strength;* to *mount up with Wings as Eagles,* to *run* and *not be weary,* to *walk* and *not faint! Isa.* 40. 30. God's continual walking with us is our Safety; The Faith of it our Comfort. 'Twas this made *David* sing so chearfully, *Tho' I walk thro' the Valley of the Shadow of Death; I will fear no Evil: For thou art with me. Psal.* 23. 4. What no Evil, *David,* in such an evil Place? No, says he, God is *with me and I fear* nothing. O the Faith of God's being With his Children, what has it carried them thro'? By this they have *overcome the World,* both in its Frowns and Smiles, I *John* 5. 4. It has made 'em bold as Lions, *Prov.* 28. 1. They have fear'd neither Men nor Devils, *Heb.* 13. 6. *Rom.* 8. 38. 'Twas this Way God strengthen'd his Servant *Joshua. There shall not any Man be able to stand before thee all the Days of thy Life; as I was with Moses, so I will be with thee. I will not fail thee, nor forsake thee. Be strong and of good Courage, Josh.* 1. 5, 6. And thus in measure he strengthens every of his Children. Let but God say to a fearful-hearted Child, *Be strong;* as I have been with others of my Children, so I will be with thee; and no Opposition shall be able to stand before thee: For *I will never leave thee nor forsake thee, Heb.* 13. 5. What Strength doth it put into the Soul? *Job* 23. 6. Now it can reason it out in Faith, against all unbelieving Fears, *Hath he said it, and shall he not do it? Hath he spoken, and shall he not make it good? Num.* 23. 19. Until it raiseth a Shout of joyful Triumph in God the Strength of *Israel,* Who's not a *Man* that he *should lie,* nor *the Son of Man that he should repent,* I *Sam.* 15. 29. God says to his *Worm, Jacob, Fear not, for I am with thee; be not dismayed, for I am thy God,* &c. *Isa.* 41. 10. Faith receives the glad Tidings, and goes on its way triumphing thro' a weary Wilderness, being persuaded, that *neither Height, nor Depth, Life nor Death, things present nor things to come, shall be able to separate* the Soul *from this Love of God which is in Christ Jesus our Lord, Rom.* 8. 38, 39.

God's continual Walk with his People is managed in such a Depth and Variety of infinite Wisdom, that his *Judgements* are oft to us *unsearchable,* and his *Ways* herein *past finding out, Rom.* 11. 33. And when the Glory of his constant Walk with us is obscured from our Sight, 'tis but a Preparation for the brighter Display of his everlasting Kindness herein; when like the Sun from under an Eclipse he breaks out upon us again, with a new amazing Glory; which is exceeding *pleasant* for our Eyes *to behold, Eccles.* 11. 7. And as God continually walks with his People in Christ, and in all the ways of his Appointment; so they also herein walk with him, according to the Exhortation, *Col.* 2. 6. *As ye have therefore received Christ Jesus the Lord, so walk ye in him.*

The Saints not only begin to Walk with God in the Person of Christ, as Mediator; and in him also as the Great Redeemer; but they go on with him continually in this Way, under the gracious Fulfillment of that Promise, *Job* 17. 9. *The righteous also shall hold on his Way, and he that hath clean Hands shall be stronger and stronger.* Tho', poor Hearts, they are often feeble; yet this *Way of the Lord is Strength to the upright, Prov.* 10. 29. And so they hold on in it, because their very Way is their Strength. And tho' Deadness and Inactivity oft seize their Spirits; yet Christ is such a Living Way, that communicates Life to 'em every Step they take in him. In this *Way of Righteousness is Life, and in the Path-way thereof there is no Death, Pro.* 12. 28. And tho' as to their continual Walking in this Way, there arise many Obstacles from their own Sinfulness and Unworthiness; yet it being a Way prepar'd on purpose for 'em in these Respects, I *Tim.* 1. 15. *Rom.* 4. 16. the Lord takes up the stumbling Blocks, and makes their way plain before them, so that they pass on safely: Yea, he makes *the Vision* of Life and Love so plain in this way, that they *run* and *read* it with unspeakable Pleasure, *Isa.* 57. 14. *Prov.* 15. 19. *Psal.* 78. 53. *Hab.* 2. 2. When God reveal'd Christ at first to the Souls of his Children, as their only Way of Walking with him, he was, as such, exceeding *precious* to their Faith, I *Pet.* 2. 7. in all his suitable Fullness to their various Wants, *Col.* 1. 19. and as they receiv'd him, so they continually Walk in him, in every Step they take with God, even to their dying Moments. Glad were they at first as poor, nothing, filthy, guilty Creatures, to *run* into this *Name of the Lord,* as their high, holy, righteous Way, where only they might Walk with God, and be safe, *Prov.* 18. 10. And they are still of the same Mind. Christ has lost no Glory in their Eye. They think they need him as much as ever. Yea, some of the Saints, the further they advance think they need him more than ever. For tho' as they pass on in Christ, their personal Holiness increaseth, yet the more holy they are, the more humble. Because the Holy Ghost, in managing this Work upon their Souls, discovers still greater and *greater Abominations* in their Hearts, *Ezek.* 8. 6. on the one hand to keep them low in their own Eyes; as on the other, he opens transcendent Views of the Glory of Christ, to keep him high in their Esteem. Hence it is, That they dare not take a Step with God in any other Way but Christ, whatever Temptations they have thereto. If Satan present a pleasing Prospect of their own Obedience, and their unbelieving Hearts cast an adulterous Glance upon it, this, under the Holy ghost's convincing work, *Joh.* 16. 9. makes them *loath themselves* so much the more in their own Sight, *Ezek.* 20. 43. esteeming themselves but as an *unclean thing;* and their best *righteousnesses* but as *filthy Rags, Isa.* 64. 6. yea, as *Loss* and *Dung,* in comparison of *the Knowledge of Christ,* as their only Way to Walk with God. Oh! *'tis in him* they would be *found, Phil.* 3. 8, 9. For as the Holy Ghost's Voice exalts Christ alone in the Soul, *John* 16. 14. so the Voice of the New Creature doth as it were eccho back the Sound: None but Christ, none but Christ, Christ is *All in All, Col.* 3. 11. *We are* (saith the Apostle) *of the Circumcision that worship God in Spirit, that rejoyce in Christ Jesus* (in him only, in him always) *and have no Confidence in the Flesh, Phil.* 3. 3. The holiest Saint on Earth, dares not set up his own personal Holiness, abstracted from Christ, as a Way to walk with God in. No, they see such Imperfections therein they dare not. Yea, they see such a transcendent Excellency in Christ, that tho' they were perfect they would not *know* their *Soul,* they would *despise* their

Life, Job 9. 21. And as they go on continually to walk with God in Christ their great Way, so in all the lesser Paths comprehended in him.

In the Way of Faith, or divine Revelation, they delightfully go on to Walk with God; Receiving his divine Testimony, and setting to their *Seal that he is true, John* 3. 33. Judging him *faithful who hath promised,* and trusting him as such even in the darkest Dispensations, *Heb.* 11. 11. *Job* 13. 15. They know and receive *the Things of God,* under the Spirit's Revelation, as the highest *Wisdom;* which are *Foolishness* to *the natural Man,* I *Cor.* 2. 6, 12, 14. Having *Fellowship* with Gospel-mysteries, they hold fast the *Faithful Word;* and Contend earnestly *for the faith once Deliver'd to the Saints, Eph.* 3. 9. *Tit.* 1. 9. *Jude* 3. They *Buy the Truth and Sell it not; Pro.* 23. 23. Counting it Dearer than their Lives, *Acts.* 20. 24. They *Love not their Lives unto the Death,* in comparison with God's Truth, *Rev.* 12. 11. If they must part with Truth or Life, they'll rather part with their own Lives, than not be found *Walking* with God *in Truth,* 2 *John* 4. *Rejoycing* that they are *counted worthy to suffer Shame for his Name, Acts* 5. 41. Knowing that they are *set for the Defence of the Gospel, Phil.* 1. 17. which is true of every particular Believer in his proper Station, as well as of Christ's Ministering Servants. For whosoever *loveth not the Gospel* above his own Life, and is *ashamed* of Christ, and his *Words,* before an *adulterous and sinful Generation,* of him will he be *ashamed,* when he *cometh in the Glory of his Father, with the Holy Angels, Mark* 8. 35, 38. And Oh how triumphantly, have many of God's dear Children walk'd with him in Truth, even to a being *Faithful unto Death!* To whom Christ has now given *a Crown of Life, Rev.* 2. 10. And tho' all the Saints are not call'd to walk with God in Witnessing for his Truth unto Martyrdom; yet the Principle of Love being the same in all, if the Lord was pleas'd to draw it out, and call 'em to it, they would rejoice to be all Martyrs.

Again, the Saints go on to Walk with God in the way of instituted Worship, whether publick or private. How do they say with *David,* Lord, *I have loved the Habitation of thy House, and the Place where thine Honour dwelleth! Psal.* 26. 8. *Our Feet shall stand within thy Gates Oh Jerusalem, Psal.* 122. 2. They go *with a Multitude that keep Holy Day, Psal.* 42. 4. to present their joint Supplications, to a God hearing Prayer, I *Tim.* 2. 1. *Psal.* 34. 15. who, as such, is *known in Judah,* and *his Name is great in Israel! While in Salem is his Tabernacle, and his Dwelling-place in Sion. For there brake he the Arrows of the Bow, the Shield, the*

Sword, and the Battle. Selah, Psal. 76. 1, 2, 3. Here they continually *sit at* his *Feet,* and delightfully hear his Word, *Luke* 10. 39. *Psal.* 119. 72. And in the midst of *Jerusalem* they offer Praises to the Lord, paying their Vows in the Presence of his Saints, *Psal.* 116. 18, 19. For *thither the Tribes go up to the Testimony of Israel, to give Thanks to the Name of the Lord, Psal.* 122. 4. Esteeming *a Day in his Courts better than a thousand, Psal.* 84. 10. As God walks in *Sion,* loving *her Gates more than all the Dwellings of Jacob,* so they walk here too: *Not forsaking the assembling themselves together, as the manner of some is, Psal.* 87. 2. *Heb.* 10. 25.

And as in Publick, so in Private Worship also, the Saints continually Walk with God. They *meditate in his Law, Day and Night, Psal.* 1. 2. Pray *always, with all Prayer, and Supplication in the Spirit, watching thereunto with all Perseverance, Eph.* 6. 18. Insomuch that it is said of them, *This is the Generation of them that seek him, Psal.* 24. 6. Among which *Cornelius* was found, who prayed to God always, *Acts.* 10. 2. They *come boldly to the Throne of Grace,* to *obtain Mercy, and find Grace* to *help* 'em in all their *Times of Need, Heb.* 4. 16. And Oh! how glad they are that they may go on to walk with God in this way at all Times, *Pouring out* their *Hearts before* him, while he is *a Refuge* for them! *Psal.* 62. 8. *The Righteous cry, and the Lord heareth them, and delivereth them out of all their Troubles, Psal.* 38. 17. And then *in every thing they give Thanks, Psal.* 140. 13. I *Thess.* 5. 18. A Saint, walking with God, runs as fast in the Duty of Praise, as he did in the Duty of Prayer. *Let* (says the Psalmist) *the sighing of the Prisoner come before thee, in the greatness of thy Power preserve thou them that are appointed to die, &c. And so we thy People, and Sheep of thy Pasture will give thee Thanks for ever: We will shew forth thy Praise to all generations, Psal.* 79. 11, 12, 13. Because to *pray without ceasing,* and *in every thing* to *give Thanks,* is the *Will of God in Christ Jesus concerning* us, I *Thes.* 5. 17, 18.

Further, the Saints walk on with God in the Way of Divine Providence, whether Prosperous or Afflictive. The wicked are *without God in the World, Eph.* 2. 12. They say unto him, *Depart from us, we desire not the Knowledge of thy Ways, Job* 21. 14. But the Saints in all their Walk would not take one Step without him. Prosperity would be a comfortless Walk to them, if God was not with 'em there. 'Tis *the Light of his Countenance* lifted up upon 'em, that *puts more Gladness* into their Hearts, than the abundant Increase of *Corn and Wine, Psal.* 4. 6, 7. The

Saints not only begin to walk with God in Prosperity, as seeing his Hand bestowing it, giving to God the Glory due to his Name, delighting themselves in his abundant Goodness, and *Honouring* the Lord with their *Substance;* but they also go on with him herein: As faithful *Stewards* improving all their *Talents* to the Glory of their great Lord, I *Pet.* 4. 10, 11. *Matt.*25. 21. And it's a higher Joy to a Child of God walking with him in Prosperity, That thereby he is enabled to glorify God the more, serve his Cause, and be rich in good Works, than all the outward Advantages which accrue to himself thereby. The Saints are the Lord's in Prosperity, as well as in Adversity: in Life as well as in Death, *Rom.* 14. 8. They interest God in all they possess. *Of thine own,* saith *David, have we given thee, Chron.* 29. 14. They receive it from him, possess it in him, and use it for him; nor do they desire any Prosperity but what may tend to the Advancement of his Glory, *Prov.* 30. 8, 9.

Again, The Saints go on to Walk with God in Adversity: Bowing to Divine Sovereignty, justifying God in all his Proceedings, attending to the Voice of his Rod, acquiescing in the Divine Will, supplicating his Throne, patiently waiting for delivering Kindness, rejoycing in Tribulation, and glorifying God in the Fires. And this not for a while only, in a few single Providences, but they thus go on with God as in a continual Course. Upon which Account the Apostle glory'd in the *Thessalonians in all the Churches* of God, for their *Patience* and *Faith* in All their Persecutions and *Tribulations* which they endur'd, 2 *Thess.* 1. 4. Hence we are exhorted, *To run with Patience the Race that is set before us, Heb.* 12. 1. To *rejoyce in Hope, continue instant in Prayer, and patient in Tribulation, Rom.* 12. 12. And to make the Saints so, the Lord *comforteth* them *in all* their *Tribulations, 2 Cor.* 1. 4. whether from himself immediately or mediately, by the Hand of Satan, or wicked Men. And O what a rare Proficient was the Apostle *Paul!* How had he learned this heavenly Skill of Walking with God, in the Way of Divine Providence, whether prosperous of afflictive? *I have learned* (says he) *in whatsoever State I am therewith to be content: I know both how to be abased, and I know how to abound: every where, and in all things I am instructed, both to be full, and to be hungry, both to abound, and to suffer need. I can do all things thro' Christ which strengthneth me, Phil.* 4. 11, 12, 13.

Again, in the Way of Conversation Holiness, The dear Saints, not only begin, but they also go on to Walk with God. They are *created in*

Christ Jesus unto good Works, which God hath before ordained that they should *walk in them, Eph.* 2. 10. They are called unto Holiness as their constant Course, I *Thess.* 4. 7. And they do go on to Walk with God, *in all manner of holy Conversation and Godliness,* I *Pet.* 1. 15. taking him for their Pattern, walking as he also walked: receiving all their Directions from his Word, and conforming their Actions herein to his holy Precepts. Thus they *walk before the Lord in the Land of the Living, Psal.* 116. 9. As *Zacharias* and *Elizabeth* are said to have Walked before God, *in all the Commandments of the Lord blameless, Luke* 1. 6. But then,

Obj. It may be objected, How can such sinful Creatures as we, be said continually to Walk with God in all these Respects?

Ans. To which I answer, That tho' the Term [Walking] doth imply a continued Course; yet when apply'd to our Walking with God, it is not to be understood strictly, as if there were no Interruptions in it: tho' it may and ought to be understood as denoting a general Course. Thus *Asa's* Heart is said to be *perfect all his Days, 2 Chron.* 15. 17. And tho' in the latter End of his Life he grievously sinn'd, for *in his Affliction he sought not to the Lord, but to the physicians, chap.* 16. 12. yet because his Heart was perfect in his general Course, he is said to be *perfect all his Days.* The Lord has promis'd, to *put* his *Fear* in our Hearts, that we *shall not depart from* him, *Jer.* 32. 40. Which is not to be understood, as if that in no single Instance we should be left to depart from him; But that we should not be left to go on in a sinful Course of departing from him. For while *an evil Heart of Unbelief* remains in us, we shall more or less *depart from the Living God, Heb.* 3. 12. Every sinful Step we take, either in Thought, Word, or Action, may be styled a departing from God. *My People,* saith the Lord, *are bent to Backsliding from me, Hos.* 11. 7. We are naturally prone to *go astray like a lost Sheep, Psal.* 119. 176. and when we are out of the Way we have no Heart, Wisdom, or Strength to return. But we have an *High-priest* that *can have Compassion on such that are out of the Way, Heb.* 5. 2. That will go after us till he finds us, and cause us to *hear a Voice behind us, This is the Way, walk ye in it, Isa.* 30. 21. Which being a Call of efficacious Grace, *restoreth* our *Souls, Psal.* 23. 3. convincing us of our Folly; and discovering the Remedy: And then again *with Weeping and Supplications,* he *leads* us *in the paths of Righteousness for his Names sake, Jer.* 31. 9. Thus there are sad Interruptions in the Saints Walk with God. And yet in regard of their general Course, they may be said so to do. There being no Place,

Relation, or Station of Life, in which they do not more or less Walk with him. Yea, according to the Mind of the inner Man, there is no Circumstance, in which they do not begin, go on, and end it with God. Their Walk with God is perfect in respect of Parts; in that they walk with him in all the parts of Obedience, both as to Faith and Practice, having *Respect unto all his Commandments, Psal.* 119. 6. But yet, even in the greatest Saint, it falls far short in respect of Degrees. And if God was to *mark Iniquity,* the Holiest Man upon Earth *could not stand before* him, as a Walker with him, *Psal.* 130. 3. But Oh! Blessed be his Name, *There is Forgiveness with* him, that he may *be feared, ver.* 4. And while *we have Fellowship one with another, the Blood of Jesus Christ his Son, cleanseth us from all Sin,* I *John* 1. 7. *As dear Children,* we Walk with God as a Father, who in infinite Grace, and boundless Compassion, pities our Weakness, pardons our shortness, and kindly accepts the Desires of our Souls to Walk with him: Calling that Walking, which we think not worth the Name; and is, indeed, rather staggering, and feeble attempting, than Walking. Oh amazing Grace! Christ will say to *the Righteous, I was hungry, and ye fed me; naked, and ye clothed me.* But what will be their Answer? Amazed at his Grace, in owning their weak Services, they'll say, Lord, when did we do this or that unto thee? We never did any thing for thee worthy of thy Notice, *Matt.* 25. 35, 37. Thus in respect of God's gracious Acceptance of their general Course, all the Saints may be said to walk with God.

But yet, there are some of whom it may be said by way of Eminence (in respect of their Uprightness, Agility, and Constancy) as of *Enoch,* That they Walk with God; while others are more uneven, flow, and inconstant in their Motion. And as there are to be found among the Saints, very different degrees in their Walking with God, as it respects different Persons, so respecting the same Soul at different Times.

Some of the Saints, walk as *Little Children,* who tho' fond of their Father's Company, yet being weak, are but slow in their Pace, and often fall. Some as *Young Men* arrived to a full Age, are nimble in their Course; being *Strong in Faith,* and *in the Grace that is in Christ Jesus,* to surmount all the Difficulties they meet with in their Way. And others there are, that Walk with God in the solid Wisdom of *Fathers. He* (saith the Apostle *John) that saith he abideth in him, ought himself also so to walk even as he walked,* I *John* 2. 6. *And I write unto you little Children, that you should walk* so (in Love) *Because your sins are forgiven you for his Name's sake, ver.* 12. *I write unto you young Men,* that you should walk so (in Manlike Strength) *because ye are strong, and have overcome the wicked one. And I write unto you Fathers,* that you should walk so (in solid and comprehensive Wisdom) *because ye have known him that was from the Beginning, ver.* 13. Thus it is with different Persons according to their different Ages in Christianity; And so with the same Soul at different Times.

At first, the Soul begins to Walk with God, in abundance of holy Fondness; tho' with a great deal of Weakness, Which the Lord takes exceeding kindly. *I remember thee* (says he) *the Kindness of thy Truth, when thou wentest after me in a Wilderness, Jer.* 2. 2.

But as it grows up in Christ to the State of Man-hood, it Walks stronger, and further with God. It can run greater Lengths with him than at first; For it goes *from Strength to Strength, Ps.* 84. 7. At first, if it did not see its Father's Smiles, it could not walk with him in the Faith of his Love. But now, tho' he should hide himself, and appear against it as an Enemy, yet it will *Trust* in Him tho' he should *Slay* it, *Job* 13. 15. And it continues to walk with him in the Faith of his Love, when there are nothing but Frowns upon his Face.

But tho' the Soul gets more Strength; yet alas! it oft wants that Keenness of Affection, that at first fill'd its heart, which the Lord complain'd of in the church of *Ephesus. I know thy Works* (says he) *and thy Labour, and thy Patience, and how thou canst not bear them which are evil: and thou hast try'd them which say they are Apostles, and are not; and hast found 'em Liars: and hast born, and hast Patience, and for my Name sake hast laboured and hast not fainted.* Here was now a great Degree of Strength in Walking with God; which therefore the Lord commends. And yet, *Nevertheless* (says he) *I have somewhat against thee, because thou hast left thy first Love, Rev.* 2. 2, 3, 4. God loves his Children, and he exceedingly delights in being lov'd by them again. Intense Love finds its greatest Pleasure in being ardently lov'd by the beloved Object. And for Creatures of the same [Make] thus to seek for, and find natural Love-Complacency in each other, is no strange thing.

But, That God, the glorious God, the Great [I AM] who is self-sufficient to his own Happiness, and needs none of his Creatures to make any Addition thereto, should yet, nevertheless, set his Heart upon such worthless, sinful Worms as we; and not only give us Leave to love him, but count himself happy in our Love, *Isa.* 62. 5. may well fill Heaven and Earth with Wonder! *Lord, what is Man that thou art thus mindful of him, Psal.* 8. 4. is a Theme fitted to the astonishing Wonder of Men and Angels, I *Pet.* 1. 12.

And if, on the other Hand, we take a View of that low, base, contemptible Worm [Man], the Sum of whose Happiness is only to be found in God, in being beloved by him, and loving him again; And yet see him fill'd with Unkindness and base Ingratitude, *Deut.* 32. 6. setting his Heart upon Trifles, *loving Strangers, and after them* he *will go, Jer.* 2. 25. It will appear to be another Wonder, at which Heaven and Earth may stand amazed! *Hear, O Heavens, and give Ear, O Earth;* (says the Lord) *for I have nourish'd and brought up Children, and they have rebell'd against me, Isa.* 1. 2. *Be astonish'd at this, for my people have committed two Evils: They have forsaken me the Fountain of Living Waters, and hew'd to themselves Cisterns, broken Cisterns, that can hold no Water, Jer.* 2. 21, 13.

And from hence will arise a third Wonder, if we take a View of God's everlasting and unchangeable Love, to this loveless, rebellious Creature. *Go yet,* (saith the Lord) *love a Woman (beloved of her Friend, yet an Adulteress) according to the Love of the Lord to the children of Israel, who look to other Gods, and love Flagons of Wine, Hos.* 3. 1. Lord, says the Soul, under the Sheddings abroad of this Love in its Heart, What not cast me off yet! No, says the Lord, *If Heaven above can be measur'd, and the Foundations of the Deep searched out beneath, then I also will cast off the Seed of Israel for all that they have done, Jer.* 31. 37. The Heaven for Height, and the Earth for Depth are to thee unsearchable; But there's a greater Unsearchableness, in the *Heights* and *Depths* of my Love, which secures thee from being cast off, *Eph.* 3. 18, 19. There's still a [Yet] for thee in my everlasting Kindness, Which reacheth beyond all thy Sinning!

But Oh! how this wonderful Grace melts the Soul, humbles it under all its Backslidings; and quickens it to walk with God, in all the Paths of obedience! Now *Ephraim* says, *What have I to do any more with Idols? Hos.* 14. 8. but doth this Fit of burning Love last? Ah! no; The Affection-part soon chills. *Thou saidst, thou wouldest not transgress* (saith the Lord) *when I had broke thy Yoke and burst thy Bonds: and yet under every green Tree thou wanderest playing the Harlot, Jer.* 2. 20. But when the soul again is made sensible of its decays in Love, Oh! how it's ashamed, and confounded in the Remembrance of all its wandering

Ways! *Ezek.* 16. 61. And sometimes it don't know whether it walks with God at all. It looks upon its defiled Feet, *John* 13. 10. *Luke* 5. 8. And is ready to faint away in Self-loathing. But then the everlasting Love of God is its Cordial, and the meritorious Blood of Christ its Bath; and so again it *goes up from the Washing clean* and strong, *Cant.* 6. 6. Thus it walks with God while a young Man, until it arrives to the State of Father-hood.

And then it walks with him in the solid and extensive Wisdom of a Father; being well acquainted with all manner of Ways of Walking with God. The Excellency of its Walk, when a Child, lies in its Love; to aim at a great deal, when it can do little. When a young Man, in its Strength; to overcome Opposition. And when a Father, in its Wisdom; to walk with God steadily and comprehensively. *When I was a Child,* says the Apostle, *I spake as a Child, I understood as a Child, I thought as a Child: but when I became a Man, I put away childish things,* I *Cor.* 13. 11.

But yet, alas! in the best of Saints there is such Imperfection in their Walk with God, that we may well wonder he'll give it the Name. The Grace that shines forth herein is amazing to us now; and will be Matter of Astonishment in the Day of Christ. When he'll open it before Men and Angels; saying, *Come ye Blessed of my Father, inherit the Kingdom, prepared for you from the Foundation of the World. For I was an hungred, and ye gave me Meat: Thirsty and ye gave me Drink,* &c. *Matt.* 25. 34, 35. *Ye are they* (say Christ) *which have continued with me in my Temptations.* And yet, poor Hearts, how did they forsake him in his last and great Trial? *Mark* 14. 50. And Christ knew this before he said so of 'em; and yet (says he) I *appoint unto you a Kingdom, as my Father hath appointed unto me, Luke* 22. 28. You have *suffer'd with me,* and you shall *reign with me, 2 Tim.* 2. 12. You have *come up* with me *out of great Tribulations,* and you shall *walk with me in white* as victorious Princes, *Rev.* 7. 14. *chap.* 3. 4. The Lord delights in the Walk of his Children now, *Psal.* 37. 23. their *Feet* being *shod with the Preparation of the Gospel of Peace, Eph.* 6. 15. Yea, he admires it, *Cant.* 7. 1. *How beautiful are thy feet with shoes, O prince's daughter!* And he'll openly shew his Grace in commending it ere long; for all our Walk by *faith* in this World, *2 Cor.* 5. 7. will be *found unto Praise, Honour and Glory* in the World to come. This *Grace* shall *be brought unto us at the Revelation of Jesus Christ,* I *Pet.* 1. 7, 13. *What manner of persons* then *ought we to be in all holy Conversation and Godliness! 2 Pet.* 2. 11. But to proceed. To Walk with God doth necessarily suppose,

Fourthly, Free Communion and mutual Fellowship. Communion, and Fellowship, which as I intend it here, consists in a free opening of Hearts, and a mutual Delight in each others Company; as is oft found in Persons walking together in Agreement. Thus of good Men it is said, *He that walketh with wise Men shall be Wise, Prov.* 13. 20. Because of that Communion that is between them in their Walk together; and so on the contrary of wicked Men, *But a Companion of fools shall be destroy'd.* And, *go not with a furious Man, least thou learn his Ways, Prov.* 22. 24, 25. And since God and his People walk together in the most perfect Agreement as *Friends, Jam.* 2. 23. *John* 15. 14. And in the sweetest Relations, as *Father* and *Children, 2 Cor.* 6. 18. as *Bridegroom* and *Bride, Isa.* 62. 5. as *Comforter* and comforted, *John* 14. 16. *Acts* 9. 31. Their Communion must needs be exceeding sweet; and their mutual Love-Delights in each other very intense, Communion with the Father in Love, with the Son in Grace, and with the Holy Ghost in Consolation, is the high and unspeakable Privilege of all the Saints, 2 *Cor.* 13. 14. The Father communes with us thro' the Son; the Son from the Father; the Holy Ghost from both. The Father opens all the Treasures of his Love to us in Christ; 'tis from off *the Mercy-Seat* he *communes* with us, *Rom.* 8. 39. *Exod.* 25. 22. The Son opens his Heart according to the Pattern-Love of the Father; having loved us as the Father hath loved him, *John* 15. 9. And the Holy Ghost opens his Grace, as proceeding from both, and co-equal with both; as *these Three are One,* I *John* 5. 7. One in Essence, and so One in Love. The Love of God our Father in Election, of Christ our Husband in Redemption, and of the Holy Ghost our Comforter in special Vocation, as co-equal Wonders of Grace, are gloriously open'd to the Saints in their Walk with God. *He* (Saith our Lord) *that loveth Me, and keepeth my Commandments,* (believing in my person, as his only Way to walk with God, and in me walking in all the Paths of Obedience) *shall be loved of my Father; and I will love him; and we will come and make our Abode with him, John* 14. 15, 22, 23. *Chap.* 15. 7, 14. And all this Love-Communion is carried on by the Holy Spirit; who, as our *Comforter, abides with us for ever,* and *takes* of the Things of Christ, and of the Father, and *shews* them unto us, *chap.* 16. 14, 15. 'Tis he *directs* our *Hearts into the Love of God, 2 Thess.* 3. 5. And O the Glories of Divine Love, which are open'd to the Saints in their Walking with God in Christ!

Here the amazing Depths of Wisdom and Grace, in Father, Son, and Spirit are display'd. The Father's in contriving, and providing the Mediator's Person, as our Way to Walk with him in, I *Cor.* 2. 7. *Psal.* 89. 20. The Son's, in assuming our Nature into personal Union with himself; that so he might be a fit *Medium* for all our Converse with God, *Heb.* 2. 16. *Job* 33. 6. And the Holy Spirit's, in becoming the *Anointing;* to fit and fill Christ's humane Nature, with all Grace, and Gifts, every way becoming the high Dignity of its personal Union with God the Son; and the full Discharge of his Mediatory Office, *Luke* 4. 18. The Spirit dwells in Christ immeasurably, *Job* 3. 34. In all his Grace and Gifts. Whence it is that he is not only *Full of Grace,* every way becoming the Hypostatical-Union; but also has *the Tongue of the Learned,* that he might *speak a Word in Season* to him that is *weary, Job* 1. 14. *Isa.* 50. 4. For which end, not only *the Lord God,* (the Father) but *his Spirit* also, did *send* him, *Isa.* 48. 16. Which is an high Commendation of the Spirit's Love. And Oh what particular Applications of this Grace of the Three-One God, are made to the Soul! *I have loved Thee,* saith the Lord, *with an everlasting Love, Jer.* 31. 3. [I have loved] thee, saith the Father. And [I have loved] thee, saith the Son. And [I have loved] thee, saith the Spirit. Ay, [Thee] particularly, personally, and individually, among the rest of my Chosen. And [Thee] also distinguishingly, from the many Thousands I pass'd by. 'Twas Thee, *Jacob, I loved,* when *I hated Esau* thy Brother; that was every way by Nature as good as thee, *Mal.* 2. 3. Aye, lov'd thee with an [everlasting] Love; That was from everlasting in Commencement, laying out itself in infinite Wisdom and Counsel for thy Good; That abides thro' Time unchangeably the same, and will run out to an endless eternity in Duration. Again, what glorious Discoveries, and particular Applications of Love, in all the Sacred Three, are made to the Soul, Walking in Christ as the great Redeemer!

"*I have lov'd thee,* says the Father, in calling my Son to be an *High Priest* for thee, *Heb.* 5. 5. To fulfil the Law, to satisfy Justice, *to make an end of Sin,* and *bring in* an *everlasting Righteousness, Dan.* 9. 24. I have lov'd thee, so as to make Him *Sin* for Thee, that Thou mightest be *made the Righteousness of God in him, 2 Cor.* 5. 21. I caus'd the *Sword* of Justice to *awake* against the *Man my Fellow,* that I might *turn* my *Hand* in a Way of Favour upon thee, *Zech.* 13. 7. Yea so great was my Love, that I took Pleasure in *Bruising* the Darling of my Heart for thee, that I might be at everlasting *Peace* with thee, *Isa.* 53. 5, 10. that I might freely, fully, righteously, and eternal pardon all thy Transgressions. Ay, notwithstanding I *knew* what an ungrateful rebellious Creature thou would'st prove," *Isa.* 46. 8. And, *"I have lov'd thee,* says the Son, in *emptying* myself of all my Glory for thee, taking upon me *the Form of a Servant,* and spending my whole Life in Service; which I thought but a *few Days for the Love* I had to thee, *Phil.* 2. 7. *Gen.* 29. 20. Yea, 'twas with the greatest *Delight* that I came to do *the Will* of my Father; though it was, that I should be made *Sin,* and a *Curse,* and give up my *Soul an Offering,* in thy Soul's stead, To *deliver* thee from *the Wrath to come,* Psal. *40. 7, 8. 2 Cor. 5. 21. Gal. 3. 13.* I *Thess.* 1. 10. And this tho' I knew that as *a Wife Treacherously departeth from her Husband,* so thou wouldest treacherously depart from Me," *Jer.* 3. 20. And, *"I have lov'd thee,* says the Spirit, in that I undertook to be an Indweller in thee, and a Sanctifier, and Comforter to thee. And this, though I knew the Contrarieties of thy Nature, to my holy Person and Work; yet in Pursuance of my everlasting Kindness (having loved thee as the Father and Son have lov'd thee) I *past by thee* when thou wast *cast out in the open Field, to the loathing of thy Person:* I saw thee *polluted in thy* own *Blood;* but none of thy Pollutions could alter my Heart towards thee; For *thy time was a time of Love;* Of [My] Love as well as of the [Father's] and [Son's] Love; And therefore I *said unto thee, Live, Ezek.* 16. 5, 6. I possest thee for Christ, having *desired* thee for my *Habitation, Psal.* 132. 13, 14. *Eph.* 2. 22. Took up my Abode in thee, as an Indweller to abide with thee for ever; As a Sanctifier to make thee Holy, by all the Changes that pass over thee; As a Comforter to comfort thee, in all thy Distresses. And though from the first Moment I began thy Conformity to Christ, thou hast been, more or less, acting contrary to my Holy Person and Design; quenching my Motions, and grieving me by thy disingenuous Carriage; yet in my unchangeable Grace, I still abide with thee; and as *the Work of* my *Hands,* I'll never leave thee nor forsake thee; But having *begun a good Work* in thee, I'll *perform* it *'till the Day of Christ,"* Psal. 138. 8. *Phil.* 1. 6. But Oh how this Love of the Three-One God, shed abroad in the Heart, forms its own Image there!

The Soul under the attracting Influence of God's first Love, afresh loves him again, I *John* 4. 19. And while, under the Holy Ghost's particular Application the *Name* of the Lord is *proclaimed,* as The *LORD, the LORD God, Merciful and Gracious, Long-suffering, abundant in Goodness and Truth, pardoning Iniquity, Transgression and Sin, Exod.*

34. 6, 7. The Soul with *Moses,* makes *haste, bows down and worships, ver.* 8. prostrating itself under the deepest Sense of its own Nothingness] before the Eternal [All;] adoring infinite Wisdom and boundless Grace, reigning to *Eternal Life,* thro' the Person and *Righteousness* of Jesus Christ the Lord, *Isa.* 40. 17. *2 Sam.* 7. 18, 19, 20, 21, 22. *Rom.* 5. 21. It *looks* afresh on him it has *pierc'd* and *mourns, Zech.* 12. 10. And with Bitterness bewails its own Wretchedness, by reason of an indwelling *Body of Sin and Death, Rom.* 7. 24. And all its Unkindness and Ingratitude to God as its Father, to Christ as its Husband, and to the Holy Ghost as its Comforter. And while it sees it has to do with a Sin-pardoning God, that will lay none of its Iniquities to its Charge. O how its Heart melts with Love! And how hateful doth Sin appear in its Sight! And as *with Weeping,* so *with Supplications* also the Lord *leads it, Jer.* 31. 9. What unutterable *Groanings* it sends forth into the Bosom of its Father, after compleat Deliverance from the Power and Being, as well as from the Guilt and Filth of Sin! Lord, says the Soul, Whatever thou dost with me, never suffer me to sin against thy Love! *Keep me from the Evil* that it may'nt *grieve* me, I *Chron.* 4. 10. And while the Child bemoans itself, the Father hears it in infinite Bowels: I *have surely heard* thee (says God) bemoaning thyself; And then breaks forth in fresh Discoveries of his Love, *Is Ephraim my dear Son? Is he a pleasant Child? I earnestly remember him still: my Bowels are troubled for him, I will surely have Mercy upon him, Jer.* 31. 18, 20. Lord, says the Soul, *what manner of Love* is thine! Is it [Me] thou call'st a *dear Son!* And a *pleasant Child!* whom thou wilt surely have Mercy upon; who am the very worst of all thy Children, and *no more worthy to be call'd thy Son, Luke* 15. 19. Aye, says the Lord, [Thou] art my dear Child, notwithstanding all thy Unkindness; And *my Grace is sufficient for thee, 2 Cor.* 12. 9. Sufficient to pardon, pity, strengthen, and at last compleatly to deliver thee. And then what Admirings of Grace, doth the Soul break forth into! *Grace, Grace* is its Cry! *Zech.* 4. 7. how unspeakably doth it *rejoyce in hope of the glory of God! Rom.* 5. 2. In believing Views of that State into which *nothing that defileth* can enter, *Rev.* 21. 27. when *Mortality shall be swallowed up of Life, 2 Cor.* 5. 4. Lord, says the Soul, then I shall love thee, and serve thee as I would, *Rev.* 22. 3. Then I'll bless thy Name for ever, for all thy Loving-kindness; when my Heart is wound up to the highest Pitch of Holiness, *Psal.* 145. 1. Mean while, pardon my Shortness, pity my Weakness, and help my Infirmities; tho' I think myself the

most ungrateful of all thy Children, thy Kindness and my Unkindness being set together; yet, Lord, since thy *Grace is sufficient for me,* even for [me] I'll go on rejoycing and glorying in it, as distinguishing, free, full, and eternal; even while I *loath* my *self* in my own Sight, for all my *Abominations, Ezek.* 20. 43. This is a little of the Talk God and his People have with each other, while walking together in Christ: and as they commune with each other in Christ the Great Way, so in all the lesser Paths comprehended in him.

In the Way of Faith, or divine Revelation, they sweetly walk and talk together as Friends. *I call you not Servants, but Friends* (saith our Lord) *for the Servant knoweth not what his Lord doth: but all things that I have heard of my Father I have made known unto you, John* 15. 15. The Gospel in all its glorious Doctrines, is a *hidden Mystery* to them that are *lost;* notwithstanding the external Revelation of it in the written Word, *2 Cor.* 4. 3. But God herein not only walks with his own in peculiar Favour, opening to them his Mind, by the internal Revelation of his Spirit, so as that they know *the Truth as it is in Jesus,* is to be walk'd in by Faith; But he herein also talks with 'em in special Grace, making particular Applications of the Truths known, as concerning them individually. So that they not only *know the Truth,* but the *Truth makes* 'em *free, John* 8. 32. They know it for themselves; and their *Hearts burn within* 'em, while the Lord talks with 'em about it, opening to them the Scriptures, *Luke* 24. 32. The Saints Knowledge of Gospel-Mysteries, is *Fellowship*-Knowledge, Eph. 3. 9. As for Instance; in the great Doctrine of Forgiveness, the Soul not only knows the Truth, by a special Revelation, as it concerns the chosen of God in general; but while the Lord communes with it herein, it knows it for its own self in particular. It's *I, even I,* saith the Lord, *that blotteth out* [thy] *Transgressions for my own Sake, and will not remember* [thy] *Sins, Isa.* 43. 25. which draws out the Soul into abundant Thanksgivings, with *David, Bless the Lord, O my Soul: and all that is within me bless his holy Name, who forgiveth all* [thine] *Iniquities, Psal.* 103. 1, 2. And so in every Doctrine of the Gospel.

But, Oh the unspeakable Sweetness of the Saints Communion with God herein! It's a *Joy* the *Stranger intermeddleth not with, Prov.* 14. 10. *Balaam* had a great Knowledge of what a Friend God was to his People; But he did not know him as [His] Friend. *I shall see him* (says he) *but not now: I shall behold him, but not nigh, Num.* 24. 17. *I shall see him, but not now,* as if he had said; "It's the Privilege of his People to have

Time-Communion with him as a Friend [Now;] But this is none of my Portion. I sha'n't see him now. I shall, indeed, behold him at last, but not [Nigh:] Not in the Nearness of Relation, as a loving Father, but as a terrible Judge." But the Knowledge of holy *Job* was attended with particular Application. *Tho'* (says he) *after my Skin, Worms destroy this Body, yet in my Flesh shall I see God: whom I shall see for my [self] and mine eyes behold, and not another, Job* 19. 26, 27. Again,

In the Way of instituted Worship, God and his People sweetly commune together. Oh what mutual opening of hearts to each other is here maintain'd! 'Tis *in the midst of the Congregation,* Christ *declares* his *Father's Name* to his *Brethren, Heb.* 2. 12. That *the Love wherewith* he has *loved* him *may be in* them, *John* 17. 26. And while the Saints *worship the Lord in his holy Mount at Jerusalem, Isa.* 27. 13. He makes *a Feast* for them, *of fat things,* of *Wines on the Lees well refined, Isa.* 25. 6. saying, *Eat, Oh Friend, Drink, yea, Drink abundantly, O beloved, Song* 5. 1. Oh! the opening of Divine Love, the Lord makes to his own, in all Gospel Provisions, while he abundantly *satisfies* them *with the Fatness of his House,* and *makes* them *drink of the River of* his *Pleasures! Psal.* 36. 8. 'Tis here God displays, and the Saints *speak of* his *Glory. Psal.* 29. 9. 'Twas this made *David pant* for God, as the chafed *Hart after the Water-brooks; To see thy Power and thy Glory* (says he) *as I have seen them in the Sanctuary, Psal.* 63. 2. 'Tis here the Lord resolves the difficult Questions of his People both in relation to themselves and others. *When I went into the Sanctuary* (says the Psalmist) *then I understood their End;* And how *I am continually with thee,* and *holden by my right Hand, Psal.* 73. 17, 23. And as God opens his Heart to his People, so with what Freedom do they open their Hearts, both in Prayer and Praise to him, as their own God in Sion! *Oh God* (says David) *thou art my God, early will I seek thee: My soul thirsteth for thee. My Flesh longeth for thee in a dry and thirsty Land, where no Water is. To see thy Power and thy Glory, as I have seen thee in the Sanctuary. Because thy loving Kindness is better than Life: My Lips shall praise thee. Thus I will bless thee, while I live. I will lift up my Hands in thy Name. My Soul shall be satisfy'd as with Marrow and Fatness; and my Mouth shall praise thee with joyful Lips, Psal.* 63. 1, 2, 3, 4, 5. A glorious Account of Communion with God in Church-Worship, which his Soul thirsteth after.

Oh what sweet and mutual Intercourse is held between God and his Children in all Divine Ordinances; while Strangers know nothing of this inside Glory of Worship; and content themselves with a bare external Form! The Saints *know* Christ's *Voice, Joh.* 10. 4. From the Voice of the Minister, and if he says nothing to 'em in the Ministry, the most eloquent Discourse will be but an empty sound. Prayer and Praise, without Converse with God in 'em, are empty things to a Soul thirsting for Him. And as the Lord creates an Appetite in the Souls of his Children, which nothing but Communion with himself can fill; so he answerably satisfies the longing Soul, *Psal.* 107. 9. *My People* (says he) *shall be satisfied with* [my Goodness] *Jer.* 31. 14. They long for the Openings on my Heart to them in my infinite Goodness; And with the Display thereof they shall be abundantly satisfy'd. And as in Publick, so

In Private Worship also, God and his People sweetly commune together. They mutually delight to open their Hearts to each other when alone. God call'd' *Abraham alone,* and *blest* him, *Isa.* 51. 2. *And Isaac* went *out into the Fields to meditate,* that he might be alone with God, *Gen,* 24. 63. To instance in the great duty of Prayer, when *Jacob* was *left alone* the Lord appears to him, and he *wrestles* with him *'till break of Day, Gen.* 32. 24. How did he open his distressed Heart to God in Prayer? *And Jacob said, Oh God of my Father Abraham, and God of my Father Isaac, the LORD which saidst unto me, Return unto thy Country, and to thy Kindred, and I will deal well with thee: I am not worthy of the least of all thy Mercies, and of all the Truth thou hast shewed to thy Servant; for with my Staff I passed over this Jordan, and I am become two Bands. Deliver me, I pray thee, from the Hand of my Brother Esau: for I fear him, lest he smite me, and the Mother with the Children. And thou saidst, I will surely do thee good, and make thy Seed as the Sand of the Sea for Multitude, ver,* 9, 10, 11, 12. With what Faith, Humility and Thankfulness doth he plead for the present Deliverance! And how did he wrestle with God for it? *Let me go,* saith the Lord, *and he said, I will not let thee go, except thou bless me, ver.* 26. And *as he wept and made Supplication to him, Hos.* 12. 4. So what Answers of Blessing did he receive! *Thy Name* (says the Lord) *shall no more be called Jacob, but Israel: for as a Prince hast thou Power with God and with Men, and thou hast prevailed; and he blest him there, Gen.* 32. 28, 29. Again, what an Instance of Communion with God, in this part of private Worship, have we recorded concerning *Abraham?* When the Lord appears to him saying, *I am thy Shield, and thy exceeding great Reward, Gen.* 15. 1. he straightway falls down and worships, opening his Heart to him, relating to his present Case. *Lord GOD,* (says he) *what wilt thou give me seeing I go childless? Behold to me thou hast given no Seed; and lo, one born in mine House is mine Heir, ver.* 2, 3. *And behold the Word of the Lord came unto him saying, This shall not be thine Heir, but he that shall come forth out of thine own Bowels shall be thine Heir, ver.* 4. And as when God drew near, he open'd his heart to him upon his own Account, so upon the Account of others also; When the Lord appear'd to him, saying, *I am the Almighty God, walk before me, and be thou perfect, Gen.* 17. 1. *Abram fell on his face: and God talked with him, saying, As for me, behold, my covenant is with thee, and thou shalt be a Father of many Nations. And I will make thee exceeding fruitful, and establish my Covenant with thee, and thy Seed after thee, in their generations; to be a God to thee, and to thy Seed after thee, ver.* 3, 4, 5, 6, 7. Particularly acquainting him with the Birth of *Isaac, ver.* 16. *Abraham* takes this Opportunity of God's opening his Heart to him herein, to intercede for *Ishmael. And he said, Oh that Ishmael might live before thee! And God said, Sarah thy Wife shall bear thee a Son indeed, and thou shalt call his Name Isaac: and I will establish my Covenant with him, for an everlasting Covenant, and with his Seed after him: And as for Ishmael, I have heard thee,* &c. *but my Covenant will I establish with Isaac. And he left off talking with him, and God went up from Abraham, ver.* 18, 19, &c. And so also, when *Abraham* was alone with God, and God open'd to him his Design to destroy *Sodom* and *Gomorrah, Gen.* 18. 20, 21, 22. *Abraham drew near and said, Wilt thou also destroy the Righteous with the Wicked: And mot spare the place for their sakes, if thou shalt find fifty there?* &c. till he comes down to ten. But O with what heavenly Freedom, godly Fear, and holy Reverence, doth he manage all his Pleas with God for the Salvation of that Place! And how familiarly and repeatedly did the Lord answer him! Nor did he leave communing with *Abraham* until he had put up his last Petition, and said he would *speak no more, ver.* 23, &c. O amazing Grace! And as Communion with God in private Worship was *Abraham's* Privilege, so likewise, *they which be of faith* are, in this respect, *blessed with faithful Abraham, Gal.* 3. 9. It being theirs also, *in every thing by prayer and supplication* to *make* their *requests known unto God with thanksgiving,* while he opens his Heart to them as their own God, *supplying* their *Need out of his Riches in Glory, by Christ Jesus, Phil.* 4.6, 19. Again,

Divine Providence, is another Way in which God and his People sweetly commune with each other. Whether prosperous of afflictive.

In prosperous Providences God not only walks with his own in Covenant-Grace and Faithfulness, and *in Blessing Blesseth* them; but he herein also doth talk with 'em. The Lord appear'd to *Jacob* at *Luz,* and told him, He would be with him in all Places whither he should go; and what great things he would do for him, *Gen.* 28. 13, &c. And he not only walk'd with him according to his gracious and faithful Engagements, as *Jacob* thankfully owns, *Gen.* 32. 10. But when God was about to advance *Jacob,* from his love and servile State in *Laban's* Family, and to take the Riches of *Laban* and bestow 'em upon him, he talks with him about it. *The Angel of the Lord spake unto him, saying, Jacob: and he said, Here am I, Gen.* 31. 11. *And he said, Lift up now thine Eyes and see, all the Rams that leap upon the Cattle are ring-straked, speckled and grizzled: for I have seen all that Laban doth unto thee, ver.*12. (I have seen all thy Affliction, and) *I am the God of Bethel, ver.* 13. (I remember what I said unto thee then; and my Heart is still the same towards thee. I am the very same God still; nor will I fail to perform ought that I have spoken to thee of) *Arise now, get thee out from this Land,* &c. So likewise, when the Lord was about to advance *Jacob,* from an afflicted starving Condition unto a State of Plenty in the Land of *Egypt; God spake unto Israel in the Visions of the Night; And said, Jacob, Jacob: and he said, Here am I. And he said, I am God, the God of thy Father: Fear not to go down into Egypt; for I will there make of thee a great Nation. I will go down with thee into Egypt,* &c. *Gen.* 49. 2, &c.

Oh happy Soul, that God thus opens his Heart to in Prosperity! Telling 'em, He will go with 'em into it, and what he will do for them there! 'Tis this affects the Hearts of God's Children, and makes 'em with *David,* break forth into Wonder and Thanksgiving. *Who am I, Oh Lord God? And what is my House, that thou hast brought me hitherto? 2 Sam.* 7. 18. (That thou hast rais'd me from the Sheepfold, from following the Ewes great with young, to the Dignity of the Throne of Israel) *For thy Word sake,* and *according to thine own Heart, hast thou done all these great things, ver.* 21. So,

In afflictive Providences, God and his People have sweet Communion with each other. He opens his Heart-Love to 'em as the Fountain-Cause of all their Afflictions. *As many as I love I rebuke and chasten, Rev.* 3. 19. *shews 'em their Transgressions, wherein they have exceeded, Job* 36.

9. Acquaints 'em with the Design of all his Chastisements, to *purge away* their *Sin,* that they might be *Partakers of his Holiness, Isa.* 27. 9. *Heb.* 12. 10. And what Honour does he put upon them herein in Conformity to Christ; that they might *glorify* him *in the Fires, Rom.* 8. 17. *Isa.* 24. 15. He opens the Grace of his Heart to 'em in the Gift of every Trial, and how exceeding precious it is; in as much as hereby the Graces of his Spirit shall be exercis'd and increas'd in order to their being own'd, and *crown'd in the Day of Christ, Phil.* 1. 29. I *Pet.* 1. 7. But Oh! how the Foundation of this Love, open'd to the Saints in Afflictions, makes 'em *Drink and forget their Poverty, and remember their Misery no more, Prov.* 31. 7. 'Tis the opening of their Father's Heart, when his Rod is upon their Back, makes 'em run into his Bosom, *humble* themselves under his *mighty Hand, Rom.* 5. 5. *Jam.* 4. 10. Acknowledge their Iniquity, justify his righteous Proceedings, *Luke* 15. 21. *Jer.* 12. 1. Adore his Sovereignty, admire his Wisdom and Grace, and delightfully submit to his Will, when it crosseth theirs, *Job* 1. 21. *Rom.* 11. 33. *Lam.* 3. 22. *Mark* 14. 36. *Job.* 18. 11. 'Tis this makes 'em *patient,* and exceeding *joyful* in all their *Tribulations, 2 Cor.*7. 4. *For this Cause* (saith the Apostle) *we faint not, though our outward Man perish, yet our inward Man is renewed Day by Day. For our light Affliction, which is but for a Moment, worketh for us a far more exceeding and eternal Weight of Glory, 2 Cor.* 4. 16, 17.

At times, indeed, it may be said of the dear Saints, as of *Israel* of old, *the Soul of the People fainted because of the Way, Numb.* 21. 4. *Psal.* 107. 5. But then the Lord, as their sweet Companion, who *comforteth* them *in all* their *Tribulations, 2 Cor.* 1. 4. graciously speaks to their Hearts, *Hos.* 2. 14. saying, *Fear not, for I am with thee; be not dismayed, for I am thy God: I will help thee, yea, I will strengthen thee, yea I will uphold thee with the right Hand of my Righteousness, Isa.* 41. 10. *Thy Shoes shall be Iron and Brass, and as thy Day is, thy strength shall be, Deut.* 33. 25. Whereby *he giveth Power to the faint, and to them that have no Might he increaseth strength,* so that they *run* afresh without Weariness, and *walk* without fainting, *Isa.* 40. 29, 31. If God doth but speak to a Child of his Affliction, and say, I am thy God still, and whatever I take from thee, I'll never take myself from thee, 'twill make it immediately to run into his Bosom, fall down at his Feet, and say, Lord, *I am thine, Psal.* 119. 94. Do with me what thou pleasest: Thou shalt *choose* my *Inheritance* for me, *Psal.* 47. 4. *Christ shall be magnified in my Body, whether it be by Life, or by Death, Phil.* 1. 20. Enable me but to glorify thee in whatever State I am, and then do with me what thou wilt. As a dear Servant of the Lord once said, "Let Christ make what he will of me, so he make but his own Glory out of me, I have enough." The Saints in conformity to Christ, are not only reconciled to take up the Cross; but they delight to do the Will of God in this respect: 'Tis their Meat and Drink. *I take Pleasure* (says the Apostle) *in Infirmities, in Reproaches, in Necessities, in Distresses, in Persecutions for Christ's Sake, 2 Cor.* 12. 10. And as God and his People walk together as Friends, so he revealeth to them his Secrets.

The Secret of the Lord is with them that fear him, and he will shew them his Covenant, Psal. 25. 14. And both Prosperous, and Afflictive Providences are particularly included in the Covenant. *Psal.* 111. 5. *and* 89. 30, &c. *Surely the Lord God will do nothing; but he revealeth his Secret to his Servants the Prophets, Amos,* 3. 7. And thus he dealt with his Friend *Abraham: Shall I hide from Abraham, the Thing which I do, saith the Lord, Gen.* 18. 17. And *Abraham's* Children partake of *Abraham's* Blessing, *Gal.* 3. 9. And as God openeth his Secrets to his People as Friends, so they also reveal their Secrets to him again, in the Faith of his being their Friend. They *open* their *Cause* unto him, and *shew before* him all their Trouble, *Jer.* 20. 12. *Psal.* 142. 2. And oh! with what unspeakable Pleasure (at times) can they trust God with the Secrets of their Hearts, and the whole of their Concerns, about which they can converse with no Creature! And as God communes with his People, opening his Heart to them in the Ways of his Providence, as all things are for their Sakes, whether Prosperous, or Afflictive; So this abundant Grace, opens their Hearts to him again *in many Thanksgivings, which redound to the Glory of God, 2 Cor.* 4. 15. Again,

In the way of Conversation-Holiness, God and his People have Communion with each other. The Lord not only accepted *Enoch's* Person, and his walk with him in Christ; but he also graciously testifi'd his well pleasedness: He *had this Testimony, that he pleased God, Heb.* 11. 5. So of *Abel* also; God, not only had *respect unto Abel, and to his Offering,* but he *testifi'd of his Gifts, ver.* 4. Manifested his well pleasedness. And when the saints at *Philippi* had professed their Subjection to the Gospel of Christ, in sending the Apostle *Paul* a full supply of his Necessities; The Lord not only accepted the same, but would have them acquainted therewith; that it was *an Odour of a sweet Smell, a Sacrifice Acceptable, well pleasing unto God, Phil.* 4. 18. And not only doth the Lord graciously testifie his well pleasedness to his Children herein; but he also , in boundless Grace, oft acquaints 'em with the great Things he designs to do for 'em. Thus *Cornelius*, a just Man, fearing God, that pray'd to him alway, and gave much Alms to the People, while he was yet Fasting and Praying before God, had a Messenger dispatch'd from Heaven, to acquaint him, that his *Prayers* and his *Alms*, were *come up for a Memorial before God, Acts.* 10. 4. *Send therefore, (saith the Lord) for one Simon, whose Sirname is Peter, who shall tell thee Words whereby thou, and all thy House shall be saved, Chap.* 11. 14. God's dear Children, under a felt Sense of their own Dryness and Barrenness, are oft saying, *I am a dry Tree.* But what will the Lord say to 'em? *Let not the Eunuch say I am a dry Tree. For thus saith the Lord to the Eunuchs that keep my Sabbaths, and choose the things that please me, and take hold of my Covenant, (that walk with* me in Christ unto all well-pleasing) *Even to them will I give in mine House, and within my Walls, a Place and a Name better then of Sons and Daughters*; (a Name for Fruitfulness, notwithstanding all their apprehended Barrenness, in my House below, yea and in my House above also.) *I will give them an everlasting Name that shall not be cut off,* Isa. 56. 3, 4. 5. And the Grace the Lord manifests to his Children, in noticing their weak Services here, and Owning and Crowning them hereafter, is so amazing great; that at times, they have hardly room enough in their Hearts to take it in. They are like the Disciples, when they saw Christ risen from the Dead, they *believed not for Joy, and wondred,* Luk. 24. 41. If the Lord tell 'em he accepts their willing Mind, *when to Will is present with 'em*, notwithstanding the weakness of their *Flesh*, which prevents their doing the Good they would, 2 *Cor.* 8. 12. *Rom.* 7. 18. *Mat.* 26. 41. 'Twill make them leap for Joy; and humble themselves in the Dust before him; acknowledging that they *are the most unprofitable Servants, Eccles.* 9. 7. *Luk.* 17. 10. If Christ say, *How fair is thy Love, my Sister, my Spouse! How much better is thy Love than Wine! And the Small of thine Ointments than all Spices! Cant.* 4. 10. 'Twill make her blush at her own Blackness; *Chap.* 1. 5. Adore his Fairness, *ver.* 16. And with ravishing Wonder, cry out, *Who is God like unto thee, That pardoneth Iniquity, and passeth by the Transgression of the Remnant of thy Heritage! Mic.* 7. 18. Lord, *not unto me, not unto* me, *but unto thy Name be the Glory, Psal..* 115. 1. Thou art Beauty, but I am Blackness. If I shine as *the Moon* in my proper Sphere, 'tis because thou

art Risen, and thy *Glory* is seen upon me, *Cant.* 6. 10. *Isa.* 60. 2. 'tis thy
Glory, as the Sun, casts all my Lustre! I shine but with the reflection of
thy Rays! In myself I am a dark Body; and if I have any Light, 'tis
deriv'd from thee, and gloriously comprehended in thee. what manner of
Love, Lord, is thine, that thou should'st call me fair! But oh! who can
express the free and mutual openings of Hearts, there are at Times,
between God and his People, in their walk with each other! And as they
freely Converse together, so they mutually delight in each others
Company.

Thou are all fair my Love, (says Christ) *There is no Spot in thee,*
Cant. 4. 7. *Come with me from Lebanon my Spouse; with me from*
Lebanon, ver. 8. *Let me see thy Face, let me hear thy Voice; for sweet is*
thy Voice, and thy Countenance is comely, Chap. 2. 14. *How fair and*
how pleasant art thou, O Love for Delight! Chap. 7. 6. *Thou shalt be*
called Hephzibah, for the Lord delighteth in thee, Isa. 62. 4. And as *the*
*Lord takes pleasure in them that fear him, Psal.*147. 11. So they in him
also: God is their *exceeding Joy, Psal.* 43. 4. *Come, my Beloved,* (says the
Spouse) *let us go forth into the Field; let us lodge in the Villages*: (I
delight in thy Company, and am unwilling to go without thee) *Let us go*
up early to the Vineyards, let us see if the Vine flourish, whether the
tender Grape appear, and the Pomegranates bud forth: There will I give
thee my Loves, Cant. 7. 11. 12. *Whom have I in Heaven but thee?* (says
Asaph) and there is none on Earth I desire besides thee, Psal. 73. 25. *My*
People are my *Portion* saith the Lord, and *Jacob is the Lot* of my
Inheritance, Deut. 32. 9. And again, they say, *the Lord is my Portion,*
Lam. 3. 24. And oh! with what unspeakable Delight, do they mutually
say of each other, *the Lines are fallen unto me in pleasant Places, yea,*
I have a goodly Heritage! Psa. 16. 6.

That the Saints indeed should rejoyce in God as their Portion, and
have their Hearts filled with exceeding Gladness in his Company, *Psal.*
46. 7. is no Wonder; But that God should call them his *Jewels, Mal.* 3.
17. And say they have *ravish'd* his *Heart,* Song, 4. 9. is an astonishing
thing! We shall wonder out Eternity at this Grace. Our Life in Heaven
will be a Life of Communion. We shall live in Love, Love and live for
ever. God's Love open'd to us in Glory-Vision, will, as an Eternal Fire,
cause our Hearts to ascend to him, in Flames of Love for ever. 'Tis the
vehement Love-*Flames* of Jehovah, *Cant.* 8. 6. will set our Souls a
Burning. But mean while, there is *fullness of Joy in his presence* now; as

well as *Pleasures at his Right Hand for evermore, Psal.* 16. 11. The Saints, in begun Communion with God here, *rejoyce with Joy unspeakable, and full of Glory, I Pet.* 1. 8. And while they know Divine *Love,* which *passeth Knowledge,* they are *fill'd with all the Fullness of God, Eph.* 3. 19. But the full Glory of Communion, and mutual Love Delights, between God and his People, is an unspeakable Thing, And better felt than exprest. I shall therefore pass on, to take a little Notice, that to walk with God, doth necessarily suppose,

In the *Fifth* and last Place, a sameness of Intention, Design, or End. Persons here among Men walking together, have often the same End in View, *Pro.* 1. 14. But God and his People always have.

God's End in walking with his People in Christ, and in all the Ways of Divine Appointment, is ultimately his own Glory; and subordinately their Good and Salvation. And this also is his Peoples End in walking with him.

Whatever God hath done, or doth do, for us in Christ, is *to the praise of the Glory of his Grace, Eph.* 1. 6. That he might *make known the Riches of his Glory, Rom.* 9. 23. 'Twas to *make himself an everlasting Name,* that the *Lord led forth his People* of old; and leads forth his People now, in all the wonderful Ways wherein he walks with 'em, *Isa.* 63. 12. And 'tis for this great Namesake, that the Lord will not forsake his People, I *Sam.* 12. 22. And such is his Grace, that he makes his People Good his End also in walking with 'em, as well as his own Glory.

The Lord will not forsake 'em, because it hath pleased him to make them [His] People: Too near and dear to be forsaken: He puts the Glory of his Name, and the good of his People together, as his End, in walking with his Rebellious Ones in infinite Forbearance. *For my Names Sake* (says he) *will I defer mine Anger, and for my Praise will I refrain for thee, that I cut thee not off, Isa.* 48. 9. It's for [Thee] my Rebellious Child, will I refrain, that I cut [Thee] not off; as well as for my own Praise. The Lord leads his People thro' all the Changes which attend their Wilderness-Way, *to do* 'em *good in their latter End, Deut.* 8. 15, 16. 'Tis he makes *all things work together for* their *Good, Rom.* 8. 28. And as he walks with 'em for their Good, so for their full and compleat Salvation; For all their time Salvations here, and for their Eternal Salvation hereafter. But 'tis the later of these I chiefly intend.

Thou went'st forth (says the Prophet) *for the Salvation of thy People, even for Salvation with thine Anointed, Hab.* 3. 13. The Lord *hath not*

appointed us unto Wrath; but to obtain Salvation thro' our Lord Jesus Christ, I *Thes.* 5. 9. And this is the End he still keeps in his Eye, in all the Ways he leads us, whether relating to Faith, or Practice. "Tis Salvation is the End, for which he leads us *thro' Sanctification of the Spirit, Obedience, and Sprinkling of the Blood of Jesus, 2 Thes.* 2. 13. I *Pet.* 1. 2.

And that God's Glory and our Salvation, should be his End in walking with us, is amazing Grace! What an Astonishing Wonder is it, that he that is [the God of Glory] *Acts* 7. 2. So far above all Praise, *Nehem.* 9. 5. That no Creature can add any thing to the Essential Glory, of his Perfect, Self-sufficient, and Immense Being, *Job.* 35. 7. *Heb.* 11. 6. Should nevertheless cast the Rays of his Glory upon the Works of his Hands! And admit Creatures to see and admire it! He might always have hid his Glory in his own Invisible Being; and never have *Shin'd into our Hearts, to give us the Light of the Knowledge* thereof *in the Face of Jesus Christ! Col.* 1. 15. *2 Cor.* 4. 6. And

Further, What a Wonder is it, that this Great God, who might have Glorifi'd his Wisdom, Holiness, Justice, Power, and Truth, in our Everlasting Destruction, as Sinners, Should nevertheless Glorify his Mercy and Grace, and all the Perfections of his Being, in our Eternal Salvation! That God should walk with us, rejoicing to do us Good now, and to save us at the last, of free Sovereign Favour, is very amazing! And so much the more, in that it is Distinguishing! And when the exceeding Riches of it are Open'd, in all *his Kindness to us thro' Christ Jesus,* it must needs be *in the Ages to come,* even to an endless Eternity, *to the Praise of the Glory of his Grace! Eph.* 2. 7. and 1. 6. And as God's End in walking with his People in Christ, and in all the Ways of Divine Appointment, is ultimately his own Glory, and Subordinately their Good, and Salvation; So also this is their End in walking with him.

the Saints walk with God by Faith in Christ, not only for their own Safety, but also for his Glory. When they *bow the Knee at the Name of Jesus,* and *confess* that *Christ is Lord,* it's *to the Glory of God the Father, Phil.* 2. 10. 11. The new Nature in their Souls, is of the same Mind with Christ, who did not *seek* his own *Glory,* but his Father's that *sent* him, *Joh.* 8. 50. and 7. 18. And those Saints that walk the closest with God, do most regard his Glory as their End. If they are *fill'd with the Fruits of Righteousness, which are by Christ Jesus,* (whether as to Faith or Holiness) 'tis *to the Glory and Praise of God, Phil.*1. 11. Christ proposes this as the highest End of his People's Obedience. *Herein* (says he) *is my Father Glorifi'd, that ye bring forth much Fruit, Joh.* 15. 8. And being *Married* unto Christ their Risen, ever living Husband, they *bring forth Fruit unto God, Rom.* 7. 4.

The Saints love the Glory of God above their own Salvation. And what a famous Instance of this have we in *Moses,* the Man of God? When *Israel* had Sinned, *let me alone Moses,* (says the Lord,) *that I may consume 'em: And I will make of thee a Great Nation, Exod.* 32. 10. But how doth *Moses* take this? Will he consent that God's People, should be destroy'd, and accept the Favour the Lord promis'd him hereupon? No verily. He saw that God's Glory would be lost, if *Israel* were Consum'd; and this lay so near his Heart, that he takes no Notice of the Personal Advantage, the Lord had told him should accrue to himself thereby; but falls a Pleading, that he would spare his People for his Great Names Sake. LORD, (says he) *why doth thy Wrath wax hot against thy People? Wherefore should the Egyptians speak and say, for Mischief did he bring them out to Slay 'em in the Mountains, and to consume 'em from the Face of the Earth? ver.* 11. 12. If thy People are Destroy'd, what will become of thy Glory, Lord? What wilt thou do to thy Great Name? Nay, he not only takes no Notice of the Personal Benefit he should reap thereby; but he goes further, and says, *O Lord, this People have Sinn'd a great Sin. Yet now, if thou wilt, forgive their Sin: If not, blot me, I pray thee, out of thy Book which thou hast Written, ver.* 31. 32. And thus *Paul,* that God might be Glorifi'd in the Conversion of his Kinsmen, could even *with* himself *accursed from Christ, Rom.* 9. 3. And tho' both these had attain'd an extraordinary Pitch of Holiness, and so their Love to God was wound up to an unusual Height; yet the Principle of Love, by which God's People walk with him, is the same in all the Saints, for Kind; tho' it riseth to a far higher Degree in some, and is more discernable than in others.

And as the Glory of God, is the Saints highest End in walking with him, so if he'll please to Glorify himself in 'em, and by 'em, they have the highest Joy. Yea, this alone, sometimes, holds the Hearts of God's People to walk with him in Ordinances and Duties; when they find no sensible Benefit thereby to themselves. Thus oft-times the Soul reasons, God had made it my Duty to walk with him here for his Glory; and if he may be Glorifi'd tho' I am not comforted, I'll go on to walk with him still.

Again, as God's Glory is the ultimate End, the Saints have in their Eye, in walking with him; So also their own Good, as a subordinate End, is regarded by 'em. God not only gives us leave, but has made it our Duty, to walk in all his Ways, and *keep* his *Commandments for* our *Good, Deut.* 10. 12, 13. *Praise ye the Lord,* (says the Psalmist) *For it is Good, yea, Pleasant, Psa.* 147. 1. To walk with God all manner of Ways, is natively sweet to the new Creature. To be *Spiritually minded,* is the Saints *Life, Rom.* 8. 6. They *draw near to God* because it's *Good* for 'em, *Psal.* 73. 28. And when they are near him, they say with *Peter, It's good to be here, Matt.* 17. 4. And as in their whole Walk, whatever they do, they *do all to the Glory of God, I Cor.* 10. 31. *That God in all things may be Glorified, I Pet.* 4. 11. And likewise for their own present Good; so also with regard to their Eternal Salvation.

The Salvation of their *Souls* is *the End* of their *Faith, I Pet.* 1. 9. Not only eventually, but designedly. And as God and his People, have a sameness of End in these Respects, in their walking with each other, so they assuredly do, and shall attain it.

God Glorifies himself, in walking with his People now for their Good. His People also Glorify his Name in their walk with him; and experimentally find it Good for 'em so to do. And when they are compleatly saved, God will be to the utmost Glorified. *The Pleasure of the Lord,* both as to his own Glory, and his Peoples Salvation, *shall prosper* in Christ's *Hand, Isa.* 53. 10. *I have Fought the good Fight,* (says the Apostle) *I have finish'd my Course, henceforth there's laid up for me a Crown of Righteousness, which the Lord the Righteous Judge will give me at that Day, 2 Tim.* 4. 7. 8. *And to all them who by patient Continuance in well-doing, seek for Glory, Honour, and Immortality, he'll give Eternal Life, Rom.* 2. 7. *There remaineth a Rest to the People of God,* (in their Father's House above, after all the Labour and Toil of the Way.) *Heb.* 4. 9. And God in infinite Grace, wisely conducts 'em all manner of Ways thro' the Wilderness, to *a City of Habitation, Psal.* 107. 7. To his own Palace Royal in Heaven. But *Eye hath not seen, nor Ear heard* the Glorious Things God hath *prepared* for them there, that walk with him in *Love* here, I *Cor.* 2. 9. *He is not asham'd to be called their God, for he hath prepared for them a City, Heb.* 11. 16. God hath made Preparation of Glory for his People, every way answerable to his own Greatness of God, and the Nearness of his Relation to them. And as he has prepar'd Glory for 'em; so he bestows it on 'em. *Enoch walked with*

God, and was not: for God took him, Gen. 5. 24. And this is the Privilege of every one that Walks with God, to be taken Home to the Lord, (either in an ordinary or an extraordinary way) to the full Enjoyment of Glory-Vision. *And so shall we be for ever with the Lord,* I *Thess.* 4. 17. Christ will come, to be *glorify'd in the Saints,* as well as to their compleat Salvation, 2 *Thess.* 1. 10. *Heb.* 9. 28. God will be glorify'd [in] his People, in making them so glorious; as well as [by] them in their Ascriptions of Glory to him. *Salvation and Glory* are put together in the Doxologies of the Saved ones, *Rev.* 19. 1. The *new Jerusalem,* the *Bride* the *Lamb's Wife,* when she comes down *from God out of Heaven,* will have *the glory of God, Rev.* 21. 9, 10, 11. But what the Greatness of God's Glory will be in the Salvation of his People, and theirs in being compleatly saved, is yet to be reveal'd, I *Pet.* 4. 13. I *John* 3. 2.

Thus (as enabled) I have said a little, of that great Abundance, which is contain'd in Walking with God, as it necessarily supposes,

First, An Agreement between God and the Soul.

Secondly, A Way in which both walk.

Thirdly, A continued Course or Series of Steps taken in that way.

Fourthly, Free Communion, or mutual Fellowship. And,

Fifthly, A sameness of Intention, Design, or End. To walk with God then, in brief,

Is, to be agreed with him; to have Christ our Way; to go on with him continually herein; to have free Communion, and mutual Fellowship, and in all to Intend, and Design the same End.

And that God and a Creature, God and a Sinner, should walk together in Agreement, familiarly as Friends; that Christ should be their Way, in his Person, Office, and Work; that herein they should go on continually with each other; maintaining free Communion, and mutual Fellowship, and in all, regard the same End, Is such a *Mystery of Godliness,* that *without Controversy* is very *great!* I *Tim.* 3. 16. *The Lord's doing,* and *marvellous in our Eyes! Psal.* 118. 23. And *this Honour have all the Saints. Praise ye the Lord, Psal.* 149. 9.

Thus having freely imparted the Light I have received; If the Lord will graciously please to make *manifest* by me, *the Savour of his Knowledge,* 2 *Cor.* 2. 14. herein, to your Soul, to your further Fellowship with the Truth; my soul shall rejoice, and my God have *the Glory:* Unto whom it is due *in the Church, by Christ Jesus, throughout all Ages, World without end, Amen, Eph.* 3. 21.

But *shall it be told him that I speak? If a Man speak, surely he shall be swallowed up, Job* 37. 20. How much more such a Babe as I, that *cannot order* my *Speech by reason of Darkness? ver.* 19. *God is great, we know him not,* and *his Ways are past finding out, Job* 36. 26. *Rom.* 11. 33. It's meet then, that his dearest Favourites, in speaking of him, and his Ways, should *serve the Lord with fear, and rejoice with trembling, Ps.* 2. 11. How much more such a Nothing sinful Worm as I? *God is greatly to be fear'd in the assembly of the Saints: To be had in reverence of all them that are about him, Ps.* 89. 7. And if Angels, in all their bright Orders, (Those Seraphs, for flaming Love of God, Cherubs, for swiftness in his Service) *vail their Faces,* as unworthy to look upon his Glory, *cover their Feet,* as unworthy to stand in his Presence; and are swift upon their *Wing* to obey his Commands, *Isa.* 6. 2. And yet he *put no trust* in these *his Saints; how much less in them that dwell in Houses of Clay, whose Foundation is in the Dust? Job* 4. 18, 19. If *the Heavens are not clean in his Sight,* when compar'd with his infinite Purity, *how much more filthy and abominable is Man that drinketh Iniquity like Water, Chap.* 15. 15, 16. With what Humility and Reverence then, should such a weak, contemptible Worm as I serve him? Even while, believing, I rejoice, that this great God, as my Father is Christ, pardons the Sinfulness, pities the Weakness, and delights to hear the broken Language of his Child; attempting to lisp out his Glory, tho' it ha'n't yet learned to speak plain! *Isa.* 38. 14. *So great are his infinite Bowels! Jer.* 31. 20.

Dear Brother, I shall commit the Whole of this my Answer to your first Request, to him that can *ordain Strength, and perfect Praise, out of the Mouth of Babes and Sucklings, Ps.* 8. 9. *Mat.* 21. 16. And next attempt the Solution of your Second: Which was, that I would give you a few Hints from *Joseph's* Blessing.

Deut. 33. 13, 14, 15, 16. Which, according to present Light, take as follows.

Deut. 33. 13. *And of Joseph he said, Blessed of the Lord be his Land, for the Dew, and for the deep that coucheth beneath.*

AND of Joseph he said] Joseph was rais'd up of God to be a Type of Jesus Christ, in his Sufferings and Glory. Which is plain to me, from *Gen.* 49. 23, 24. *The Archers have sorely griev'd him, and shot at him, and hated him. But his Bow abode in Strength, and the Arms of his Hands were made strong by the Hands of the mighty God of Jacob. From thence is the Shepherd, the Stone of Israel.*

God had design'd to advance *Joseph* to Royal Honour in *Pharoah's* Court; to be the very next in the Throne, set over all the Land of *Egypt.* Which was apparently done, when in Royal Apparel, with kingly Majesty, *Pharoah* made him ride in his second Chariot; while they cry'd before him, *Bow the Knee, Gen.* 41. 41, 42, 43. This wonderful Effect of divine Providence, was to render *Joseph* a lively Type of Christ, in his Mediatorial Glory and Kingdom: Whom God hath *highly exalted,* even to *sit down with him in his Throne, Rev.* 3. 21. aray'd with Glory and Honour, as Sovereign Lord of Heaven, Earth and Hell; and caused to *ride prosperously* upon the Word of Truth; while the Royal Proclamation's made before him, in all the Places of his Dominion, *Bow the Knee, Phil.* 2. 10.

But before *Joseph* was advanc'd, God made some Intimations thereof to him; Which, when he acquainted hid Brethren with, they *hated* him for it; tho' the Salvation of their temporal Lives depended thereon, *Gen.* 37. 5. so Christ, when he came unto his own Nation the *Jews,* acquainting them, That he was by his Father advanced to be their Messiah; they *received him not, John* 1. 11. And the more they saw the Glory of his Messiahship break forth, the more they hated him, *chap.* 15. 24. altho' it was impossible for them to have *Salvation in any other, Acts* 4. 12.

Joseph was shot at, and sorely griev'd, hated and sold by his Brethren, before his Advancement: And Christ first *suffer'd,* and then *enter'd into his Glory, Luke* 24. 26. The *Jews* reject him, *John* 18. 40. *Judas* selleth him, *Matt.* 26. 15. his Disciples forsake him, *ver.* 56. *the Assembly of the Wicked inclose* him, *Psal.* 22. 16. Thus was he hated and sorely grieved, in this *Hour and Power of Darkness, Luke,* 22. 53.

But, as *Joseph's* Bow abode in Strength, the Arm of his Hands being made strong by the Hands of the mighty God of *Jacob;* so did Christ's. His Father strengthned him by his supporting Presence, even when his comforting Presence was with-held; and he call'd him to conflict with the combined Wrath of Heaven, Earth and Hell.

Joseph's Brethren thought they had done enough to hinder his Advancement, when they had sold him into *Egypt:* And Men and Devils thought when they had got Christ crucified, they had fully put an End to his Glory and Reign. But Oh, how did the infinite Wisdom of Jehovah, *take the Wise in their own Craftiness, Job* 5. 13. And not only disappoint the Designs of the Enemy, but effectually over-rule them for his own Glory, and his People good.

From thence is the Shepherd, the Stone of Israel: From [thence], from
the Wisdom and Power of God ever-ruling the Malice of *Joseph's*
Brethren; and from that very Time of their hating, and selling him into
Egypt, did God begin to advance him, as the Typical Shepherd, and Stone
of Israel; (Upon which Account *Joseph* has the Name) to Sustain and
Feed the Church of God in *Jacob's* Family. Who when the Time of
Famine came on, must have died for Want, had it not been for an
advanc'd *Joseph.*

But when they were reduced to a starving Condition, having heard
that there was *Corn in Egypt,* they come bended Suppliants to *the Lord
of the Land;* who not only supplies their Wants, but to their amazing
Wonder, opens himself in the Nearness of his Relation. *I am Joseph your
Brother, whom ye sold into Egypt. Now therefore, be not grieved that ye
sold me hither: for God did send me before you to preserve Life: to
preserve you a Posterity in the Earth, and to save your Lives by a great
Deliverance, Gen.* 45. 4, 5, 7. You thought *evil* against me, but *God
meant it for good, to save much People alive. Now therefore fear ye not,
I will nourish you and your little ones, chap.* 50. 20, 21.

And as it was with *Joseph* the Type, so with *Jesus,* the glorious
Antitype. *From thence is the Shepherd, the Stone of Israel,* really. From
[thence] from the infinite Wisdom of *Jehovah,* over-ruling the Rage of
Hell; and from that very Time when Men and Devils, in their Hatred,
triumph'd over Christ, God began to exalt him: The Foundation of his
kingly Throne, being now laid in his priestly Blood. *He humbled himself
onto Death, even the Death of the Cross. Wherefore God also hath highly
exalted him, and given him a Name that's above every Name: That at the
Name of* Jesus *every Knee should bow, Phil.* 2. 8, 9, 10. This crucified
Jesus, *God exalted as a Prince and a Saviour, to give Repentance unto
Israel, and Remission of Sins, Acts* 5. 31. And God having rais'd him
from the Dead, set him at his own Right Hand, and sent down the Holy
Ghost from the ascended Saviour, to glorify Christ in the Church: Now
he's openly laid as the Foundation Stone in *Sion,* and declared to have *all
Power in Heaven and Earth given* him, as the great Shepherd of *Israel.*

And when there ariseth a mighty Famine in his Brethren's Land,
and they come bended Suppliants to this great Lord, having heard of Life
for 'em, in an once crucify'd, but now exalted Jesus, when they are just
ready to perish; Oh with what Gladness they receive this Word, *Acts* 2.
41. And how transcendent is their Joy when he manifests himself to

them, as their Friend and Brother; telling 'em, That because he *lives, they shall live also! John* 20. 17. *and* 14. 19. Yea, with what an amazing Glory, doth infinite Wisdom and Grace, shine in their View, while they see Jesus their Brother, that's now Alive, was once *deliver'd* unto Death for Them, *by the determinate Counsel and Fore-knowledge of God;* even when by *wicked Hands* he was *crucified and slain, Acts* 2. 23. Thus it appears that *Joseph* was a Type of Christ. To proceed then,   *Blessed of the Lord be his Land*] *Joseph's* Land, was *Joseph's* Inheritance, *Josh.* 16. 4. Christ's Inheritance is his People, *Deut.* 32. 9. *Joseph's* Land was eminently blest, in relation to him, as His. And Christ's People are transcendently blest, in relation to Him, above all the World beside, *Deut.* 33. 29. And this by JEHOVAH; Who, alone is that Self-existent Being, which is infinitely able to give Being to all his Creatures, and to all their Happiness, *Psal.* 83. 18. *Isa.* 26. 4. And by Him also, as having engag'd himself by Covenant; and so infinitely faithful to all his gracious Engagements, *Exod.* 6. 3, 6.

For the precious Things of Heaven.] A comprehensive Phrase, wherein are summarily contain'd the particular Blessings after mentioned. *Joseph's* Land, was bless'd, as His, with all the natural Influences of the Heavens. Christ's People are *blest* in Him, with *all spiritual Blessings in the Heavenlies, Eph.* 1. 3.

For the Dew,] the natural Dew, which fell upon *Joseph's* Land, to refresh the Plants and Herbs almost scorch'd up by the Heat of the Sun, was a great Blessing, conducing to its Fruitfulness. But the Heavenly Distillations of Christ's Spirit and Grace, which fall upon the Saints, to refresh and keep them green and flourishing, under all the scorching Heat of Persecution, they meet with from Sin, Satan, and the World, are a more transcendent Blessing, conducing to their more abundant Fruitfulness. For while God is *as the Dew to Israel,* he *grows as the Lilly, Hos.* 14. 5.

And for the Deep that coucheth beneath] the Natural Waters of the Sea, that great Deep, conveying themselves thro' Veins and Caverns of the Earth, were a further Blessing unto *Joseph's* Land. Which sets forth the transcendent Blessedness of Christ's People, in that the infinite, unfathomable Deep of Divine Love, thro' the crucified flesh of Jesus, conveys itself into their Souls, to water their Roots. And the Blessedness of the Saints herein, is, indeed, unspeakable; even when, as *the Deep that coucheth beneath,* it runs under-ground out of their Sight. 'Tis the secret

Conveyances of this Love, that keep the Saints Roots full of Moisture. 'Tis this supplies 'em with a Sufficiency of Sap, to endure the scorching Heat of Persecution, which not only withers the Leaf of others, but dries 'em up at the Roots. At Times, indeed, in its exuberant Fullness, and freeness, it breaks up above-ground in our Sight, and flows forth abundantly: but even then, it's a *Deep* that still *coucheth beneath.* Beneath all Dispensations, and beyond all our Apprehensions. 'Tis but the Surface of this great Deep that we behold; or rather a visible Effect of that Love, that abides in the Heart of God towards us; which in the Infinity of its *Depth,* will for ever be beyond the Search of created Understanding, *Eph,.* 3. 19. O who can set forth the Saints Blessedness, as interested in this unfathomable Knowledge-passing Love! They are for ever secured from drying up at Roots, because this immense Deep that waters 'em is inexhaustible; and the Channels thro' which it runs, (the Merits of Christ, the everlasting Covenant, the free and absolute Promises) can never be stopt.

Ver. 14. *And for the precious Fruits brought forth by the Sun*] *Joseph's* Land was greatly bless'd with the sweet, warming, quickening Influences of the natural Sun; to bring forth and ripen the precious Fruits that grew thereon. Which sets forth the unspeakable Blessedness of the Saints, under the transcendent Influences of Christ *the Sun of Righteousness, Mal.* 4. 2. by whose supernatural Life and Heat, arising upon 'em in bright Beams of glorious Light, all the precious *Fruits* of the Spirit are brought forth, and ripen'd in their Hearts and Lives for God, *Phil.* 1. 11.

And for the precious Things put forth by the Moon,] *Joseph's* Land was bless'd, not only with the sweet warming Influences of the Sun, but also with the moistening Influences of the Moon; some precious Plants and Fruits being brought forth more eminently by the Moon, as others by the Sun, (as Naturalists tell us;) which may set forth the Saints Blessedness, under the Influence of that Light the Lord is pleas'd to afford when it's Night with 'em. They bring forth a Variety of precious Fruits in various Seasons. Some are Winter, others Summer-Fruits. Some are brought forth by the warming Day-Light Influences of the Sun of Righteousness; others by the cooling Influences of the Moon, or the lesser Light afforded in the Night Dispensation. The Jewish Church in the Night Dispensation of the Old Testament, under the Moon-like Influences of Types and Shadows, brought forth Fruit to God. But the New Testament Church, in a more eminent Way, under the Transcendent Influences of the

Risen *Sun of Righteousness,* in the broad Day-Light of the Gospel. Thus *John,* saw a *Wonder in Heaven, a Woman cloath'd with the Sun, having the Moon under her Feet, Rev.* 12. 1. Which might be a Representation of the Gospel Church, Shining forth in the Glory of Christ, the Sum and Substance of all Shadows; having the Moon of Old Testament Ordinances under her Feet, (As some Great Men of God have thought.) But tho' the Privileges of the Church under the Gospel Day, are much advanc'd, when compar'd with what it enjoy'd under the Night of the Law; yet even the Gospel Church hath it's Nights, as well as Days still. It's needful for them, at Times, to be in *Heaviness, thro' Manifold Temptations,* I *Pet.* 1. 6. And when it's *Night* with 'em, *Psal.* 30. 5. The Lord doth not leave 'em without Light, suitable to the Dispensation they are under; their *Moon shall not withdraw it self* in such Seasons, *Isa.* 60. 20. And the Church is bless'd by the Heavenly Influences of the Night, as well as those of the Day: For both jointly conduce to her abundant Fruitfulness.

Ver. 15. *And for the chief Things of the ancient Mountains, and for the precious Things of the lasting Hills. These Mountains* and Hills, tis very probable, were *Mountains of Spices,* said to be *Ancient,* as being from the beginning of the Creation cast up by God himself; and *Lasting,* for their Perpetuity: And as such were an eminent part of the Blessing of *Joseph's* Land. And fitly serv'd to represent the transcendent Blessedness of the Saints, as standing upon the high Acts of God's Grace, in his Covenant Settlements; which Gloriously secure their Fruitfulness. These may be compar'd to *Mountains.* for Firmness; to *Ancient* Mountains for Antiquity, in as much as they bear upon 'em the Date of Everlasting, as it denotes Eternity before Time commenc'd; and to *Lasting* Hills, because they endure thro' Time and to Eternity the same. And oh the unspeakable Blessedness of Christ's Land, this People, as standing in the Grace of the Everlasting Settlements! *Rom.* 5. 2. The Saints are blest for the chief Things of these Ancient Mountains, for the precious Things of these lasting Hills; such as Adoption, Justification, Sanctification, and Glorification, *Rom.* 8. 29, 30. And oh, the fragrant Fruitfulness of Christ's Land, as blest in these Respects! What Revenues of Glory arise to him thereby! As they are adopted, he inherits a *People near* to God, *Psal.* 148. 14. As justifi'd, a *Righteous People, Isa.* 60. 21. As Sanctifi'd, *an Holy Nation, a peculiar People,* I *Pet.* 2. 9. And as Glorifi'd, in the absolute Settlement of it upon 'em, he inherits a People that he shall possess for ever, as *a Crown of Glory, and a Diadem of Beauty, Isa.* 62.

3. And as Christ's Glory is great, so the Blessedness of the Saints is unspeakable herein: And the *Fruit* they are *ordain'd to bring forth* hereby, to the glory of God, is effectually secured, *Joh.* 15. 16.

Ver. 16. *And for the precious Things of the Earth, and the fullness thereof. Joseph's* Land, was not only bless'd for the chief Things of the ancient Mountains, which were precious by way of Eminence; but also for the precious Things of the Earth, and the fullness thereof; for all kinds of Influences and Productions, the rich Soil of the Earth affords. And so Christ's People, are not only *blest with all Spiritual Blessings in the Heavenlies,* suitable to the Glory of their Heavenly State, as the Offspring of Christ the Heavenly Man; but also with all the precious Things of the Earth. In being *Heirs with Christ,* they are *Heirs of God;* and of all that he Is and Has. *The World* is theirs, and the fullness thereof, I *Cor.* 3. 22. It was made for Christ and the Saints; and they with him *Inherit all Things, Heb.* 1. 2. *Rev.* 21. 7.

And for the Good-Will of him that dwelt in the Bush. This was a Blessing [Indeed,] which extending to all the rest, did exceedingly enhance their Worth. And is last mentioned, as the *Coronis,* and Glory of them all. This distinguish'd *Joseph's* Land from the common Earth, and put a peculiar Glory upon it. And as in the Type, so in the Antitype, all the Saints Blessings as flowing from, nourish'd by, and crown'd with, *the Good-Will of him that dwelt in the Bush,* (their own Covenant-God and Father, dwelling in Christ and them for ever,) makes 'em Transcendently Full, and Glorious. This is a Blessing so high, that it even puts a Glory upon Divine Love it self. While the Boundless Love of Jehovah's Nature, appears cloath'd with the Sovereign good Pleasure of his Will, with what an amazing Glory doth it Shine! How doth Grace Shine in its Absoluteness, Sovereignty, Freeness, and Distinguishing Glory; while Jehovah, proclaims all his Goodness to his People, and says, I [Will] *be Gracious, to whom I will be Gracious! Exod.* 33. 19. Here it appears to be not of Necessity of Nature, but, of the highest Freedom of Will; which begets the highest Admirations, and Adorations in the Saints. In God's dwelling in the Bush, there was a Display of an high Freedom of Will, and great condescending Love. Which put together, might well be call'd Good-Will, [Good] for the exceeding Kindness of it, and [Will] for the absolute Freedom of it, and [Good-Will,] as the highest Love was cloath'd with the highest Freedom. And for this Good-Will of him that dwelt in the Bush, are the Saints bless'd in all their Blessings. Oh! The unspeakable Sweetness, this puts into every Favour, whether of *the Upper,* or *Nether Springs, Jos.* 15. 10.

Let the Blessings come upon the Head of Joseph,] Or *coming, Let it come upon the Head of Joseph;* and so upon his Land in Relation to him. Which sets forth the Order, in which God Communicates all Blessings to his People, as well as the abundant Freeness, and Fullness thereof. They are first given to Christ, as the prime *Heir of all Things,* and then to us in him, as *Heirs with* him: we are bless'd in his Blessedness. The Father hath *bless'd us with all Blessings in Christ, Eph.*1. 3. So that our Right depends upon his Title, and is thereby exceedingly secured to us. And as we are blest in him in respect to Right, so also in respect of Communication. God communicates all Grace and Glory, with every good Thing, to the Man Christ first, and then thro' him to all his Seed. And our highest Blessedness, is but a Derivation out of his Fullness; which heightens it yet the more. And as all Blessings come first upon Christ, and then upon us, in and thro' him; so in this way, coming they come, freely, fully and perpetually.

And upon the top of the Head of him, that was seperated from his Brethren.] The Blessings being said, to come upon *the Top,* or *Crown* of *Joseph's* Head, may denote the utmost, and highest Degree thereof. And as it comes upon the Top, or Highest part of his Head, (so that he's all over blest,) so also upon him, as *seperated from his Brethren:* First, by God's special Designation, setting him apart to an exalted State of Glory above 'em; and secondly, as seperated from 'em in his Sufferings. Which God ordain'd, both to go before, as also to be a Means of his future Advancement; that so the Glory thereof might shine the more Conspicuously. And as the Blessing came upon the Head of *Joseph,* the Type, as seperated from his Brethren, in both these Respects, so upon Christ the glorious Antitype: First, upon his Person, as seperated from his Brethren, being by the Father *chosen from among the People,* set apart, and exalted to the Office, and Glory of Mediator, and High Priest, *Psal.* 89. 19. *Heb.* 5. 5. Upon which Account he's *most blessed for ever, Psal.* 29. 6. But then Secondly, the Blessing comes upon Christ's Head, not only in the right of his being the alone Mediator, but also in the right of his Mediatorial Obedience unto Death; when seperated from his Brethren, as the one great Sacrifice of Atonement: for *of the People there was none with him, Isa.* 63. 3. And in both these Respects, as Mediator, and Head of the Church, as Redeemer, *and Saviour of the Body, Eph.* 5. 23. How doth the Blessing coming, come upon Christ, and his for ever! *To every one of us,* says the Apostle, *is given Grace, according to the Measure of the Gift of Christ, Eph.* 4. 7. (The Gift to Christ, as well as the Gift of Christ; for he first *Receiv'd,* and then *gave Gifts, Psal.* 68. 18. *Eph.* 4. 8.) *And now that he Ascended, what is it but that he first Descended into the lower parts of the Earth. He that Descended, is the same also that Ascended far above all Heavens, that he might fill all Things, Ver.* 9. 10. God having so order'd it in infinite Wisdom, that he who was *Lord of all,* as God-Man Mediator, the great Head of the Church, should yet *empty himself* of all his Glory, and become *Obedient unto Death, even the Death of the Cross, Phil.* 2. 6, 7, 8. That hereby he might, not only satisfie Justice, but also Ascend to Glory, and take Possession of all Blessings for us, in order to communicate to us, in the right of his Meritorious Obedience; which being superadded to his Personal right, was, as for the more abundant Glory of the Mediator, so for the *Strong Consolation,* and more abundant Security of the *Heirs of Promise.*

Thus the Type, and the Antitype agree; in that *Joseph* was first separated from his Brethren, by God's special Designation of him, to an exalted Glory above them, and again by peculiar Sufferings; and in both these Respects the Blessing came upon his Head. So Christ, was first seperated from his Brethren, when *set up from Everlasting,* in the Office, and Glory of Mediator, *Prov.* 8. 23. And again, when God smote *the Shepherd, and the Sheep* were *scatter'd, Zech.* 13. 7. And upon both these Accounts the Blessing comes upon Christ, and his for ever. But yet there was this Difference between *Joseph,* and Christ: *Joseph's* Afflictions preceded his Advancement, only as Means, wise Providence made use of to bring about and illustrate the same. But Christ's Sufferings preceded his Glory, not only as Means to bring it about, and as a Foil to set it off, but also as a Meritorious Cause thereof: so that upon the account of his being seperated from his Brethren in this Respect, the Blessing coming, comes indeed!

I shall attempt to give a few Hints upon the next Verse: It being also a part of *Joseph's* Blessing, or rather a Prophetic Description of his Blessedness.

Ver. 17. *His Glory is like the Firstling of his Bullock]* all *Joseph's* Glory was *like the Firstling of his Bullock,* the Lord's, and offer'd up to him; which was the prime excellency thereof, *Exod.* 13. 12. And all *the Glory* Christ *had with* God, as Mediator, *before the World was, Joh.* 17.

5. How did he offer it up in Flames of Love to his Father, when with Delight, he came to *do* his *Will? Psal.* 40. 7, 8. Did God Glorify him, in calling him to be *an High-Priest? Heb.* 5. 5. He faithfully laid it out to his Honour, *chap.* 3. 2. He *magnifi'd* his *Law, and made it honourable, Isa.* 42. 21. both in it's preceptive, and penal Part, by his great Obedience to it, both in Life and Death. Did the Father *Crown* him as High-Priest, with Glory and Honour? he Dedicates it unto the Lord; offers up himself a Sacrifice; tastes Death for every Man: that God might be Glorifi'd, and his People saved. *Heb.* 2. 9. And as Christ's Glory was the Lord's on the Cross, so also on the Throne: there's no Glory Christ possesseth now in Heaven, at God's Right Hand, but what he employs in his Father's Honour. When he told his Disciples, what great Things he would do for 'em in his exalted State, he gives the Glory of God as the Reason of it. *Whatsoever* (says he) *ye shall ask in my Name, that I will do, that the Father may be Glorifi'd in the Son, Joh.* 14. 13.

And his Horns like the Horns of Unicorns:] *Horns,* especially the Horns of *Unicorns,* which are eminent for Strength, *Num.* 23. 22. Are an emblem of Power, and Kingly Majesty, *Psal.* 89. 24. and 92. 10. which Literally, may denote, the Strength and Greatness of *Joseph's* Glory; and Spiritually, the Glory and Strength of Christ's Kingdom.

With them he shall push the People together to the Ends of the Earth,] which sets forth Literally, the Victory, *Joseph* in his Offspring, should obtain over his Enemies the *Canaanites,* in driving them out, and possessing their Land; and Spiritually, the compleat Conquest, Christ and his People, obtain over all his and their Enemies.

And they are the Ten Thousands of Ephraim, and they are the Thousands of Manasseh.] Which Literally, sets the Strength of *Joseph's* Glory, in his numerous and victorious Offspring; and also may point it out as an encreasing Glory: in that Ten Thousands are ascrib'd to *Ephraim,* his younger, and but Thousands to *Manasseh,* his first born Son. Which when apply'd to Christ, sets forth the Strength and Glory of his Kingdom in the Abundance of his Spiritual Seed. *Solomon* says, that *in the Multitude of People is the King's Honour, Prov.* 14. 28. And King Jesus has a Multitude of Loyal Subjects, so Great, that *no Man can Number, Rev.* 7. 9. It also sets forth the encreasing Glory of his Kingdom. The *Jewish* Church, like *Manasseh,* was the firstborn, and Christ had his Thousands among them; But he hath his Ten Thousands in the *Gentile* Church, tho' like *Ephraim,* the younger Son; Christ had his Thousands under the Law, but his Ten Thousands under the Gospel; *from the Womb of this Morning* he had the *Dew of his Youth, Psal.* 110. 3. And more eminently will have, as the glorious Day dawns, when *the Fullness of the Gentiles* shall be brought in, and *a Nation born at once, Rom.* 11. 25. *Isa.* 66. 8. *For of the Increase of his Government, and Peace, there shall be no End, Isa.* 9. 7. And as they, the Ten Thousands of *Ephraim,* and the Thousands of *Manasseh,* were the *Horns,* by which *Joseph* push'd the People, his Enemies; So it sets forth the Honour Christ puts upon his Children, in employing them under him, as *the Captain* of their *Salvation,* to fight all his Battles, and the Victory he obtains in 'em, and by 'em. For *Jacob is his Battle-ax, and Weapons of War, Jer.* 51. 20. *With thee* (says he) *will I break in pieces the Nations, and with thee will I destroy Kingdoms: and with thee will I break in pieces the Horse and his Rider; and with thee will I break in pieces the Chariot and his Rider; with thee also will I break in pieces Man and Woman, old and young, the young Man and Maid, the Shepherd and his Flock, the Husbandman and his Yoke of Oxen; and with thee will I break in pieces Captains and Rulers. And I will render unto Babylon, and to all the Inhabitants of Chaldea, all the Evil that they have done in Zion, in your Sight, saith the Lord, ver.* 21, 22, 23, 24. O then Christ's enemies, shall be push'd together to the Ends of the Earth indeed! And his Horns in the Thousands and Ten Thousands of his Saints, appear like *the Horns of Unicorns;* And his Glory in that great Day, openly shine forth as the Lord's; When *the Son* delivers up *the Kingdom to the Father, that God may be All in All,* I *Cor.* 15. 24, 28. Again,

I look upon *Joseph* to be a Type of the Church. Which appears from *Psal.* 80. 1. *Give Ear, O Shepherd of Israel, thou that leadest Joseph like a Flock.* As a Type of Christ, *Joseph* had this Name of *the Shepherd of Israel* given him, *Gen.* 49. 24. And here, as a Type of the Church, the Name of the Flock, that *Israel's* Shepherd leads. And the church goes by the Name of *Joseph, Amos* 6. 6. and 9. 18. as in several other Places. And if taken in this Sense, then *Joseph's* Land, sets forth the Saints Lot, or Portion of Privileges, both in the Church, and in the World. And the Blessing in every part of it, may fitly be apply'd thereunto. In as much as the Saints are blessed in all their Blessings; and what they seem to enjoy in common with others, is under a peculiar Blessing to them. And the Thousands and Ten Thousands of *Joseph's* Off-spring, may set forth the abundant Fruitfulness of the Saints, both in Grace and good Works:

And their being compar'd to *Horns,* sets forth their Royal Dignity, as made *Kings and Priests unto God, Rev.* 1. 6. And also the Royalty and Strength of Faith, and every Grace of the Spirit, with all the Weapons of their spiritual Warfare; by which, as being mighty *thro' God,* they obtained a compleat Victory over all their Enemies; even to the captivating of *every high Thought into the Obedience of Christ,* I *John* 5. 4. 2 *Cor.* 10. 4, 5. And in that *Manasseh* the elder had Thousands, and *Ephraim* the younger Ten Thousands, It may set forth the extensive Fruitfulness of the Saints, both as to Nature and Grace; and also the increase Fruitfulness thereof. Nature, or the natural Endowments of the Man, (which in respect of Grace is the First-born Image) the Saints imploy for God; and Nature, as us'd by, and for Grace, has its Thousands, But Grace, in the pure and high Actings thereof, its Ten Thousands. Again, it may set forth the rich Increase of Grace in the Saints: The First-Fruit they bring forth to God, when Grace is young, hath its Thousands; but the Productions of its elder Years, Ten Thousands. And all the Saints Glory, both in Nature and Grace, here and hereafter, is the Lord's, and by them dedicated to him; which they esteem the highest Part of it: For as *of him and thro' him,* so *to him are all things. To whom be Glory for ever, Amen. Rom.* 11. 36.

Dear Brother, your last Request, which is implicit, contain'd in these Words, [I shall be glad to hear how my Lord dealt with you] (I suppose you mean, How he brought me into some Measure of Gospel-Liberty) I shall now attempt to answer in general, as briefly as I can. It being my Duty to *be always ready to give a Reason of the Hope that is in me, with Meekness and Fear,* I *Pet.* 3. 15.

It pleased the Lord, after that he had *call'd me by his Grace, and reveal'd his Son in me, Gal.*1. 15, 16. to favour me with frequent visits, and much communion with himself; by which I was oft-times fill'd with unspeakable Joy, quickly after I had pass'd thro' the New Birth. But yet, for about 2 Years or little more, (as near as I can remember) I remain'd in an unsettled State as to the Faith of my Interest. When the Lord broke out upon my Heart with the sweet enkindling Beams of his glorious Favour, in a Promise, or in an Ordinance, in his *Light* I saw *Light, Psal.* 36. 9. And then I could believe my Int'rest in his Love, and my eternal Security therein. And while my Heart burn'd with Love to him, being set on Fire by the Discoveries of his Love, I have been so transported with Joy at the Manifestation of Divine Favour, That I have thought Eternity little enough to praise the Lord for such a Visit. But tho' *my Mountain* stood *strong* in my own Sight, while the Lord's *Favour* shone bright upon my Soul; yet when he *hid* his *Face,* I was *troubled, Psal.* 30. 7. When the Sun was withdrawn, Clouds and Darkness return'd: It was straightway Night with my Soul, and the *Beasts* of Prey came out upon me, *Psal.* 104. 20. Satan with his Temptations, together with my own Corruptions, which threatned to devour me; and then my Life hung in doubt, and I question'd all the former Discoveries of Kindness I had receiv'd from the Lord, whether they were indeed from him or no. I thought what I found in my Heart was inconsistent with a State of Grace, and Int'rest in the Favour I before had rejoyc'd in. And thus, with *Peter,* when his Eye was off his Master, upon the *boistrous Waves* he was encompass'd with, beginning to *sink,* I cry'd, *Lord, Save me: And immediately Jesus stretch'd forth his Hand and caught him, and said unto him, O thou of little Faith, wherefore didst thou doubt? Matt.* 14. 30, 31. Thus by some Word of Promise or other, omnipotent Grace has saved my soul from sinking many a Time. And thro' rich abundant Grace, the Lord never left me long without a Cordial in my fainting Fits: But yet, while I mainly took up God's Love to me, in the Light of my own Sanctification, I never came to Establishment. As my Love to him was high or low, so my Faith of his Love to me, was strong or weak; Because I so strictly adhered to the Witness of *the Water,* (Sanctification in me) rather than to the immediate Testimony of *the Holy Ghost,* in the Word of Promise, I *Joh.* 5. 8. But such was the superabundant Grace of my God, to me a sinful Worm, That *after* I had *believ'd,* I was *Seal'd with the Holy Spirit of Promise, Eph.* 1. 13.

Which was done by the Holy Ghost, as a *Comforter,* opening God's Heart in the Declarations and Promises of Grace; setting on a powerful Impression of his Love upon my Soul, in its Sovereignty, Freeness, Fullness, and Eternity; in particular to [Me]: While my Heart under his mighty Operations, heated with the heavenly Fire of divine Love, receiv'd the same as the melted Wax the Impress of the Seal: Love was set in upon me, and taken in by me. And being thus Seal'd by the Holy Spirit of Promise, *my Feet* were not only *set upon* Christ *the Rock,* but *my Goings* also were *establish'd, Psal.* 40. 2.

Yea such a Flood of Divine Love was pour'd out upon my thirsty Soul, that overflow'd every Corner of it; and refreshfully soak'd to the Bottom of my Heart; which made me *spring up* in Faith, as a *Willow by the Water Course,* even to the rich and *full Assurance* of my being the Lord's, *Isa.* 44. 3, 4. *Heb.* 10. 22. Which I was enabled to take up from the immediate Testimony of the Holy Spirit in the Word of Promise; and to hold fast, because of his Veracity and Truth, I *Joh.* 5. 6. And upon this Consideration alone, my soul was held up from yielding to unbelieving Fears for some Time together. There was, I remember, such an Impression made upon my Heart, of the Faithfulness and Truth of the Holy Spirit as *the Witness,* and also of the Reality of what he had witness'd to my Soul; which were so joyn'd together, that I might not, durst not question my own Interest, unless I first question'd the Truth of the Holy Spirit that witness'd it; which I was held in an awful Reverence of. And now, tho' I had an high Veneration for, and was more confirmed by, the Witness of *the Water and the Blood,* (Justification and Sanctification) which together with *the Spirit* agree in one joynt Testimony, I *John* 5. 8. yet being made primely to adhere to the supreme Witness of the Spirit, and to these as subordinate Evidences in the Spirit's Light; I was mightily establish'd hereby. For tho' my holy Frames were subject to Change, and the Sense of my Justification by what Christ had done, was not always alike upon my Heart; yet the Spirit's Witness abiding at such Times, which I was enabled to give Credit to, I was greatly reviv'd again, and held up in Faith; which made me long for, and press after the highest Holiness, in Conformity to Christ my holy Head.

And now *my Goings* were *establish'd* indeed. Oh with what Freedom could I go to God, as my own God and Father in Christ! I had indeed some Interruptions of Communion; but in those Intervals, I was made by an efficacious Word of Power, to *stand fast by Faith, in that Liberty wherewith Christ* had *made me free, Gal.* 5. 1. when I had not spiritual Sensation. Being *rooted and grounded in Love, Eph.* 3. 17. My Faith of Interest was not soon shaken, by the contrary Winds of Temptations and Corruptions that arose against it. The Holy Ghost had given me such Views of God's free, unchangeable Favour in Christ; of the Immutability of his eternal Counsel; and the Unalterableness of his sure and everlasting Covenant; together with my unchangeable Standing in all this Grace, from Eternity to Eternity; that tho' I had not always the immediate Flowings in of it upon my Spirit, yet my Faith was kept clear and steady as to personal Interest and full Propriety.

And I must say from felt Experience, that even the Children of God themselves, before they arrive to the full Assurance of God's Favour, are very much unacquainted with the glorious Heights of that unspeakable Joy which fills the Hearts of sealed Saints; or those that have been more eminently seal'd with the Holy Spirit of Promise. If *Perfect Love* hath not *cast out Fear,* it has *Torment;* and so much Bondage-Fear, so much Torment and Disquietude there is in the Heart of a Child of God, I *John* 4. 18. 'Tis by *Believing* the Saints *enter into Rest, Heb.* 4. 3. And further, I must say as one of God's Witness, That full Assurance of Faith, is an unspeakable Privilege, and exceedingly tends to promote the highest Holiness; notwithstanding the unbelieving Cavils Men make against it. For, so far as the Faith of Believers in weakned in God's Kindness, so far they become weak to every holy Performance: God's *Love, shed abroad in the Hearts,* is the Strength of a Believer's Spirit, *Rom.* 5. 5. 'Tis this excites 'em to an universal Respect to all God's Commandments; and makes them loath and abhor themselves, for the Imperfection of all their Obedience. When God's Kindness and their Unkindness are set together in the Holy Ghost's Light, O how their Hearts melt into Gospel-Repentance! And for my own Part, I must say, That God's Love manifested to, and taken in by Faith, has carried me comfortably thro' innumerable Trials, in every of which *I had fainted, unless I had believed to see the Goodness of the Lord in the Land of the Living, Psal.* 27. 13. But to return.

The Lord having thus, in some good measure, *drawn* me *from the Breasts,* and *wean'd* me *from the Milk* of sensible Enjoyments, in respect of drawing my Faith of Interest from thence, *Isa.* 28. 9. He was yet, nevertheless pleas'd in the rich aboundings, and superaboundings of his Grace, to add Abundance of spiritual Sense to my Faith; By giving me frequent Communion, and sweet Fellowship with himself, in his Three glorious Persons; in the infinite, free, full, unchangeable and eternal Love of the Three-One God, display'd in and thro' the Man Christ Jesus; as that which gloriously encompass'd me in one eternal Round. Thus highly was I favour'd for many Years.

And I must say from abundant Experience, That Jehovah's Love is free, Free in itself; and free also in its Manifestation. I have found reigning Grace, thro' a crucify'd Jesus, in its glorious Superaboundings over all my abounding sinfulness, to be infinitely free indeed. For I have ever been a favour'd Child; and yet, I think one of the most ungrateful, of all my dear Father hath. The rich Bounties the Lord hath shewn, and the great Things he hath done for me, have call'd for great Returns of

Duty, and Thankfulness to him. But, alas! I have not render'd to the Lord, according to what he hath done for me; but have evil requited him for all his Kindness. If I had had to do with all the Grace of Creatures united in One, I had long since exhausted it. But *Jehovah's* Grace has been, and still is, infinitely *sufficient* for me, To bear with all my Provocations; to pity my Weakness; to pardon all my Sinfulness; and still to *rest in his Love, rejoycing over* me *with Singing:* O adorable Grace! It's well for me, That my God is the Lord *Jehovah,* that *changeth not;* else I had long since been *consumed, Mal.* 3. 6. But O! his Love holds still towards me, notwithstanding all my Unworthiness, as infinitely full and free as ever! And will continually flow out upon me, in rich Streams of Loving-Kindness, to and endless Eternity, without the least Waste or Diminution! And while I have Communion with this free, unchangeable, and everlasting Love, my Heart falls down and adores it; and is broken in pieces at the Remembrance of all my unanswerable Carriage; longing for the Time when I shall be freed from this hateful Thing [Sin;] and love God perfectly, and without Interruption for ever.

And tho' it has pleas'd my dear Father, in a great measure to with-hold the Manifestations of his Love, that were wont to flow in upon my Soul in the Joys of spiritual Sense; yet thro' rich abounding Grace, he still maintains my Faith in his everlasting Kindness; and helps me to believe, that his Love, when it runs under-ground out of my Sight, still keeps a steady Course, in that Channel infinite Wisdom has ordain'd; in order to its triumphant Rise above Ground ere long, with a more glorious Display than ever. And the sweet Remembrance of those *Full Joys,* I have had *in* God's *Presence* here, makes me long, at Times, for those *Rivers of Pleasures* that are *at* his *Right Hand for evermore:* When in that State of immediate Presence, the bright Beams of divine Favour, like an eternal Sun, shall shine out upon me with uninterrupted and transforming Rays. Thus rejoycing in Hope of the Glory of God, and waiting for his Salvation, *I come up out of the Wilderness leaning on* my *beloved, Cant.* 8. 5. whose everlasting Arms of Kindness, both support and inclose me: And will delightfully, without the least Weariness, conduct me safe Home, to that Glory which is prepared for me in my Father's House in Heaven; Where *holy, and without Blame before him in Love,* I shall be, *to the Praise of the Glory of his Grace* for ever, *Eph.* 1. 4, 6.

Thus I have given you a brief, tho' broken Account, how the Lord has dealt with me. And if he will please to get himself any Glory, and give you to reap any Benefit by what I have written, I shall esteem it a rich and full Reward of my weak Attempts to perform this Service. *The Grace of our Lord Jesus Christ be with your Spirit, Amen.*

Desiring your Prayers, That much of the Holy Spirit may be poured down upon me, to enable me to bring forth much Fruit, to the Glory of God by Christ:

In him I rest,

with dear Christian Love,

your unworthy Sister,

A. D.

A

NARRATION

OF THE

WONDERS OF GRACE,

IN SIX PARTS,

I. OF CHRIST THE MEDIATOR, AS SET UP FROM EVERLASTING IN ALL THE GLORY OF HEADSHIP.

II. O GOD'S ELECTION AND COVE-NANT—TRANSACTIONS CONCERNING A REMNANT IN HIS SON.

III. OF CHRIST'S INCARNATION AND REDEMPTION.

IV. OF THE WORK OF THE SPIRIT, RE-SPECTING THE CHURCH IN GENERAL, THROUGHOUT THE NEW TESTAMENT DISPENSATION, FROM CHRIST'S ASCEN-SION TO HIS SECOND COMING.

V. OF CHRIST'S GLORIOUS APPEARING AND KINGDOM.

VI. OF GOG AND MAGOG: TOGETHER WITH THE LAST JUDGMENT.

TO WHICH IS ADDED,

A POEM ON THE SPECIAL WORK OF THE SPIRIT
IN THE HEARTS OF THE ELECT.

ALSO,

SIXTY ONE HYMNS COMPOSED ON SEVERAL SUBJECTS.

By ANNE DUTTON.

A NEW EDITION.
REVISED, WITH A PREFACE AND COLLECTED MEMOIR OF THE AUTHOR,

By J. A. JONES,
MINISTER OF THE GOSPEL, MITCHELL-STREET, LONDON.

London:

PUBLISHED BY JOHN BENNETT,
4, THREE TUN PASSAGE, IVY LANE, PATERNOSTER ROW.

1833.

[Reverse titles page transcription]

W. M. KNIGHT AND CO., PRINTERS,
BISHOP'S COURT, OLD BAILEY.

EDITOR'S PREFACE.

Reader,

Before I commend to thy notice this volume, I would enquire of thee, what wantest thou? What art thou seeking after? What will please thee; yea, rather, what will *satisfy* thee? Honest answers to these queries, would enable me to say, "*read,* and the blessing of the Lord accompany the reading to thy soul;" or, lay the book aside, it will by no means *suit* thee."

The author of the *lines* contained in this book, was a great saint. Her renewed mind was largely led into *truth.* The great and glorious doctrines of the everlasting gospel, she delighted in beyond expression. She had a deep insight into the native depravity of her heart; and, her experience of the grace of God upon her soul, with the *soul-liberty* granted her, was so blessed, that the plenitude thereof, as *she* experienced it, very rarely falls to the lot of the Lord's family, at least not in these days of "small things." —Zech. iv. 10.

But who, I say, are those that will *prize* this book? Not the lovers of *modern* divinity: the doctrinal truths herein stated are *altogether out of their line.* Not those who, in reading *verse,* are delighted principally with a *critical exactness* in the harmony of *sounds.* Good versification is not here. If it may be termed *poetry* at all; it is indeed *rugged* poetry. Alter it, I could not, 'twas beyond my art; and if I could have done it, I *would* not. All I can say for it, in this respect, is, the reader must bear in mind that it was written *one hundred years ago;* and penned in the *style* of verse *then* in vogue. Zion's pilgrim's in *those* days (and especially in the *midland* countries) were "plain and homely folk." In those parts they mostly sang (if they sang at all) "*Davis's* Hymns:" a seventh edition, *recommended by Dr. Gill,* is now before me. *It is, in my esteem, beyond gold.* Years past I would have reprinted it, but for its awkward poetry. Reader, figure to yourself a cluster of the Lord's people (round-frocked, and red-cloaked) in a retired country village, and in an humble *thatched* building, on a Lord's day; after having been *fed* with the finest of the wheat, with the pure wholesome truths of God in the ministry of the word, from a *labourer* raised up of the Lord amongst yourselves, ("rude in *speech,* yet not in knowledge," 2 Cor. xi. 6,) *then,* sitting down at the Lord's table, with a rich enjoyment of the presence of Jesus, they sing—

> "How fat the feast! how rich the wine!
> How pleasant was the company!
> We fed on Christ, we drank his blood,
> Whilst with us sat the glorious Three!

> To heaven our faith was mounted up,
> We were impatient of delay;
> Thy coming hasten, Lord, to us,
> Or, let us haste to Thee away.   *Davis's Hymns.*"

Now *as* Dr. Gill wrote concerning *those* hymns; *so* I write of Anne Dutton's *lines* and *verses*. "They may be thought, by *nice* and *critical* judges, to be destitute of those poetical *flights* and *beauties*, which adorn and recommend *verse* to men of *polite* taste; yet, these *supposed* deficiencies are abundantly made up to *those who have tasted that the Lord is gracious*, by that spiritual devotion and affection, and by those *gleams of gospel light* which appear throughout the whole."

Well, then, the *bookseller* has risked the republication of this volume, in the *hope* that there are *yet* to be found persons, who, having "tasted that the Lord *is* gracious," will not *reject* Anne Dutton *because* of the inharmoniousness of her verse; but, blessing God for "those bright gleams of gospel light" shining in every page; will kindly listen to her *own* voice; for though long since fallen asleep in Jesus, she "yet speaketh." For myself, I just step on one side, and (quoting from a *Preface* of her's to *another* choice piece) say, let *us* hearken to our sister, whom one day we hope to meet in glory:—"Dear saints, what you shall see of the *truth* of God in the following pages, receive in the *love* of it: what of *weakness* appears, pass by, and cover, in brotherly kindness; remembering that these lines are but the chatterings of a *child* that cannot speak, Jer. i. 6. If the Lord shall please to use the hints I have given, to any of *His* children, for their further fellowship with the Truth; as it will be an addition to my *joy*, so I desire that *He* may have *all* the honour, who *alone* doth build the Temple of the Lord, and is worthy to bear the glory."

Christian reader! Buy the Truth, and, sell it not. If you should meet with *diamonds* in your way, cast them not from you, *because* they have not come under the *polishing* hand of the skillful lapidary.

I have sought the *glory* of God, and the *profit* of his people, in looking over, and just here and there *(in very few places indeed)* removing an unsightly word or so; *altering* no where—adding *none*. This done, I have prefixed thereto the best collected account I could of the Author. And *now*, looking up to *Him*, who alone *can* bless, that *He* will condescend *to* bless His *own* Truth contained herein to *His own people*,

I subscribe myself,
An unworthy servant to the best of Masters,

JOHN ANDREWS JONES

London,
March 29, 1833.

A
MEMOIR
OF
MRS. ANNE DUTTON.

The subject of this Memoir was born at *Northampton*, somewhat *about* the year 1695. She says, "It pleased the Lord to order it so, that I had the advantage of a religious education, my parents being both *gracious*. I attended with my parents upon the ministry of Mr. *Hunt*,* who was the pastor of a church of Christ at Northampton. From a child I was acquainted with the Holy Scriptures, and took pleasure in reading the same, with other good books, especially *hymn* books, which I greatly delighted to learn and commit to memory. It pleased the Lord to work savingly upon my heart when I was about *thirteen* years of age. There was a mighty impression made upon my heart, of the reality and consequence of a future state either of *misery* or of *glory*, of unspeakable happiness, or inconceivable torment; together with the nearness of its approach. O, eternity! eternity! was ever before mine eyes! And the worth of mine own soul, as an immortal spirit, was strongly impressed upon my mind. Again, the misery of my natural estate was set before me, as a transgressor of the holy law: I thought all the curses in God's book belonged to *me*. Now I needed none to tell me, that *I* was the person that was undone by sin; and that if *I* died in a state of unbelief and alienation from God, I must be damned for ever!

"This raised a cry in my soul (though I kept it as close as I could from others,) 'What must *I* do to be saved?' Now I set about religion in good earnest. I *prayed, read,* and *heard* in a very different manner than I had ever done before. *But my wound was too deep to be healed by my own doings now.* The law of God pursued me with its *curses*. notwithstanding all my religious *duties*. Before, I was a *beautiful* creature in my own eyes, as wrapt round with my fine doings; but now I saw myself a most *deformed* object. I saw sin, now, in another light than before. I now saw myself guilty by reason of *heart-sins*. Yea, my eyes were now

---

*Mr. Hunt wrote a book, entitled, *"The Saint's Treasury, or, Christ the most excellent."* And the celebrated Mr. *Joseph Hussey's* sublime work, *"The glories of Christ vindicated, in the excellency of his Person, Righteousness, Love and Power,"* was none other than his *Reply* to this book of Mr. Hunt's.

opened to see the *filthy fountain*, whence all the defiled *streams* both in heart and life did proceed. I now no longer thought myself to be better than others; but one of the vilest creatures the earth bore. Yea, I thought myself to be the very chief of sinners. I saw that I was held as in chains under the dominion of sin; and the power and being, as well as the guilt and filth of sin, was now a great burden to my soul. I saw, that nothing less than an *omnipotent* arm could pluck me out of those amazing deeps! And now I was undone indeed! Just ready to perish, in my own apprehension; being filled at times with terrible fears of approaching wrath: so that I have been in dread in the evening, when I went to bed, lest I should lift up my eyes in hell before morning.

"Though what I heard of salvation, at times, was but, as it were, in *general* propositions: as that, Christ died for the chief of sinners; and He that believeth shall be saved, &c.; from whence a *possibility* of salvation for *me* was *hinted* at; yet so powerful as influence had it on my soul, that it kept me from *despair*, and held my heart at the throne of grace. So that those *glimmerings* of salvation by Christ, together with a *possibility* of its being for *me*, were so intermingled with my aforesaid convictions, that I was kept form sinking into desperation.

"Now, to know whether I was *elected*, was my chief concern. For the *notions* I before had of the *doctrines* of the gospel, were not sufficient to comfort me *now*. I could no longer rest satisfied with knowing that God had chosen a *remnant* in his Son unto eternal life; unless I knew *my own interest* in electing grace: nor, that Christ had died for *sinners*, without knowing that he loved *me*, and gave himself for *me*, &c. *I wanted to know these things for my own soul.* God's election-grace stood forth before mine eyes in an amazing glory; but O to know whether or not I was one of God's chosen! The blessedness of those who were interested in Christ's person, love, life, death, and glory. Yea, I saw the inexpressible blessedness thereof; but O the tormenting *fears* which at times racked my heart, lest I should stand *excluded* from all this grace! I remember once reading in the seventeenth chapter of St. John, and when I came to those words, 'I pray not for the world, but for them which thou hast *given* me, for *they* are thine;' my heart was as it were struck with a dart, fearing that *I* was none of the Lord's, but of the world; and, as such, was excluded from Christ's prayer. But through rich grace, everlasting arms being underneath me. I was not left to sink into despair; nor was I long without *hopes* that I should find mercy. As a poor perishing sinner I waited at the throne of grace, with *earnest longings* and *some hopes* that *mercy* would bid me *live*. I saw there was grace enough in God to save me; and I have said, 'Speak but the *word*, Lord, and my soul shall be saved: bid me *live*, and I shall live in thy sight.' But O! though I doubted not his *ability*, yet I questioned his *willingness*. I was surrounded with *a crowd of discouragements*. Yet though attended with so many fears, I pressed through all difficulties, and *cast myself at the foot of free grace in Christ*; resolving that if *I did* perish, it should be at *Mercy's feet*.

"Here I would just *sum up* the effects of this work of the Holy Ghost upon my soul. By *this*, He took me off from old *Adam's* bottom, of self-dependence and doing, for life. By *this*, He laid all my hopes of eternal happiness on a *new* foundation, even the free grace of God in Christ. By *this*, He made me *low* and *loathsome* in my own eyes; and Christ exceeded *high* and *precious* in my esteem. By *this*, He made me *long* for, and *seek* after *holiness* as much as *happiness*, yea to esteem it as an *essential* part thereof: insomuch that I once thought, 'Well, if I must go to hell at *last*; I desire I may be holy *here!*' This, though I can hardly account for, I yet *well* remember. In a word, by *this*, He made *God in Christ all and all to me*; and, every thing else *nothing*, in comparison of Him.

"The blessed Spirit took me, as it were, by the hand, and led me to take *a survey of Christ*. He led me to take a view of Christ on the cross; in the agonies of his soul, and torments of his body, as bearing *my* sin, enduring *my* hell, giving up himself a sacrifice in *my* room and stead, to redeem *me* from endless misery, and raise me to eternal glory! *I viewed all my sins meeting on Jesus!* In the finished work of redemption, I viewed my salvation wrought out; and a perfection of peace, pardon, life, and glory, came flowing down to me in free grace, through the blood of Christ! I looked, and *loved!* Yea, I looked and *mourned!* The fire of divine love melted down my soul, and made mine eyes a fountain of tears! This was the *sweetest*, and yet the *bitterest* mourning that ever my soul felt. 'O hateful sin, (cried I,) thou art the most loathsome abominable thing in my sight. It was *me* the dear Lord loved; and yet it was I that *pierced* him.' This was one of the sweetest days I have enjoyed in this world. It was the time of my espousals, and the day of the gladness of my heart.

"I was, as it were, brought forth into a new world. I conversed with new objects; I felt new affections, desires, delights, &c. I was delivered from Mount *Sinai*, and brought to Mount *Zion*, the city of the living God. Religious duties were now very precious to me; such as hearing, reading, praying, meditation, and converse with Christians; and much of God I enjoyed in them. The saints were now my own company; I esteemed them the excellent of the earth, in whom was all my delight. *Lord's days* were the very joy of my heart; yea, Sabbaths indeed to me. And the *soul-rest* which I enjoyed thereon, received an additional sweetness, as I viewed it as an *earnest* of my *eternal rest* in the bosom of Jesus. In short, my conversation was in heaven; and the world, sin, and Satan, under my feet. But, alas! I soon found that I was not got out of the reach of my spiritual enemies."

After the relation of some severe temptations, soul plunges, and dreadful Satanic assault; occupying several pages in our Author's own account of herself, she then proceeds. "All this while, *babe-like*, I rather lived upon *promises given in*, than upon *Christ* in those promises. I knew not how to believe without sight. So long as *God's* love flowed into my soul, and *my* love flowed out to him again; *just so long I could believe*. But, when the sweet sensation *abated*, my faith began to *sink* with it. But my kind Lord always brought me some *cordial* or other, to support me in my *fainting fits*. And after this manner I was carried on for a year, or little more (as near as I can remember) before the Lord brought me to some *stability* and strength of faith in the *dark*.

Mr. *Shepherd's* 'Penitential Cries' were of great use to me. O how has my soul breathed out its desires to God in some of those hymns! Particularly that *one* for 'Communion with God.' And though I could not say, '*My* God and *my* Christ;' yet I saw such a ravishing glory in Jesus, as made me *thirst* after the knowledge of *interest* in Him. That my impatient longings for Christ may be discerned, I shall transcribe the Hymn; and truly my soul was in it.

I.

Alas, my God, that we should be
Such strangers to each other!
O that as friends we might agree,
And walk and talk together!
Thou know'st my soul does dearly love
The place of thine abode;
No music drops so sweet a sound,
As those two words,—*my God*.

II.

I long not for the fruit that grows
Within these gardens here;
I find no sweetness in the *rose*
When *Jesus* is not near.
Thy gracious *presence*, O *my* Christ,
Can make a *paradise*;
O what are all the goodly *pearls*,
Unto this *pearl of price!*

III.

May I taste that *communion*, Lord,
Thy people have with Thee!
Thy spirit daily talks with *them*,
O let him talk with *me!*
Like Enoch, let me walk with God,
And thus, walk out my day,
Attended with the heavenly guards,
Upon the King's highway.

IV.

When wilt thou come unto me, Lord?
O come my Lord most dear!
Come near, come nearer, nearer still;
I'm *well* when thou art near.
When wilt thou come unto me, Lord?
I languish for Thy sight;
Ten thousand *suns*, if Thou art *strange*,
Are *shades* instead of *light.*

V.

When wilt though come unto me, Lord?
For till thou dost appear
I count each *moment* for a *day*,
Each *minute* for a *year*.
Come, Lord, and never from me go;
This world's a darksome place;
I find *no pleasure* here below,
When thou dost veil thy face.

VI.

Those falsely call'd "the *sweets* of sin,"
Are *bitter* unto me;
I loathe the state that I am in,
I long to come to Thee.
But O wilt thou receive me now,
I'm coming to thy door;
I bring thee *nought*; no *dowry*, Lord;
I come *extremely* poor!

VII.

There's no such thing as pleasure here,
My *Jesus* is my *all!*
As Thou dost *shine*, or *disappear*,
My pleasures *rise*, or *fall*.
Come, spread thy savour on my frame,
(No sweetness is so sweet,)
Till I get *up*, to sing Thy name,
Where *all thy singers meet*.

"It pleases the Lord, in the fifteenth year of my age, to incline my heart to join with the Church of Christ in *Northampton*, over which the late Mr. *Hunt* was pastor. Under his ministry I was often laid to the breasts of consolation, and, being fed with the milk of the word, which was suited to my present case, I *grew* thereby. In this house of the Lord I oft *sought* for, and found my beloved; both in his more *general* and *special* ordinances. So that the experience of God's power and glory in the sanctuary, was precious to my soul; and fellowship with his dear saints was sweet. But yet, I too much lived upon *enjoyments*, I delighted to have my *interest* in Christ tried, by all the *marks* and *signs* of a believer, which were continually laid down in the ministry. When I could *find* them, my heart was filled with *joy*; but, if there were any I did not clearly *discern*, I sunk down in *sorrow*. So foolish was I, that I looked for the *effects* of faith, when faith was not in *exercise*. Just as if a person should look for the beauty of the *spring* in the *winter* season; or seek to know what o'clock it is by the sun-dial, when the sun does not *shine* on it. And while I went *this* way to work, I never attained to *settled* *assurance*. No! the soul that enters into REST by faith, must have somewhat more *firm* and *stable*, than *fleeting frames* to *lean* upon.*

"At length it pleased the Lord to take me by the arms, and teach me to go in the way of *faith*, when I had not spiritual *sense*. I had been once, I remember, at a meeting of *prayer*, but not meeting with *God* in it, I returned very *sad*. And as I was lamenting my *case*, that word was brought to my mind, 'Rejoice in the Lord *always*; and again I say rejoice.' But my heart straightway replied, 'I have not *enjoyed* God to-night, and how can I *rejoice?*' Then the *word* brake in again upon my heart with such a *ray* of glorious *light*, that directed my soul to the true and proper *object* of its joy; even, *the Lord himself.* I was *pointed* hereto,

---

*Dear Christian Reader! I charge thee to read the above *remarks* over and over again; yea, read them more than *seven* times; and may the Lord the Spirit, graciously condescend to open up to thy spiritual mind the vast importance (so far as real *establishment* of soul is concerned) of the *distinction* here pointed out, between resting *on*, living *upon*, and centering *in* Christ *alone* by faith; and, *leaning* on, and taking *comfort* from, uncertain *"fleeting frames;"* as Anne Dutton here, very justly terms them.

Most blessedly has my great favorite *William Romaine*, stated it;—"Whatever the sinner seeks *to rest* in, the Spirit of Jesus detects the *false* foundation, till he leaves him no resource but to believe in the only begotten Son of God. So that when he comes to Jesus, he is stript of *all*, quite *naked*, and *blind, money-less*, and *friendless*, and as empty of *good* as the Devil and sin could make him. *This is all the fitness and preparation for Christ, which I know of.* And when Christ is thus *received*, the same Spirit which would let the sinner bring nothing *to* Christ, will now make him bring all *from* Christ. He will teach the believer, daily, more of his poverty, weakness, unworthiness, vileness, ignorance, &c. that he may be kept *humble*, without any *good* but what he is forced to fetch out of the *fullness* of Jesus. And, when he would go any where else for *comfort*, such as to duties, frames, gifts, and graces, (for *pride* will *live* and *thrive* too, upon any thing but *Jesus*)—the Spirit makes them *dry* and *lean*, and will not let him stop short of the *fountain-head* of all true comfort. In short, He will *glorify nothing but Jesus*. He will stain the pride of all greatness, and of all goodness, excepting what is derived from the fullness of the incarnate God." Reader! form thine own conclusions; but for *my* part, blessed be God, my soul has long been at a point in these matters. Jesus saith of God the Holy Ghost,—"He shall glorify *Me*." Amen! let Jesus be glorified, says

J. A. Jones.

as with a finger—In the *Lord*, not in your *frames*. In the Lord, not in what you *enjoy* from him, but in what you *are* IN Him. And the Lord sealed my instruction, and filled my heart brimful of joy, in the faith of my *eternal* interest and unchangeable standing *in Him:* and of His being and infinite *fountain of blessedness* for me to rejoice in *always*; even when the *streams of sensible enjoyments* failed.

"But yet I was often ready to stagger through unbelief; and at such times and seasons I was for putting forth my hand, to lay hold on *past experiences*, the remembrance of which, at times, had been precious to my soul. But when I sought for my *satisfactions* from hence, instead of deriving all my *life* and *comfort* from Christ by fresh acts of faith; the Lord, in great mercy, was pleased to draw a *veil* over his work upon my soul, and direct me to *stay myself upon my God*, even when I walked in the dark as to present *enjoyments*, and had not the light of past experience. And this was to make me die unto *a life of sense*, in order to raise me up to a *higher life of faith* upon the Son of God. The Holy Spirit shewed me my everlasting standing in Christ's person, grace, and righteousness; and gave me to see my *security* in his *unchangeableness*, under all the *changes* which passed over *me*. And then I began to rejoice in my dear Lord Jesus as *always the same*, even when my *frames altered*. Thus the Lord began to establish me, and settle my faith upon its proper basis."

"Mr. Hunt, my first pastor, was removed, and another minister succeeded him. The ministry of *this* servant of Christ was of use to me in *some* respects, though I did fall in with his judgment in several points. But he not insisting much upon them at *first*, I was willing to content myself, and *pass by* what I did not like: but some time after this, not finding myself edified under his ministry, and my dissatisfaction increasing, I thought it my duty to acquaint him with it, and accordingly I did so, after having sought the Lord about it. I thought I should meet with opposition if I attempted it, and much indeed came on. But I saw such an excellency and preciousness in the *Truths* I contended for, that I thought at that time I could not only bear the *reproaches* I might meet with on this account, but *even lay down my life in the defence of them*, if the Lord had called me to it. Many were the trials, and great the supports I met with. A mighty spirit of prayer was upon me; the liberty of God's bosom was afforded me in the day of my distress; frequently were the answers I received from him; and great was the familiarity I had with him. I found the truth of what the prophet asserts by way of interrogation, 'Can two walk together except they be agreed?' Amos iii. 3. Having received full satisfaction that it was the Lord's mind, I should *remove my communion* from that church to which I was then related, to that over which Mr. *Moore* was pastor,* I accordingly did it."

"This providence of God in removing me from one church to another, I have great reason to bless his name for; as he made it an introduction to all that great glory which I have since beheld in *Zion*. Upon my being anew *planted*, the Lord watered me, I cast forth my roots as *Lebanon*, and my branches did spread. The Lord Jesus, my *chief* shepherd, led me by the ministry of his servant and *under* shepherd, Mr. *Moore*, into *fat* green pastures. The *doctrines* of the Gospel were *clearly stated*, and much insisted on in his ministry. The sanctuary-streams ran *clearly*, and the sun shone gloriously. I was abundantly satisfied with the fatness of God's house; made to drink of the river of his pleasures, and, in his light, I saw light.

"The next providence I shall give some hints of, relates to the Lord's removing my habitation from *Northampton* to *London*; which was occasioned by my entering into the marriage state when I was *twenty-two* years of age.**

---

*I would, in a note, inform the reader, that Mr. *John Moore*, above alluded to, was born in 1662 at Kighly in Yorkshire. He was awakened and convinced at sixteen years of age; and continued *nine* years in great distress of soul. He became Pastor of the Baptist church at Northampton in 1700. No doubt but he was the very blessed free-grace gospel preacher, which Mrs. Dutton has described him to be. I have in my possession, a small volume of his sermons printed in 1722, which I most highly value. It is rarely to be met with; and for richness of gospel truth it can scarcely be exceeded by any writer. Under this well-taught divine, Anne Dutton grew in grace; and increased in the knowledge of Him, whom to know is life eternal.

Mr. *Moore* died January 14, 1726, aged 64. His daughter became the wife of Mr. *John Brine*, whose funeral sermon for her, with and account of her *choice* experience, is yet to be met with.

**She was married to Mr. *Benjamin Dutton*, who after living some time in London, removed to *Evershall* in Northamptonshire, and from thence in 1733 to *Great Gransden* in Huntingdonshire; being chosen Pastor of the Baptist Church in that place. The church increased much under Mr. Dutton's ministry. They built a new meeting-house, and a minister's house, in the year 1743. Mr. Dutton went

"The privileges I enjoyed in Zion were very valuable in my esteem. And when the Lord was about my removal, I was afraid it might be attended with some loss; and that my *small improvement* of the favours I had enjoyed, might have provoked the Lord to *take them away* from me. But the Lord's design in removing me, was the more abundant display of his great goodness, notwithstanding all my unworthiness. And upon my being fixed in London under the ministry of the late *Mr. Skepp*, I soon found the truth thereof. The waters of the sanctuary were indeed *risen* waters, which filled my soul with wonder and joy. I found the *same doctrines* of the gospel maintained and vindicated in the ministry of *Mr. Skepp*, as I was wont to hear under *Mr. Moore*, with abundance of glory, life, and power.*

"Upon my removal to London, I had *transient* communion with the church under the care of Mr. Skepp; but my *abode* being fixed, it was thought proper, after a time, that my *communion* should be so too. Being *dismissed* from Northampton, I was received into full communion by this

---

to *America* in August in that year, for the purpose of soliciting assistance towards the cause at Gransden. His applications were successful, he obtained all the money he wanted; but, on coming home, having nearly reached the English coast, the ship was cast away, and *Mr. Dutton was lost*, to the inexpressible grief of his people; leaving his *widow*, then about forty years of age.

*Perhaps it will hardly be needful to inform the reader, that, Mr. *John Skepp* was a most excellent servant of Christ. He had been a member of the Church at *Cambridge*, under the ministry of the famous Mr. *Joseph Hussey*. He became pastor of the Baptist Church meeting in Currier's Hall, Cripplegate, somewhere about the year 1715, perhaps before; and died in 1721. He wrote only one work; and which was not published till after his death. This was entitled, "Divine Energy; or the efficacious operations of the spirit of God upon the soul of man, in effectual calling and conversion." *It is a most blessed book.* Dr. Gill wrote a recommendatory preface to the second edition, in 1751, saying, "The worthy author was personally and intimately known by me, and his memory is precious to me." Mr. James Upton, much to his honour, put forth a *third* edition, well printed, with an excellently written preface, in 1815. This work ought to be constantly preserved in print, especially in the present day; for, according to Mr. Skepp's own words, "A sad day it is, when men, to make themselves *popular*, take upon them to hector, and to run down the Spirit's work in regeneration and conversion," &c. Mr. *Brine* was Pastor of the Cripplegate Church from 1730 till 1765.

church; and my fellowship with them was sweet. The Lord dwelt in this Zion for *me*; he abundantly blessed her provision, and my poor soul was satisfied with bread: He clothed also her *minister* with salvation, and I, with her saints, did shout for joy; O the glory of God, that I saw in this house of his! In this *garden of God* I sat down under the shadow of my beloved with great delight, and his fruit was sweet to my taste: yea, the enjoyment of the same did quicken my appetite, and set my soul a longing for that happy *day*, when I should feast upon his *glory-fulness*, as 'the Tree of Life in the midst of the paradise of God.'"

Reader, I now pause and inquire of thee—Hast thou, in reading thus far, at all entered into the *truth* of the blessed things treated of by this mother in Israel? Lest any should suspect her of at all underrating, much less despising, good spiritual frames, she goes on to state,—"Though I did not take up my faith of interest principally from *frames*, yet I had abundant *experience* of the rich overflowings of God's love upon my soul, and of the blessed *fruits* of it in my *heart* and *life*. The Holy Ghost opened to me such glorious views of all that vast grace wherein I stood; as gave me to see my *everlasting standing* in it, and to have frequent access *into* it. The doctrines of the everlasting Gospel were daily opened to me in their amazing glory: now *one* was opened to me, then *another*, and oftentimes *many* to explain *one*. Delightfully I viewed over the wonders of infinite grace displayed therein, and *feasted of all as my own*; as having an *entire* and *eternal* interest in the God of all grace, and all the glorious *provisions* of his grace for the salvation of sinners through Jesus Christ."

"In vain do the enemies of the grace of God malign it with their *old odious calumny*, that '*it leads to licentiousness.*' So long as God has a people in the world, he will have *witnesses* to stand on the side of free grace, *as it constrains to holiness*. And among them *I will cast in my mite, and bear my witness for God* that the *more* his glorious grace in my salvation did appear to my soul, the more I was efficaciously TAUGHT to deny ungodliness and worldly lusts, and to live soberly, righteously, and godly, in this present world: looking for that blessed hope, and the glorious appearing of the great God, and our Saviour Jesus Christ, who gave himself for us, that he might *redeem* us from all iniquity, and *purify* unto himself a peculiar people, *zealous of good works.*' Titus ii. 11-14.

"Thus, as enabled, have I given *some* account of the Lord's loving-kindness to my soul;—of my manner of life from my childhood;—of the

work of divine grace upon my heart, in a saving conversion to Christ;—
and of my being brought to some *establishment* in Him. I would address
myself *now* to the people of God in *two degrees of experience:*—First, *to
such saints as have a comfortable knowledge of the work of grace in their
own souls*, I would say with the Psalmist, 'O magnify the Lord with me,
and let us exalt his name together. I sought the Lord, and he heard me,
and delivered me from all my fears.' Psalm xxxiv. 3, 4. You have heard
something, dear saints, of the Lord's lovingkindness to *my* soul: 'Glorify
God in me,' Gal i. 24.

"Secondly, to such of God's people as have *not*, as yet, *a full
persuasion* of a special work of grace in their hearts. *You* also have heard
what the Lord has done for *me*; and I know you are apt to *listen* how it
has been with *others*, whom you *judge* are *believers*, and *to compare your
experience with theirs*, in order to form a *judgment*, whether the work of
God upon your *own* soul be indeed *genuine* and saving. But, dear heart,
be not too critical herein; for know this, that the experience of the saints
in *many* particulars may *vary*, though in the general it *agrees*. Do not say,
then, upon the reading of this narrative, 'I have *not* been in *all respects
thus*, and therefore I fear that I am not right.' Hast thou been convinced
of the misery of thy natural estate, that thou wast in a perishing condition
without Christ? Hast thou had a discovery of Christ's beauty, excellency,
and *suitability* to thee in all thy *wants*; so as to draw out thy soul into
earnest desires after an *interest* in this precious Jesus? And, under a deep
sense of thy *perishing* condition, hast thou been encouraged by God's
free grace in Christ *to cast thyself at his feet*, in *hope* of finding mercy?
Committing thyself into the arms of his grace and power for all life and
salvation, with an holy *venture*, saying, 'I will unto the king, and if I
perish I perish?' 'I *see* there is *no other* way of salvation; *here therefore
I will wait as an undone sinner*; it may be *free grace* will save *me*, if *not*
I can but die; and *if I perish* it shall be at the foot of God's free mercy
in Christ.' Hast thou, I say, at any time experienced such *resolutions*
wrought in thy soul? Thou art then exceeding *safe*, and thy *state* eternally
secure; though thou mayest not have so much *comfort* in it, or *satisfaction* about it, as *some* of God's children *enjoy*. What though thy *Father*
may not have *indulged* thee with such *love-feasts*, such sensible mirth and
rejoicing, as *some* of thy brethren, poor *prodigals*, have met with at their
return; yet thou art *ever* with him, and *all that he hath is thine!* thou hast
Christ, and, in him hast *all!* Be *content*, then, that infinite wisdom should

carve out thy TIME-*portion of comfort.* The Lord leads thee in a *right* way; a way that is *best* for thee NOW: thou shalt see it to be so, ere long. It is but a little while, and the *sun* shall rise upon thee, and no more go down, for *night* and *darkness* shall be swallowed up in *eternal day!* In the mean time go on, trusting thy soul in the hands of Christ, taking him at his word; counting him *faithful* that has promised; thus glorifying of him in the *dark*, until taken up to be glorified *with* him in the enjoyment of thy *inheritance in light."*

"But I would say something to *poor sinners*, and that of *three* sorts.

"1. To such as are *openly profane*, if any such may read these lines. Ah, poor souls, your condition is exceedingly *miserable*, and so much the more because you *know it not.* I have declared somewhat of that concern I was under about my eternal estate: what think you of *yours?* I ran not such lengths in sin as perhaps *you* have done; and yet I saw that I must perish for ever, if God's free grace and mercy in Christ was not extended to my soul. How do you think to escape the wrath to come? It may be thou wilt say, 'I know that hell will be my portion if I live and die in my present case; but, after I have had *a little more pleasure in sin*, I purpose to leave my sinful course, to amend my ways, and *make my peace with God."* Ah, poor soul! but what if *death* should overtake thee suddenly, and *hell* swallow thee up in a moment? Poor soul! thou art under the *dominion* of sin, and thy *lusts* are so many *lords* over thee. Satan, the prince of darkness, possesseS thy *heart* as his *throne.* Thou art so far from *groaning* under thy bondage, that thou likest it, and yieldest thyself a *willing slave* to the *drudgery* of *hell.* It is a very great *mistake* for thee to think thou hast *power* to leave thy sins *when thou wilt.* Alas, poor soul, there is such a *power* in the kingdom of *darkness* in which thou art *held*, that *no power in thyself*, nor in any other creature, *can* rescue thee from it. Thou hast *destroyed* thyself by thine iniquity; and if thy help is not in the Lord, thou art undone for ever. Thou art sunk *too low* for any *created* arm to reach thee; and if the *omnipotent* arms of divine grace and mercy do not snatch thee from the powers of darkness, and pluck thee as a brand out of the *burning*, thou wilt perish for ever in thy own deceivings.

"But supposing thou couldst *reform*, and amend thy ways; yet, 'by *the deeds of the law* shall no flesh be justified in the sight of God,' Rom. iii. 20. And suppose thou couldst, from this time, even to thy dying moments, *walk exactly* as the holy law of God requireth, (which is an utter impossibility,) suppose it, I say, yet what wilt thou do with thy *past* sins? All thy *future* obedience is but thy duty, but none of *that* can pay *a mite* towards thy *old* debt. In vain then thou dost think to bring thy *external* reformation and *legal* repentance to stand before God, and *make thy peace* with him. Such is the flaming holiness and justice of his *nature*, as well as of his *law*, that he cannot endure the least sin, but will break forth, like devouring fire, upon every soul where sin is found. No; the work of *making peace* with a sin-avenging God, was too great for all the creatures, either in heaven or earth, to perform.

"There is full, free, and everlasting salvation, already wrought out by Jesus. This complete salvation is proclaimed in the glorious Gospel. The Holy Spirit of God is given to attend the *ministry* of the gospel; even of *that* ministry which exalts the free-grace of God *alone*, as the foundation of a sinner's salvation; the righteousness of Christ *alone*, as the matter of his justification; the blood of Christ *alone*, as cleansing the sinner from all sin; and the Spirit of Christ *alone*, as the applier of this great salvation. Wait under the ordinances of divine appointment. I *know* thou canst not quicken thine own heart; but there is *an almighty energy* attends the Gospel: the *all-creating power of God* goes forth in 'the words of this life,' to quicken *dead* sinners, and to make them stand up upon their feet *alive* as a exceeding great army. Ezek. xxxvii. 2-10. Be encouraged then to *wait* where God *works*; all things are possible with God; there is nothing too hard with Jehovah.

"2. A word or two to you, poor sinners, who are *self-righteous*. I have told you also somewhat of my experience; such as, that I had *a religious education*; and was kept from those *gross* evils which many run into: I attended divine worship in public, and had some notional knowledge of the truths of the Gospel. I thought myself to be fair for *Heaven*, and *better than others*; and yet, if infinite mercy had not prevented, I had gone to *Hell* with a lie in my right hand. But when God came to shew me the infinite purity of his nature, and the spirituality of his law; I then soon found *my own righteousness* to be but as filthy rags. The Spirit of the Lord blowed upon all my performances, and then, those which looked *green* and *beautiful* before, soon withered as the grass: my *comeliness* was turned in me into *corruption*: and a sight of God's *holiness* made me cry out—Woe is me, I am *undone*, because of my *uncleanness!*

"And how dost thou, *poor self-righteous creature*, think to stand before this Holy Lord God? If thou trustest to thy *performances*, either *moral* or *evangelical*, as the matter of thy *righteousness* before God; I tell thee, the bed is *shorter* than a man can stretch himself upon it, and the covering *narrower* than he can wrap himself in it. All hope of safety from any of thine own *performances*, shall be *cut off*; and thy *trust* therein shall be as the spider's web, swept away as *poisonous dust*, by the besom of destruction. Never think, then, to stand before God in the filth and rags fo thy own righteousness; for, if thou *dost*, thou wilt surely be found naked; and with this additional weight which will *increase* thy condemnation, that, *thou hast rejected the righteousness of Christ*. They that are incensed against *Him*, shall be ashamed; they shall go into confusion together, that are makers of *idols*; that have set up the idol of their own righteousness, instead of submitting to the righteousness of God; but, Israel shall be saved in the Lord with an everlasting salvation; in *Him* shall they be *justified* and shall glory; they shall not be ashamed nor confounded world without end."

"3. A few words to such poor sinners, as are, *in some measure*, sensible of the misery of their natural state; have had *some* discoveries of Christ; and yet are afraid that he will not save *them* in particular. Dear souls, I have told you that this was once *my* case: I saw myself to be a chief sinner; and in my perishing condition I came to a throne of grace to find mercy; allured by *some hopes* that I *might* obtain, but also attended by innumerable *fears* that I should *not*. And yet, *I obtained mercy*; yea, I found Jesus to be as infinitely *willing* to save me, as he was *able*. Be *encouraged* therefore to come to the throne, to come to God, in and through *Christ*, where thousands have found mercy; yea, *where never any soul was denied its suit*. I know thy *weakness* and thy *fears*; and I also know the *weights* which hang upon thee; thou art *heavy-laden:* all these greatly hinder the *swiftness* of thy motions toward Jesus. But, in the Lord's own time, he will greatly strengthen thy weak faith, encourage thy hope, take off thy burdens, and give thee access with freedom to Jesus, and through him, by one Spirit, to the Father.

"Meanwhile *come as thou canst*; though with a trembling heart, attended with ten thousand fears, and under the guilt of innumerable transgressions. There is an infinite ability in Jesus to save. Yea, *by one word of his mouth he can speak full salvation to thee in an instant—* enough to take up an eternity of time for thy *enjoyment* of it. Come then, with all thy *wants*, and prostrate thyself at his feet: there is *enough* in Christ to supply them all. Yea, there is infinitely *more* than enough! Were thy wants ten thousand times greater than they are, *it is all one*, when thou comest to this *infinite ocean*. The fullness of Christ is an immense, an inexhaustible ocean, that can never be drawn dry, or in the least *wasted*, by all innumerable multitudes of needy sinners that have been, are now, and shall be *supplied* thence, to all eternity! O who can *conceive*, much less express, the unsearchable riches of Christ's *ability* to save sinners! To know it fully, is beyond the reach of created understanding. And he is as *willing* as he is *able*. The infinite *willingness* of his *heart*, is as large as the almighty *power* of his *arm!* Poor sinner, thou canst not *ask* grace, *more* grace, than he *has* to give, or than he is *willing* to bestow. He *delights* to fill such needy, empty souls, as *thou* art. Now the bitter work of his death on the cross is over, dost thou think his heart is changed? No, as he *died* for thee on the cross, so he lives for thee on the throne. In denying *thee* it would be to deny *himself:* not only to deny thee the grace of his heart, but also it would be to deny (in denying *thee*) the very *end* and *design* of his *death.* What hinders thee then, from an immediate running into Christ's bosom, since there is such *room* for thee in his *heart?* I dare say that nothing but thy *unbelief* hinders; and, blessed be God, even *that* shall not hinder thee *always*, neither. Would it be an unspeakable joy to *thee*, to get into Christ's arms? let me say, *it would be much more so, to him.* The day of his espousals with a poor sinner, in the day of the gladness of his heart!"*

Having now presented the reader with the *substance* of Mrs. Dutton's own account of the Lord's gracious dealings towards her, &c. I proceed to notice her last *most sever affliction*, which ended in her death. And this will be narrated from the account of "one who was an eye and ear witness of the whole."

Perhaps there are but *few* instances where death has made such slow, sensible, and gradual approaches. Anne Dutton was a great saint; she had

---

*I had not intended, in compiling this *Memoir*, to have inserted the above encouraging *addresses*. But I found them, on perusal, so truly sweet and blessed to my own soul, that I *could not refrain* from drawing out the *essence* for the reader's profit; though the limit of pages forbad inserting the whole. May a signal divine blessing, accompany the same, to the several characters addressed—

EDITOR.

great grace; she was greatly tried; she glorified the Lord; she was satisfied with all the Lord's procedure towards her; she rested the *whole*, for body and soul, for time and eternity, with *Him*.

> Pleas'd with all the Lord provides,
> Wean'd from all the world besides.

Near twelve months before her dissolution she complained of a soreness in her throat, as if something stuck in the passage: she used several means to remove it, but all in vain; it kept slowly increasing, till she thought it felt as if much swelled, and would have me often look at it, though I could perceive but little swelling outwardly. At length the obstruction to her comfortable swallowing so far increased that she began to be apprised it might be the pleasure of God to remove her by it in the end. For she would often say, *"Who can tell but it may be the will of my heavenly Father to love me home to himself by this affliction?"* During all this time she continued (as she had for years before done) unweariedly writing to her numerous correspondents, both in this and in other Nations: so that it has been often thought that Psalm civ. 4, was never in any mere mortal more verified than in her. I have often known her to write sixteen or eighteen hours out of the twenty-four; and I suppose all her other avocations of the day scarcely had *one* hour. She would often lament over the time lost in eating, drinking, and sleeping, and *long for immortality*, when she should serve the Lord without let or interruption! And would often express, with more than common emphasis, "And his servants shall serve him."

About the sixth or seventh month after her disorder began, she published her thirteenth volume of Letters; and, understanding by a corresponding friend at Norwich, that Mr. Sandiman's unscriptural notions were embraced by one Mr. N_____n of that place, and that many unstable souls, both there and at Wymondham, were corrupted from the simplicity of the gospel, she was spirited to write and publish, as her *last* public testimony to the truth, an attempt to prove that saving faith is more than a bare assent to gospel truth.

Her difficulty to swallow increasing, she was yet unable to set about her work of writing with great vivacity; for as her outward man decayed her inward man was renewed day by day. Having eight volumes of unpublished letters by her, she was willing to peruse, and fit them for the press, if the Lord should in his providence, by any means, bring them out of after her decease. All this was a considerable addition to her usual work; for all this while, her writing to correspondents rather increased, they being very solicitous to hear from her often, being impatient to know how the Lord would deal with their dear, and never enough valued friend. How constant and large must those divine communications have been which maintained her holy flame, causing it to blaze forth still stronger and brighter, and she in the midst of the waters of a more than common affliction! So that she would often in the evening of a day, when she had been able to take little or no *bodily succour* all day long, bless and praise God, who had supplied and strengthened her to write such and such things for his glory, to such and such of his children; and with her once humbled, obedient, suffering Lord, esteem it her meat and drink to do the will of her heavenly Father.

About three months before her death, being sensible of her duty to try all probable means, and to wait on the Lord for his blessing, she employed a skilful apothecary in the neighborhood, who in a very few days, after practising the utmost of his skill, judiciously and honestly declared her case very dangerous, and that her life was too precious and valuable for him to proceed on his own judgment; desiring her to consult with an eminent physician of Huntingdon, which as she chose not to do, a beloved friend of hers in London procured her advice from an able doctor there, which was duly attended to: but her disorder baffling all skill and means, she cheerfully left herself in her Father's hands, rejoicing that it was, and would be, *eternally well with her.*

From about this time I have an opportunity, from her own pen, to give an account of several things relating to the Lord's dealings with her during the remainder of her very painful disorder; which I choose to do, as being better done than I am able, and more satisfactory, in her own words.

August the 17th, 1765, she thus expresses herself to a dear and worthy friend, "If the Lord spares me, I will write you the effects of the present applications; whether I live or die, your life is not bound up in *me*, but in the Lord Christ, your God, by the Father's everlasting covenant: and as long as *he* lives *you* shall never die, nor want in the wilderness a tender friend to your joy. When *creature-streams fail* and are *dry*, the Lord, the ever-lasting fountain, will be your continual supply. And I have often seen that when one creature dies, he raises up and fills another to my joy. You see, my dear Madam, that mercy and misery, or rather joy and sorrow, follow us through the wilderness, and miseries are *mercies* to *us* that believe in Jesus. If all things were to be smooth and pleasant we should be too much *elated*; and if all things were afflictive we should be unduly dejected."

August the 24th she thus expresses her case: "I am ill and weak, and no better in my throat; it is very difficult for me to swallow any thing; but, blessed be God, he helps me to get something down. Last Saturday night I was almost choaked, but much delighted to think, that *when my breath was stopt, I should be with Christ*, for ever with my dearest Lord; which is far better than this distant state. God grant that Christ may be glorified in my body, whether it be by life or death; that in faith and patience I may endure his good pleasure to his honour. Before the affliction rose to this height the Lord said to me, 'When thou passest through the waters I will be with thee, and through the rivers they shall not overflow thee: when thou walkest through the fire, thou shalt not be burnt, neither shall the flame kindle upon thee.' And, blessed be my gracious, faithful God, He is with me; and will never, never leave me, nor forsake me. If by this affliction He designs to *love me home to glory*, it will be in the best time and way: and if he designs me to abide awhile longer in the body, with means and without, he will give some relief; *I choose that which is most for his glory.* He has said unto me, "Be it unto thee even as thou wilt.' And indeed I have no will but *his for* life or death. It is marvelous kindness that he hath continued me so long in the body, and enabled me in some measure to seek his glory. Which ever of us, Madam, is taken to glory *first* will be the *happiest*; and the other shall find an immutable God, infinitely kind. and soon we shall meet in a perfect state, to celebrate the praise of salvation-grace, and to bless God that made us of mutual use in the wilderness. Let us rejoice, Madam, to put off sinful mortality, that we may put on the image of Christ in perfection of purity and immortal glory!—What have we in this distant state? Surely no joy but to see the Lord by faith, and serve him by love. But, oh, our imperfection! never shall we be as we would and should be until faith is turned into vision, and love is raised into a perfect endless flame! Let us not fear death; the sting is gone; and the Lord our life will be with us in it. The further we enter into death's dark valley, glory will beam upon our spirits more brightly. And as soon as ever the soul is out of the body it will at once be made perfect in purity." In another letter, some days after: "As to myself, Madam, I was nearly choaked yesterday, in attempting to eat a bit of roast veal, though I could not get down *half a mouthful in all.* To-day my throat is bad, but through the Lord's mercy I have got down *a little milk.* The Lord is still very gracious to me in supporting and comforting me. In the present state we are compassed about with sin and death; sin, in God's just vengeance, brought death in upon our nature; and death, through the death of Christ, by the omnipotent power of the Holy Ghost, shall be the outlet of sin for ever. Through the Lord's goodness I had a very comfortable night the last night, by many exceeding great and precious promises given to me. Besides my poor throat, I have some degree of fever; and, from the great weight I feel in my forehead, with heaviness and inclination to sleep, I fear a stupor will seize my brain. When our time of departure draweth nigh, how kind is it of the Lord to cause various diseases to lend their influence to *dissolve* the body, that he may bring us soon up to *glory!"*

About the middle of September she could take nothing down for two or three days together, no, not so much as a *drop* of milk or wine, and then her passage would be a little open to take down, with difficulty, a few spoonsful of some liquid, without the smallest crumb of bread, or any thing substantial in it. And then her language was, "In all this my God is to me a God of infinite kindness! He conducts me by a right way to the city of habitation, and for the conduct of his grace and wisdom I shall shortly praise him perfectly and eternally in the heights of Zion." About this time that seasonable word was brought to her mind, "Let patience have its perfect work, that ye may be perfect and entire, lacking nothing." On which she thus sweetly speaks, "If the greatest, the longest affliction, under divine agency, is to work our perfection, what a solid ground this for patience? Yea, for strong consolation!" About this same time she heard of an instance of a woman in the neighborhood who died lately of the same disorder, and who lived a quarter of a year after she could eat nothing, by only putting a little sugar in her mouth now and then, until she was quite wasted and spent. "And, if this should be my lot," she said, "*the Lord can make it pleasant:* my Jesus has said to me, My grace is sufficient for thee; afflictions are as waters which pass away."

September the 20th she thus writes to a dear friend: "It is the good pleasure of my all-wise, all-gracious Father, still to keep me in the furnace of affliction; but glory to his name, I am favoured with his presence therein: This strengthens my faith and patience in and for their exercise; this gives me hope of deliverance in way and time, as infinite wisdom and goodness see best. This makes me choose what my father chooseth, and love and bless him for that which to frail nature is grieving. While the Lord says, I know thee by name, and thou hast found grace in my sight, my faith is strengthened in my eternal interest in the God of Grace and peace in and through Christ. While he says, It is given you on the behalf of Christ not only to believe, but also to suffer, I see my sufferings to be gifts of infinite mercy, to exercise my graces to spiritual felicity, and as a further preparation for eternal glory. A sense of God's love in every stroke makes the affliction light, and sweetly reconciles me to it. A little while since, when distress was threatening; to keep me from verging towards self-care, the Lord caused that word sweetly drop in, "Casting all your care upon him; for he careth for you:" hence my heart was drawn to cast all my care upon him; his care I saw was all productive of help, and that mine could effect nothing for myself; and I thought, If my dear Lord Jesus careth for me, what need I, in any misery, to care for myself anxiously? If he cares for me who is infinite in love, received me at the Father's hand as his own, to redeem me from all misery, and to bring me up to all glory; if he cares for me, who in love unknown died for me, and lives for me, if he cares for me, who in everymisery hath with me an infinite love-sympathy; he will see that the affliction shall not abide too long, nor rise too high; not one degree beyond what in infinite wisdom and goodness is appointed. Let me therefore cast all my care upon him with complacency, and bosom my soul in his all-wise, all-gracious disposal. I am much troubled, dear Madam, to swallow any thing, but 'God help me' is my name; and his mercy shall be upon me according as I trust in him. It is no wonder that such a *favoured* child as I have been, through so long a life, should have some sharp trials to meet with so long before death. But, as nothing overtakes us by hap or chance, but the Lord is now performing the thing which was appointed for me, and many such appointments are with him for others of his dear children; so there was grace laid up for us in Christ, to carry us through all our trials, to the Lord's praise and our bliss: and soon we shall see what need there was for us at seasons to be in heaviness.

"As I was much afflicted with my throat, Madam, yesterday, that word sweetly dropt on my heart, "Who art thou, O great mountain? before Zerubbabel thou shalt become a plain, and he shall bring forth the headstone thereof with shoutings, crying, Grace, grace unto it!" By this

I was blest with a sweet glance of the Lord's delivering kindness, that he would either rebuke my disorder, how proud soever it might appear; or suffer it to rise to its height, ad *loose me thereby from all misery* to the heights of joy and glory: and either way I shall cry 'Grace, grace' to the Lord's deliverance. I was much pleased last night and this morning to think that I have a God that changeth not; a God that is as full of wisdom, grace, and power, to help and save, now as ever. There, my dear Madam, under the shadow of his wings, let us both make our refuge, until all our calamities are overpast. I am taken with a straining cough, and prodigious wheezing from my throat, which makes my stomach very sore, and has much interrupted my sleep for five nights past. Yesterday I tried to get down a little milk three or four times, but could not compass it, most of it coming up again, and occasioning great pain. This morning, to my amazement, I was able to take down almost half a pint, with but little pain: thus the Lord has dealt with me several times, my stomach much wanting food, and after that my throat has again been open a little. I wait to see which way the Lord will save me to his glory."

Her long inability to take any food, and but little liquid, had by this time greatly enfeebled her. Her flesh was now much sunk; her colour, which was lively in health, was gone; and her visage, which used to be round, was now grown long; but her spirits were to a wonder constantly cheerful. She would receive her visiting friends as freely and vigorously as ever; and they were amazed to see with what vivacity and spirit she would walk up and down the house. Her conversation was always spiritual, instructive, and profitable; and while she was telling any one how she was, with the particulars of her painful disorder, she would frequently break out, "Glory be to God, all is well! Blessed be his name, his wisdom cannot err! It is best as it is!—I would not have it otherwise."

About the latter end of September she thus writes, "Is any thing too hard for the Lord? If he speaks the healing word, I know I shall be restored, and then, oh for grace to be doubly his! But, if by affliction he brings me down into death, by that he will raise me to glory's height! Sweetly he said to me yesterday, 'I am God—all-sufficient: walk before me, and be thou perfect.' He is all-sufficient to support, relieve, and deliver, in such a way as shall most advance his glory, and my felicity: and oh, that in respect of humble submission, sweet acquiescence, and steadfast confidence, to, and in, his all-wise, all-gracious disposal, I may abound continually! Then should I give to God my Saviour glory; then would rise my spiritual felicity; and soon the Sun of righteousness, with healing in his wings, would arise upon me!" In a letter, the beginning of October, she thus speaks: "I have been this last week marvellously supported, and blest with some comfortable sleep: when for a considerable time I can swallow nothing, all on a sudden the Lord helps me to take a little milk down, and now and then a little balm wine.—How great is his goodness in this; and that I have so many parts of my body in health and at liberty! Yea, let me say, how great is his goodness in that he thus favours me! If in this affliction I may but give God glory, I shall have the joy of it to a blest eternity. A thought of giving him glory makes me, at times, lose the smart in that ineffable sweet! He bids me stand still, and see the salvation of the Lord with me! and I trust he will strengthen my faith and patience, cheerfully to wait the time of his delivering kindness. When all is done for me, upon me, and by me, which the Lord designed, then instantly he will love me into his bosom. I wait upon my God; my soul doth wait to see which way he will glorify himself, and save me. Glory to his name, I am sweetly borne in love's unwearied arms: and this God, my dear Madam, is your God for ever and ever; he will be your guide, even unto death; unto, through, and beyond death; and your soul's portion to a glorious, endless duration! My illness often changes; that will be the most glorious change, to be made perfect in Christ's image."

October the 12th she thus writes to a dear friend: "I am much as I was as to my affliction; am favoured with divine consolations, and patiently and cheerfully kept waiting for the God of my salvation. The Lord helps me continually, and every day and night I am made a partaker of new mercies. A little milk, or home-made wine, now and then, the Lord helps me to receive; but I cannot eat a bit of bread or meat, or any thing of substance for my support, which makes my stomach very windy and *craving*; and, should the affliction continue, perhaps it may bring on a consumption: but whatever comes to me will come as the happy product of my heavenly Father's wise and gracious decree; will come as a blessing to bring me to Him, who of all my felicity is the total sum!"

About this time, under the exercise of an empty and craving stomach, she would be often cheerful saying, *"My poor stomach, how it does crave! it prays me to give it something, but I can get nothing to it!"* One by her, being affected with her case, and she perceiving it, said, "You think my affliction very heavy, and so indeed it is to flesh and sense! but my dearest Lord bore the penalty of it for me! and glory to his name, he strengthens me to bear it cheerfully! I esteem it light, and bless him for it." About the same time a friend by her, eating heartily and comfortably, said to her, "My dear child, is there no envy in your mind prevailing, at seeing me eat thus freely, with a secret wish that you could do so? To which she replied. "No, I bless God, there is none prevailing; I am glad to see you eat, and may you be helped to prize the mercy! but, for my part, I bless God the affliction is just as it is; I would not have it otherwise; I would neither have it in the least degree lighter, nor deliverance from it come one moment sooner, than my heavenly Father sees fit! Glory to his name, he doth all things well, nothing could be better than it is."

October the 17th, in a letter she thus expresses herself, "Blessed be my good God, another week hath he borne and carried me in the sweet strong arms of his eternal love, and ever-enduring mercy! A sweet view he gave me the first day of the week, that this great affliction,, which I am called to endure, was not cast upon me in wrathful displeasure, but in infinite favour, as an honour. And sweet was that word to me, "Behold, we count them happy which endure." Nature calls its affliction *misery*; but the grace of Christ, which enables us to endure affliction to God's praise, in our afflicted state, makes us happy. And, though there is much imperfection and weakness in my attempts at filial duty, my gracious Father tells me that he forgives my iniquity, and will spare me as a man spareth his own son that serveth him. This comforts my heart and strengthens my faith in his infinite grace; this excites me to greater obedience. I have not been wholly without grievous suggestions from the enemy; but through grace I have been enabled to resist them vigourously, and tell him to his head that I would hear no slanders cast upon my gracious god, but trust in him for his glory if he was to slay me, and wait upon him cheerfully for his delivering mercy; which I know will come in the best time and way: and thus the enemy has been made to flee. There is an appointed measure for my affliction, and when that is full, deliverance will come. I was apprehensive this week that I should *swallow no more*; but the Lord has helped me again to take a little liquid out of a tea-spoon for two days. This God is our God for ever and ever; he will be our guide even unto death; and the strength of our hearts when all nature faints."

By this time her bodily weakness was so great she could no longer attend the public worship of God in his house, though her dwelling was *close to the meeting:* this was a great addition to her affliction; for, though she was so eminent in grace and gifts, yet she conscientiously attended all opportunities; and perhaps not one in the whole auditory so frequently edified, strengthened, and comforted, and happy she. And now, when confined, her soul so longed for the word of the Lord, that she prevailed on the minister, after worship, to repeat to her as much of the heads, particulars, and other parts of his discourse, or discourses, as he could remember; and even in this the Lord was good to her, as she would often declare.

October the 25th she thus writes her case: "My affliction seems to be appointed to end in my dissolution, and the humour in my throat to be too stubborn to yield to any attempts to divert it, and still grows worse and worse, whatever I try. I thank my dear tender friend for her advice to try panada and broths. But I cannot swallow thin panada; I think milk goes down rather easier than any thing; but after I try, and cannot get that down, the Lord so *quiets my stomach*, that it does not *rage* for want of food as it used; so that goodness and mercy still follow me, and I can say in faith, they shall follow me all my days. I must needs be weak, as I can take but little for nature's support, and as my old disorder, the fever on my spirits, makes its fresh attack. This mortal frame must be sown in weakness but, glory to my saviour, he will raise it in power! Then I shall be no more unfit ardently, constantly, and perfectly to love and praise the Lord; for mortality of every kind shall be swallowed up of life! And, mean time, how great a comfort is this, that as a father pitieth his children, so the Lord pitieth them that fear him! He knoweth our frame, he remembereth that we are dust. The bowels of God in Christ have been a sweet relief to my heart this week. I trust to him as my Father; and a Father infinitely kind and tender he will prove unto me for ever. Indeed, when he seems to defer answers of prayer, and puts us to cry unto him day and night, till we think it a long time, it is very trying to our faith and patience; but, when trials *pinch* us most, they are to do us the greatest kindness; and our God will avenge us speedily, however long it seems to be; and will not stay one moment beyond the time appointed, till when he bears or suffers together with us, by love-sympathy; so that when his way is in the sea, and his footsteps are not known, we are called in humble faith and holy adoration to say, 'O the depth of the riches both of the wisdom and knowledge of God! how unsearchable are his judgments, and his ways past finding out!' And yet, Madam, when we cannot trace the Lord's ways, let us believe them to be ways of mercy, which shall open shortly with a surprising glory in his infinite wisdom! For this will give praise to our chastening Father when he hideth himself as the God of Israel the Saviour; and bring sweet peace to his children in the roughest storm. Oh, how sweet is it, when tossed with tempest in a trying dispensation, and assailed with blasts of temptation, to lie at anchor by faith in God's bosom! for, till the enemy can get us thence to launch out among the surges, we shall not be in great distress, however trying is our case; and indeed, come whatever may, we must say, "O Lord of hosts, blessed is the man that trusteth in thee!" It was to me, Madam, a surprising expression of your kindness in your last, in that you *wished to nurse me in my illness*; the Lord reward your wondrous kindness of his Godlike grace! And, if such an instance of condescension is admirable in a superior to an inferior creature, how should we adore that infinite grace, which to us in our unworthiness makes that great promise, "The Lord will strengthen him upon a bed of languishing: thou wilt make all his bed in his sickness."

Her bodily weakness was now so increased, that every one who saw her was amazed how she could arise from her bed at all, which she still continued to do, and sit up ten or twelve hours a day. Those hours were filled up with her private duties, and writing to her correspondents, though want of strength compelled her to much greater brevity than she was wont. She could now only once a week answer two or three of her most dear friends. She would often turn her eye upon many unanswered letters that lay by her, and say, "If it were the will of my heavenly Father to give me a little strength to write a few lines to such and such, how glad should I be! The spirit is willing, though the flesh is weak." But, as her light in this world had but a little longer to shine, how amazing were the displays of divine wisdom and power, that, instead of the waters of her heavy affliction quite extinguishing it, it was made, if possible, to shine brighter and clearer; as may be seen a little by the following extract of a letter, wrote Nov. 2, to one of her dearest friends.

"Hitherto the Lord hath helped; glory to his name for his supporting and comforting hands, which are underneath, and embrace me! My afflictions are light, short afflictions: Oh for some happy fruit to the glory of God, which shall be to his honour and pleasure for ever! I have been,

Madam, for several days this week so bad, that I could take nothing till just night, and then most kindly enabled to take a little with great difficulty. Both the fever and disorder in my throat are increased; and it seems to me that, unless the Lord is pleased to give me a little more relief, *my weak tabernacle must fall before another week.* I have a desire to depart and be with Christ, which is far better; but I am willing to stay the Lord's time, and to endure the whole of his good pleasure, for his honour. He gives me to see this affliction coming down on me as a fruit of my Father's love, my Saviour's blood, and the grace of the Holy Ghost; and I am enabled to receive it with humble submission, approbation, and thanksgiving. The Lord frequently tells me of his delivering kindness; and last night those words were sweet, "For the oppression of the poor, and for the sighing of the needy, now will I arise, saith the Lord, and set him in safety from him that puffeth at him." And this is "even the time of Jacob's trouble, but he shall be saved out of it." These strengthen my faith, excite my praise, and patience of hope to wait. Mourn not for me, Madam, but rejoice in the Lord, your eternal portion, in whom you are so well provided with all supplies for your time necessities, that in the most trying of cases you cannot, shall not, want any good thing. *If I am taken to glory first, Madam, it will be to welcome you Home.* O with gladness shall I receive you into the city of habitation, when the Captain of your salvation has brought you safe and triumphant through Jordan into the heavenly Canaan and delivered you for ever from your cruel enemies, that so often have put you in fear! There in perfect bliss we sill recount the wonders of Jehovah's grace, and jointly celebrate his praise to endless ages! I was much pleased yesterday, Madam, to think that, after my long natural *fast,* I should shortly have a most delightful, spiritual, and eternal *feast*; when my gracious God will make me sit down to meat at his table in his kingdom, and will gird himself and come forth and serve me! Then, Madam, there will be nothing to hinder our *free feasting upon new dainties*, with new *appetites*, and raising praises to the days of eternity. I have you cheerfully in the heart and arms of your dear Lord Jesus, who loves you infinitely, cares for you tenderly, and will save you eternally."

Most surprising was it to all who now saw her, that she could either write or sit up; but her conversation was so cheerful, edifying, spiritual, and refreshing, as filled the hearts and eyes of many that visited her with wonder. Her case, expressed by herself in the following letter, which was written November the 8th, and the *last* she was able to write, will give some idea of the state both of her body and mind.

"Honoured and dear Madam, I am extremely weak; but would fain, if I possibly can, once more write you a line, to thank you for all your great kindness, and for your last dear and tender letter. I have been so very bad, dear Madam, this last week, that I could not write one line to any of my dear friends. My speech faltered two days ago, and I rattled in my throat as if dying, but the Lord gave a little reviving. Yesterday my strength seemed quite exhausted, and I was parched up with the fever. It is very little I can swallow this day; that little the Lord gives me to receive: but my stomach now turns sick at every thing. It is marvellous that my life should be preserved for so long a time, without any thing of substance, and very little liquid to support the animal frame. *My moisture seems dried up, and I am as if I had no blood in me*; and my flesh is so wasted, that I am almost like a skeleton; and yet, glory to my good God, this has been, and is, a blessed affliction! I hope has been attended with some fruit, to the glory of his worthy name; and the Lord hereby has exercised my graces variously, and blessed me with divine consolations abundantly, which shall turn to my salvation. I am enabled now at last to triumph in Christ, who makes me more than a conqueror over sin, death, and hell, and all spiritual enemies. Though I walk through the valley of the shadow of death, I fear no evil, but am expectant of the greatest approaching good; because with me is the Lord my life; on his strong arm I lean; in his sweet bosom I rest; and thus cheerfully I come up from this grievous wilderness to Immanuel's land of full joy and eternal bliss! And there, oh how sweetly shall I drink, and bathe, and dive, in and into that pure river of water of life, which proceedeth out of the throne of God and of the Lamb! How delightfully will the Lamb in the midst of the throne feed me, and lead me to living fountains of waters, while God my father wipes all tears from my eyes!—And this bliss, my dear sister in Christ, shall you and I together possess, after a few more troublous days in the wilderness. God grant you strong faith, that you may be confident of this very thing, that of the infinite love of the Lord your Saviour you shall never be forgotten nor forsaken. Then the feet of your faith being well fenced, and your shoes iron and brass, in roughest places, your strength shall be equal to your trying days, to God's praise and your bliss.

"I forget not you and yours before the God of all grace; *pray for my salvation out of all distress.* Now I leave you, the Lord will take you up, and nourish you as his own child for himself. To his love, care, and power, I commit my beloved sister; and in him, with the most tender love, and great esteem, bid you *farewell for a little, very little time."*

After this she had no strength to hold her pen any longer; but for two or three mornings would arise as usual, though it was expected, by all who saw her, she would die every hour in her chair; but her consolations in Christ abounded. She spake of her disease, and gave orders to a particular friend of the manner of the laying out and internment of her body, with the greatest cheerfulness, satisfaction, and pleasure. On the 12th of November she took to her bed, and then it was expected every hour would be the last. The Lord gave her in mercy to sleep pretty much; but, when awake, she would often say, "How my poor heart beats! but God is the strength of my heart, and my portion for ever." Thus she continued till Lord's day, the 16th of the same month, when many friends going in to see her, and every one expecting to see her *last*, she, with her finger pointing upwards, could only be heard to say, "Glory, glory!" and then, laying her hand on her breast, would express the same with a smiling and cheerful countenance.

A letter from a friend, who knew nothing of her dying condition, coming to hand Lord's day evening, she signified her desire of a brother's sitting on the bed's side to read it; which he doing, and on reading the death of a well-known friend, and she taking no notice of it, he said, "Do you not hear, my dear child? the Lord hath removed by death Mr. C_____ll before you." Upon her recollecting who the deceased was, she said, "Ah! he has got the start of me.—*He is gone before*, to welcome *me* home to glory." About midnight she could speak no more; but her mouth, eyes, and hands, loudly expressed the joys and consolations of her soul. The next day, about noon, a particular friend going to her bed-side, she opening *the corner of one eye*, and perceiving who he was, put her hand out of bed to take hold of him; which he doing, and holding her hand in his, some little time, he then put it into bed, laying it on her breast, in which posture she lay till near nine in the evening; when the same friend, being by her bed, and perceiving her soul to be quivering on her lips, put up with his whole heart, the following ejaculation, "Lord Jesus, receive thine handmaid's spirit!" And immediately her long imprisoned spirit took wing, and made its joyful flight; at which instant those words dropt upon his mind with power: "Are they not all ministering spirits, sent forth to minister for them who shall be heirs of salvation?" From which he had such a realizing view of those blessed spirits doing their kind offices to this honoured saint, in conveying her safe and triumphant through the regions of the air into the glorious presence of God and the Lamb, as enabled him, under his present inexpressible loss, greatly to rejoice; the savour of which he hoped would never wear off his mind.

Thus this truly eminent, godly woman, finished her course at Great Gransden, Huntingdonshire, on Monday, the 17th of November, 1765, aged about 70 years. Her body was decently interred the Thursday following at the same place, in a burying-ground belonging to the church of Christ, of which she was many years a very useful and honourable member. A funeral discourse, agreeably to her request, was preached at the same time, from I Thess. iv. 17. *"So shall we be ever with the Lord,"* to a very considerable and truly affected auditory; the greater part of which were sensibly touched with the loss which they, and a dear Redeemer's interest, had sustained in her; but to whom it is a matter of comfort that they, with her, and all that sleep in Jesus, shall at his coming be ever with him.

It was amazing, to all who personally knew her, that her eyes, which were naturally weak, should hold for so many years at such constant writing! But the Lord, who encouraged her heart, strengthened her visive faculty to almost an incredible degree. She met with opposition and discouragement from some, from whom others things might have been expected; but her God encouraged her under all; for, her bowels being drawn forth to the lambs and weak of Christ's flock, he so attended her letters with his blessing, that the accounts she frequently received of their use for instruction, strength, comfort, and joy, animated her heart always to abound in the work of the Lord.

Perhaps very few, if any, of the children of God, or servants of the Lord, in our days, are favoured to walk so close with God as she did, or to have such frequent communion with God in Christ as she had; and, as she was enabled in the most minute thing and circumstance to acknowledge the Lord, so he, always to her safety, profit, and joy, directed her path. She was amazingly ready at both doctrinal, casuistical, and practical divinity; and her conversation the most spiritual and profitable of any I ever heard.

Failings and imperfections, attending all the saints in the present imperfect state, she had; but as none knew so much of them as herself, so no one ever groaned more under their burden; and humility on their account was her continual clothing.

But what need of saying more? She, being dead, yet speaketh, by her many excellent published works. I shall close with giving, in the words of one, her just character, which will shew the high estimation all her numerous friends had of her: "I bless and praise the Lord that I ever knew and corresponded with her; I never knew her equal. So able to advise—so ready to assist—so kind, faithful, constant; always the same; unwearied in diligence; a real pattern of Christian friendship; a true mother in Israel! Blessed be God for shewing me such a pattern of himself, through the power of his sovereign grace!" May all that love our Lord Jesus in sincerity and truth be daily earnest at the divine throne, for grace and gifts, to fit precious souls to fill up the place of this, and others his eminent servants now with him in glory. And that the all-productive AMEN of the Three-One God may be pronounced, shall be the constant prayer of him who prays and longs for Zion's prosperity.

It may not be amiss just to add, that Mrs. Dutton left at her death, for the use of all succeeding pastors of the church at Great Gransden, houses and lands worth 25l. 5s. per annum; also a small library of books (no doubt *very* choice) for the pastor's use.

Her epistolary correspondence was most extensive, throughout England, Scotland, Wales, Holland, America, &c.; so that after her death, several sacks, full of letters, were found, which were all burnt. she published many volumes of *letters* full of the sweet savour of Jesus, also some very choice treatises; such as, 1. A Discourse on Walking with God. 2. On God's Act of Adoption. 3. On the *Inheritance* of the Adopted Sons of God: with some others. These sterling pieces of the *old-school* divinity, are intended for publication in the succeeding parts of this gospel library, in the event of the publisher meeting with suitable encouragement.

PREFACE.

It may be expected, that I should give some account of my publishing this volume; some hints of which take as follow: It pleased the Lord, after he had called me by his grace, and revealed his Son in me, to make great manifestations of his love to me, under the sealing work of the Lord the Comforter; which filled my heart with joy unspeakable and full of glory. Soon after this, the Providence of God cast Mr. Hussey's book, "The Glory of Christ Unveiled," into my hands, which was abundantly blessed for my further instruction, confirmation, and consolation. I may say, concerning the doctrines of the Gospel, which are there opened in such a glorious light, as the Apostle did to the believing Thessalonians, "For our Gospel came not unto you in word only, but also in power, and in the Holy Ghost, and in much assurance." By means of which I was made to drink deeper into the freeness, fullness, eternity, and unchangeableness of God's love, under the Spirit's witness of personal interest. But, Oh! the ravishing joys my soul felt while swimming in love's ocean; in diving into its unfathomable depths. I have often thought, that as the natural man is utterly a stranger to that spiritual joy, which filleth the hearts of the new-born, so likewise believers themselves, while under a prevailing spirit of *bondage,* are greatly strangers to that glorious joy which fills the hearts of *sealed* saints. Oh! how sweet is Gospel-liberty! And how doth it constrain to *holiness!* I can experimentally say, That when the love of God, like a mighty deluge, overflowed every corner of my soul, being shed abroad by the Holy Ghost, it had no such effect upon me, as the carnal minds of men imagine; who think, that the discovery of free grace gives liberty to sin. No, but on the other hand, my soul was sweetly drawn by the powerful influence of God's love, to love him again, to hate sin, to thirst after the highest holiness, in conformity to Christ; and so to give up myself to serve him, from the freest principle, whilst drawn by the strongest motives, as being under the highest engagements. And, sure I am, that if the souls of the saints don't live under the quickening influence of God's grace, their obedience is too much mercenary, lifeless, and formal; not at all becoming that nearness of relation, and dearness of love in which they

Gal. i. 15, 16.

I Pet. i. 8.

I Thes. i. 15.

Prov. xiv. 10.

Rom. v. 5.

Jer. xxxi. 3.

stand. The *servant* works for wages out of a principle
of fear, knowing, that if he don't please his master he
must turn out of doors; but the ingenuous *Son* serves
his Father out of a principle of *love* and *gratitude,* as
having settled an inheritance upon him, even whilst he
knows his relation cannot be broken. And though it is
true, that all the saints serve God out of a principle of
love; yet their filial obedience riseth proportionably with
their faith of relation. If perfect love has not cast out   John iv. 18.
fear, the performance of duty springs too much from a
principle of self-love, fear of Hell, or the like; for it's
nothing less than the love of God, manifested by the
Spirit (in all the perfection of its nature, as it shines in,
and flows through the Mediator) and so apprehended by
faith, that can engage the soul to serve the Lord in the
freedom of a Child. But to return,

The Lord having (as was said) filled my heart with joy
unspeakable, I sought to express my thankfulness in
some hymn of praise (in which I had many precious
seasons) but not finding one that did fully express the
comprehensive views I then had, I set about making one,
which I chiefly designed for my own private use. But
when my beloved had taken me by the hand, and led me   Cant. vii. 11.
to take some turns with himself in the vast field of
boundless grace, he there shewed me a variety of wonders,
which so multiplied upon me, that I soon saw I
could not contract them into the narrow bounds of an
hymn, and therefore gave myself further scope; and
when I had finished my verses, I communicated them to
some intimate friends, that so we might mutually rejoice
together. But in some space of time many *copies* were
taken, and through the heedlessness of transcribers many
errors crept in, which was one motive with me to print
them. But I hope, the main-spring that has set all the
wheels in motion, in order to bring about this work, is,
the glory of God, and the good of souls. Since they were
designed for the press I have made some considerable
alterations and additions. I have also placed the Scriptures
in the margin which are glanced at in the line.

I have, indeed, met with some discouragements in my
own mind, as to making them public, from my own

weakness, unworthiness, &c. which has made me reject
the motion of some that importuned me to it. And,
perhaps, Satan has not been wanting to dissuade me from
it, by suggesting, this work both as needless and useless.
But I have been encouraged, from the acceptance of the
widow's mite, which was in itself (like this little piece)   Luke xxi. 2, 3.
very inconsiderable, if compared with those large gifts,
which others, out of their abundance, had cast into the Treasury.

I expect that I shall meet with reproaches, and that
the Truths herein contained will meet with opposition, not
only from common professors, but, perhaps, from some
of the saints themselves, we not being, as yet, come up
to the unity of the faith, in the knowledge of the Son of
God, and so don't see eye to eye; this being a glory   Eph. iv. 13.
reserve until the latter day, which is very desirable to   Isa. lii. 8.
the souls of the saints; for they all love Christ's
appearing and kingdom, though they have different   2 Tim. iv. 8.
apprehensions about the manner of it. And, doubtless,
the glory of that bright scene will be surprisingly new to
all its expectants.

I trust, my eye has been single to my one Lord and   John xlii. 18.
master, Christ: and, may I, at last, have but one accepting *smile*
from him, I shall esteem it an abundant recompence of reward,
should I meet with ten thousand *frowns* from others.   Heb. xi. 26.

I would not be mistaken by any, when, in the first part,
I speak of the glory Christ had with God before the world
was; as if, thereby, I thought that either his body or soul
was then created; for I have no such apprehensions.
This being all I intend by it; that Christ, as Mediator,   Prov. viii. 23.
"was set up from everlasting" in God's covenant; and, as   John xvii. 5.
such, had all "glory" then settled upon him. When God,
the eternal Son, engaged from everlasting to take our
nature into personal union with himself, the Father looked
upon it as if done; for he "calleth the things which be   Rom. iv. 17.
not as though they were." So of Abraham, Christ's type,
the Lord said, "I have made thee a father of many nations," Gen. xvii. 5.
when as yet he had no child. I [have] made, &c. It is
put in the past tense, because it was then done to God in
his sure covenant, though it was not yet done to men;
and, therefore, in this respect, it is put in the future tense,
"I [will] make thee exceeding fruitful." And its being   Verse 6.

done to God in covenant, secured its being done to men in
the fulfillment of covenant-engagements. Thus, when
Christ was set up from everlasting in God's covenant, it
was done to God; and the divine person of the Son, in
the covenant capacity of Mediator, was so reputed by the
Father in all those covenant-transactions which then mutually
passed between them concerning the elect. And
Christ's taking our entire mature from everlasting in the
covenant, was the foundation of his taking it in the fullness
of time in the womb of the Virgin; and, as I conceive,
Christ's being thus set up from everlasting, as the Head of
the creation, in the beginning of God's way, is, what is
intended, where he is called "the First-born of every   Col. i. 15.
creature," and "the Beginning of the creation of God."   Rev. iii. 14.
      Satan, in all ages, has shown his malice in using the
utmost of his power and policy against Christ, (the
"Rock of the Church,") as God-Man, in two entire distinct   Matt. xvi. 18.
natures, and one person for ever; and also against
the church built upon him as such. And, blessed be God,
our Christ abides still the "same," as the immoveable Rock Heb. xiii. 8.
of Ages; and the church still abides immoveably fixed
upon him, amidst all those awful "shakings" which over-   Chap. xii. 27.
turn the faith of others. And, O what a mercy it is
to God's people, that they are, and shall be, enabled to
"hold the Head," in whom alone salvation is; when others   Col. ii. 19.
cast off their first faith to the utter ruin of their souls, and
are left to set up a mere creature instead of the Christ of
God; who, "according to the flesh," or human nature,   Rom. ix. 5.
"came of the Fathers," and yet, according to his divine
nature, is "God over all, blessed for ever. Amen."   1 Tim. iii. 16.
Without controversy, great is this mystery of godliness; God
manifest in the flesh. The diversity of natures, in the
unity of the Mediator's person, is a doctrine of the
Gospel to be believed by the saints with the highest
joy and deepest reverence. The person of Christ, God-
Man, as the "Foundation" laid in "Sion," is "a Stone   1 Cor. iii. 11.
of stumbling, and a Rock of offence" to many, who dash   1 Pet. ii. 8.
against it, and are broken to pieces; but "unto them
which believe, he is precious." And whosoever believes   Verse 7.
in the person of Christ as such, trusting the whole of his
salvation in the hands of this mighty Saviour, shall

never be "confounded." "In this Lord," Jehovah-Jesus, "shall all the seed of Israel be justified, and shall glory." "Our Maker is our Husband, the Lord of Hosts is his name." "O this is our Beloved, and this is our Friend, O ye daughters of Jerusalem." Verse 6.
Isa. xlv. 25.
Chap. liv. 5.
Cant. v. 16.

As to the poem on the special work of the Spirit, which I have placed at the end of the "Wonders of Grace," I would not have any from thence think, that I esteem that part of the Spirit's work as a wonder of grace *inferior* to the rest. No; I believe that all the acts and works of the three Persons in God, as they have a joint hand in the salvation of the elect, shine forth with as equal splendour. But when my soul was first drawn out to speak something in the fourth Part, about the work of the Spirit, I saw this subject naturally divided itself into these two branches, viz. His *general* and his *special* work, both which I designed to have taken in; but in going over the first, I found it to be such a large field, that I could not (without swelling this Part too big to bear any proportion with the other five) make any progress into the latter; and, therefore, contented myself with only giving some general hints as I went along.

But sometime after this, my heart was again drawn out, to speak somewhat particularly about the special work of the Spirit, which I thought might not be amiss to place by itself, in that order in which it now stands, since it is such a copious subject.

I hope the Hymns may be of use to some saints.

I commit the whole of these lines to the blessing of God, who can "ordain strength out of the mouth of babes;" earnestly desiring, that many souls, in reading, may drink of that "River, the streams of which made me glad" in composing them; and that all the praise may redound to the sovereign grace of Jehovah, "unto whom be glory in the Church, by Christ Jesus, throughout all ages, world without end." Amen.

Psal. viii. 2.

Psal. xlvi. 4.

Eph. iii. 21.

ANNE DUTTON.

A

NARRATION

OF THE

WONDERS OF GRACE.

PART THE FIRST.

OF CHRIST THE MEDIATOR, AS SET UP FROM EVERLASTING IN ALL THE GLORY OF HEADSHIP.

The wonders of God's ancient love,	Psal. lxxxix. 5.
Which Being had in Heaven above	Psal. xxxi. 19.
To us they are amazing great,	Psal. xxv. 6.
And bear their everlasting date.	
May we be led in the Spirit's light,	
To see by faith, love's mystery bright,	
As in Christ's face it radiant shines,	2 Cor. iv. 6.
In all Jehovah's vast design!	
Come, my beloved, let's go forth,	Cant. vii. 11.
Let's take a turn beyond the Earth,	
Into the field of boundless grace;	
For that's our pleasant feeding place.	
Our pastures are exceeding wide,	
There let us still by faith reside;	Psal. xlix. 9.
Whilst with their fatness we solace,	Psal. xxiii. 2.
And rest in settlements of grace.	
There let us, as it were, entranc'd,	
Behold our glorious Lord advanc'd,	
To all those heights of glory, He	
With God had from eternity.	
God's glorious wisdom first begun	Rev. i. 11.
To lay the project of his Son:	Col. i. 15.
And then ordain'd God-Man to be	1 Pet. i. 20.
The brightness of the Deity.	
First, the man-nature of our head	Heb. i. 3.
Was taken up and advanced,	
In the vast thoughts of our great God:	
There was our glorious Lord's abode.	
Christ's person is a mystery,	1 Tim. iii. 16.
And was so from eternity;	Eph. iii. 9.
When he engag'd before all time	
To take our nature upon him,	

God look'd upon it as if done;	Rom. iv. 17.
And thenceforth did repute his Son,	Zech. vi. 12.
As the great Mediator, who	
Should one day openly be so.	Verse 13.
His holy flesh here let us see,	
Advanced from eternity,	
Who then, as man of God's right hand,	Ps. lxxx. 17.
By cov'nant, in his Son did stand.	
Christ was before the mountains' birth,	Prov. viii. 25.
In God's eternal thoughts brought forth;	
Before the lofty hills were made,	
Or Earth's decreed foundations laid.	Verse 26.
Christ brought up with his Father, then	Verse 30.
Rejoiced in the sons of men;	Verse 31.
Those chosen from among the rest,	
On whom all his delights were plac'd.	Psal. xvi. 3.
This is the man God pitch'd upon,	
To stand in God the eternal Son;	
In whom he makes the bright display	
Of all his glory every way.	
Here grace shines in its native rays,	John i. 14.
To all the Chosen, for its praise;	Eph. i. 4, 5, 6.
And just severity is shown	Acts xvii. 31.
To heirs of wrath, through Christ the Son.	2 Thes. i. 8.
This is the man, the Lord's delight,	Isa. lxii. 1.
In whom all glories ever meet;	Col. i. 19.
In whom the Father's soul doth rest,	Matt. iii. 17.
The man, in whom we're fully blest.	Eph. i. 3.
This wisdom-man, possess'd of old,	Prov. viii. 12, 22.
Whose glory-heights can ne'er be told,	
God's image was, e'er time began,	Col. i. 15.
By which he form'd his creature man.	Gen. i. 26.
Yea, all things both in Heaven and Earth,	
From Christ the Lord derived their birth:	
The creatures all by him were made,	Col. i. 16.
Both as Creator, and as Head.	
And for his glory were design'd,	
Each in their proper place, and kind.	
Thus God set up the glory man,	Prov. viii. 23.
In covenant e'er time began;	
Who was the glorious wisdom-draught,	

Of all the works Jehovah wrought.
As nature-head Christ was ordain'd,   1 Cor. xi. 3.
To the vast body of mankind;
But to a remnant, head of grace,   Eph. iv. 15.
And glory, Christ ordained was.   Col. i. 18.
This was the glory which he had
With God, before the world was made.   John xvii. 5.
But, O bold word! what did I say?
Christ's glory is beyond display   Eph. iii. 8.
Of the most raised saints below;
Yea, saints above, and angels too.
What can I say then, who am weak,   Jer. i. 6.
A child, alas, that cannot speak?   Is. xxxviii. 14.
To chatter's all that I can do,
The theme's so high, and I so low!
Yet with Christ's glory set on fire,
(To lisp his praise is my desire.)   Matt. xi. 27.
God trusted Christ with all his grace,
To bring his great design to pass: Ps. lxxxix. 19.
God knew he was the mighty One,
And fitted for this trust alone.
The creatures all, alas! were weak,   Job. iv. 18.
No sooner trusted but they break:
But Christ is God as well as man,   Isa. ix. 6.
And therefore change he never can.   Heb. xiii. 8.
God set the Mediator high,
In council, from eternity;   Phil. ii. 10.
And did resolve that all should pay   Verse 11.
An homage to his kingly sway;   Col. i. 16.
Angelic glories from Christ flow,   Isa. vi. 3.
Of him they hold, to him they bow;
The highest angels round the throne,
Subjected were to Christ the Son.   John xii. 41.
But Satan, with his rebel train,
To stoop to Christ they did disdain;   Is. xiv. 13, 14.
Thus lifted up in pride they fell,
And heavy wrath sunk them to hell.   Jude, ver. 6.
Yet the infernal spirits below,
Were put beneath Christ's power too: Rev. i. 18.
Christ's revenues of glory rise,
Even from his worst of enemies.

In Christ, good angels were preserv'd
From falling, when the other swerv'd;
Because they chosen were for him,   1 Tim. v. 21.
He kept them from the devil's sin.
Thus was our Lord exalted high,
Far above principality.
Christ is the great foundation-stone   Psal. lxxi. 3.
The whole creation's built upon;
It's he that by his power doth   Heb. i. 13.
Upon the fabric of the earth:
Christ as the corner stone doth lie,   Job xxxviii. 6.
Or the world would soon in pieces fly.   Col. i. 17.
As *Alpha,* God began with him,   Rev. i. 11.
Before the early dates of time;
When he went forth in his decrees,   Prov. viii. 27, 28
To make the Heavens, Earth, and Seas.
Yea, Christ is the *Omega* too,   Rev. i. 11.
Of all things God did ever do;
And all that yet shall come to pass,
Ordained for Christ's glory was.
God's glory was the highest end,   Prov. xvi. 4.
For which all creatures were design'd;
But next, Christ was the end of all,
That was, or are, or ever shall.
Thus Christ our head's exalted high,
To whom be praise eternally.

A

NARRATION

OF THE

WONDERS OF GRACE.

PART THE SECOND.

OF GOD'S ELECTION, AND COVENANT-TRANSACTIONS CONCERNING A REMNANT IN HIS SON.

From everlasting God went forth,	2 Tim. i. 5.
In Christ, who was his chosen path,	
To Us, in glorious acts of grace;	Eph. i. 3.
Which brightly shine in Jesus' face.	
Jehovah, from eternity	
Had all his creatures in his eye,	Acts xv. 1.
Which he determined to make	
By Christ, for his own glory sake.	
These in one lump, like potter's clay	Rom. ix. 21.
Before the mighty Former lay	
Who, doubtless, had a sovereign right	
To fashion them as he thought fit.	
Vessels of honour some were made,	
Design'd for Christ their glorious head;	Verse 23.
Others Jehovah did refuse	
To set apart for sacred use	
Nor good, nor evil, did appear,	Rom. ix. 11.
When first the vessels fashion'd were;	
But each his make entirely	
Owed to the Former's sovereignty.	
'Tis true, when God beheld them in	
The guilt and filth of *Adam's* sin,	
The vessels were again design'd	
To different ends, in God's own mind;	
Those that for Christ were set apart,	
On whom Jehovah fixt his heart,	
Of further grace, were made to be,	
Vessels to hold his mercy free.	Verse 23.
The rest, that only were ordain'd,	
As creatures for a lower end;	
When they were view'd in all their sin,	
And filthy as an unclean thing	Psal. xiv. 3.

These then, by just severity,
Were made for wrath eternally.   Rom. ix. 22.
But when our God at first did choose
Part of mankind, and part refuse,
They were beheld in the pure mass,   Verse 11.
Which greatly magnifies free grace.
The greatest of electing love
Did first embrace our head above;
And then we chosen were in him,   Eph. i. 4.
By the same grace, before all time.
And as we're chosen, so we're blest,   Verse 3.
And in the heaven lies share with Christ.
Infinite wisdom saw it meet,
That Christ, who stood in glory great,
In Heav'n advanc'd to highest state,
Should have with him his glory-mate.
For the glory of the sacred Three,
Christ was as man, ordain'd to be
And for the glory of this man,
God chose a bride e're time began
Adam and *Eve* a figure were
Of Christ, and of his bride most dear;
And in the state of innocence
Their marriage-union did commence.
God took a rib of *Adam's* side,
Of which he made his lovely bride,
Who was his very flesh and bone
That so he might not be alone.
And when to *Adam* she was brought,   Gen. ii. 22.
What sweet surprise did strike his thought,
While he, with joy, beheld her in
The beauties which she had from him!   Verse 23.
He view'd her, and immediately
His heart, as in an extacy,
Was to his lovely helpmeet knit,   Verse 24.
As for his social pleasure fit.
This marriage did resemblance bear,   Eph. v. 31.
Of Christ's, who *Adam's* elder were;
For this ordained was to be
A shadow of that mystery.   Verse 32.
God set Christ's human nature high,   Psal. viii. 1.

Advanc'd him to that dignity,
In which the man in God doth stand,
Plac'd at his father's own right hand.
As Mediator, God him fill'd,   Col. i. 19.
No after glories he beheld,
But first in Christ he made to meet,
As in their proper glory-seat.
A world of creatures God would make,
By Christ, for his own glory sake.
Electing love did then bring forth,
A bride for Christ, O wond'rous birth!   Cant. vi. 9.
This bride to him presented was
Complete in his own glory-dress:
He ravish'd was with Wisdom's choice,
And in his love doth still rejoice   Zeph. iii. 17.
In nature, grace, and glory, we
Part of himself appear'd to be:
Christ's perfect likeness we did bear,
With which he then transported were   Cant. iv. 9.
His heart was ravish'd with this sight,
His soul o'ercome with strong delight,
His father's gift, this lovely one,   Hos. ii. 19, 20.
He took to cleave to her alone.
The marriage settlements were made;   John xvii. 22.
Her glory-jointure cannot fade;   1 Pet. i. 4.
An uncomputed one it is;
A right to share in all that bliss,   Rom. viii. 17.
Her glorious husband doth possess,
With which the Father did him bless.   1 Cor. iii. 22.
Her riches great, settled of old,   Eph. i. 3, 4.
By men nor angels can be told.
Our Father then a portion gave,
To answer all the need we have;
No less than his great self in Christ,   Ps. xxxiii. 12.
'Twas this that made us fully blest.
Electing grace in Christ our head,
Secured to him the chosen seed;   Ps. lxxxix. 36.
By settlements in cov'nant made,
And in Jehovah's counsels laid.
This was the firm foundation strong,   2 Tim. ii. 19.
The spouse of Christ was fixt upon;

'Twas this upheld the elect all,
From perishing in *Adam's* fall.
We thank thee, Lord, for sovereign grace,
Abounding in the chosen race,
That so in Christ secured us all,   Jude, ver. 1.
That we from him could never fall.
Who could not fall, as did the rest,
Who only were in *Adam* blest:
Our portion lay in safer hands,
With Christ we stood in union bands.   John xiv. 19.
And therefore could not lose our all,
In the first *Adam's* woful fall.
In him we lost what others did,
But grace and glory-life were hid   Col. iii. 3.
In Christ, as our transcendent head,
For the elected holy seed,
Ordain'd for higher happiness,   Acts xiii. 48.
Than the first *Adam* did possess.
Let's deeper drink into this love,
That in the Father's heart did move;
Astonish'd at its early rise,
Before the man of Paradise!
We bless our God for reigning grace,   Rom. v. 21.
That so secures our happiness,
In its own everlasting rounds,
As it through Christ o'er sin abounds.   Verse 19, 20.
Here's all things wisely carry'd on,   Eph. i. 11.
To serve God's ends in Christ his Son;
Each in their order rightly move,   Verse 8.
To serve the great designs of love;
In raising up Christ's royal mate,
To that triumphant glory-state,
For which she ever was design'd,   2 Thes. ii. 13.
In the deep counsels of God's mind.
Yet in the world she was to meet
With changes manifold and great;   Job x. 17.
Although her glory ever was,
Of old secured in faithfulness.   Titus. i. 2.
Our Father swore to Christ our head,   Ps. lxxxix. 3, 4.
To give to him the chosen seed;
With Christ his cov'nant standeth sure, Verse 28.

By which his seed shall e'er endure.	Verse 29.
God's counsels are immutable,	Heb. vi. 17.
He is of one eternal will:	Job xxiii. 13.
In all his thoughts of boundless love	Ps. xxxiii. 11.
He is not subject once to move.	
'Twas love that in the Father lay,	
That gave our vast security:	
His love's the fountain of our bliss;	Eph. ii. 4, 5, 6.
The source of all our happiness!	
'Twas in our everlasting head,	Heb. xiii. 8.
All stores of grace were treasured;	Col. i. 19.
That now through Christ, the only way,	John xiv. 6.
Our Father doth to us convey.	Ch. i. 16.
Jehovah's love, richly indeed,	Eph. i. 3.
Provision made for all our need,	
In cov'nant, from eternity,	Phil. iv. 19,
Whence we receive a full supply.	*with* Ps. cxi. 5.
Early our Father did provide,	
The Lord our shepherd, and our guide;	Isa. xl. 11.
To bring back all his straying sheep.	Ezek. xxxiv. 12.
And the whole number safe to keep.	
Though in the fall Christ's bride from him,	John xvii. 12.
Departed treacherously by sin;	Jer. iii. 20.
She was too dear for him to lose,	Hos. iii. 1.
Because her union was so close.	
for ever Christ betroth'd his bride;	Chap. ii. 19.
And though she fouly turn'd aside,	
He freely did engage to pay,	Chap. xiii. 14.
All that vast debt that on her lay.	
Like Judah, he engag'd to bring	Gen. xliii. 9.
Her back again from death and sin;	
And set her in his Father's sight,	
An object fit for his delight.	
Rather than lose her he'd come down,	Mat. xviii. 11.
He would not stay in heaven alone;	John xii. 24.
That in his glory she might share,	
His Father's wrath for her he'd bear.	
Amazing grace to such as we,	
Must Christ be bound to set us free!	
Our Creditor then call'd upon	
The Surety, for the debt alone:	Isa. l. 4.

Thus, when our Father took a view,
Of us in our depraved hue,
His boundless love to us the bride,
Resolv'd to flow thro' Christ's pierc'd side.   Zech xiii. 7.
And Christ's engagements to fulfil,
He said, I come to do thy will;   Ps. x. 7, 8.
My God, thy law is in my heart;
And I for mine will bear the smart.   Prov. xi. 15.
That body thou'st prepared for me,   Heb. x. 5.
I will assume to set them free;
In which I'll do the work thou'st given,
And serve the great designs of heav'n.

A

NARRATION

OF THE

WONDERS OF GRACE.

PART THE THIRD.

OF CHRIST'S INCARNATION AND REDEMPTION.

AND when th' appointed time came on,	
Behold, the Father sent his Son!	Gal. iv. 4.
In which his great love did appear	John iii. 16.
To his elect, that sinners were.	Rom. v. 8.
A glorious work Christ came to do,	Dan. ix. 24.
To save his fallen spouse from woe;	
To ransom her from death and grave,	Hos. xiii. 41.
This was the work his Father gave!	
He came to work a glorious robe,	
In which we stand before our God;	Rom. v. 19.
Presented spotless in his sight,	Col. i. 22.
With an unspeakable delight.	
By nature, Christ was God most high,	Rom. ix. 5.
The second in the Trinity:	1 John v. 7.
Co-equal with his Father, he	Phil. ii. 6.
Thought it not robbery to be.	
But, lo! he took the servant's form,	Phil. ii. 7.
Which was the nature of his own;	Heb. ii. 14.
Into the personal union high,	
Which is a glorious mystery.	
God manifested in the flesh,	1 Tim. iii. 16.
The faith of saints doth much refresh;	
Christ is Immanuel, God with us,	Mat. i. 23.
And let us glory in him thus;	
For as such, he, and he alone	
Could work out our Salvation	
As God, he could not serve or die,	
He was so infinitely high;	
He therefore did a man become,	John i. 14.
That he might stand in sinners room:	1 Pet. iii. 18.
And if that man had not been one	
In person, with God's only Son,	
His service could not profit us;	
Nor his death save us from the curse.	Ps. xlix. 7, 8.

Christ's Godhead puts infinite worth,
On what his human nature doth;
As man, he doth obey'd and dy'd,   Phil. ii. 8.
As God, he fully satisfy'd.   Acts xx. 28.
This Person is the mighty One,
Salvation-help is laid upon.   Ps. lxxxix. 19.
Oh! this is our beloved friend,   Cant. v. 16.
On whom we safely may depend
Th' immediate object of our faith, Acts xvi. 31.
There's none like Him in heav'n nor earth! Ps. lxxiii. 25.
Though Christ was rich in glory great,
He laid aside his royal state,   2 Cor. viii. 9.
And with the greatest joy came down
To make our poverty his own.
What condescending love was this,
To raise us to the highest bliss! Eph. v. 25.
In love he serv'd, in love he died, Verse 26, 27.
And thus he did exalt his bride.
Let's stand astonish'd at his love,
That such a vehement flame did prove Cant. viii. 6.
That many waters could not drown; Verse 7.
Victorious love the conquest won.
Herein our husband's love did shine,
And every way appear'd divine;
When he endur'd God's curse and wrath,
That he might shelter us from both. Isa. xxxii. 2.
Here boundless love all reigning round, Rom. v. 20.
Did to the chosen one's abound;
When God made Christ sin and a curse, 2 Cor. v. 21.
That thence he might deliver us:
For when the holy law found sin,
By justice charged upon him,
As standing in the sinner's room,
Its curses all upon him come. Gal. iii. 13.
His Father spar'd him not a jot, Rom. viii. 32.
But all his wrath he poured out, Mat. xxvii. 46.
When Christ was made a sacrifice,
Well-pleasing in Jehovah's eyes. Eph. v. 2.
And now free pardon from God's heart,
Flows to us through our Surety's smart, Eph. i. 7.
Which he hath underwent for us

In th' garden, and upon the cross.   Luke xxii. 44.
Pardon and peace, and full discharge,
Of all our many debts at large,   Rom. v. 10.
The father gave to Christ our head   Isa. 1. 8.
When, lo, he rais'd him from the dead.   Rom. iv. 25.
And now the Lord the Spirit brings
Glad tidings of these glorious things;   1 Cor. ii. 12.
And witnesseth unto his own,
Their interest in what Christ hath done,
Let's triumph in our risen head,   Rom. viii. 34.
Who hath a glorious conquest made,
O'er all the powers of sin and death,   1 Cor. xv. 55. &c.
With Satan, and his train beneath!
He's now ascended up on high,   Col. ii. 15.
Sat down in royal Majesty;   Eph. iv. 8.
And while he wears his glory-crown   Chap. i. 20, 21.
As head, he represents his own.   Verse 22.
Oh! may the Lord the Spirit fill,
Our souls with heavenly art and skill,
That we in love's vast sea may swim,   Ezek. xlvii. 5.
That delug'd hath o'er all our sin.   Rom. v. 20.
For now in mighty grace's reign,   Gal. v. 1.
A glorious freedom we obtain,
From law and death, from sin and wrath,
A liberty of greatest worth!
More of thy Spirit give us, Lord,
His quick'ning influence afford,
That we may live on things above,   Col. iii. 2.
As drawn by everlasting love.   Jer. xxxi. 5.
Uphold us by thy mighty grace,   Ps. cxix. 117.
Till we have run our Christian race;
And give us new supply alway,
For every duty of the day.
Oh teach us looking still to be,   2 Pet. iii. 12.
With stretch'd out neck, hasting to see
The coming of that glorious day,
When Anti-Christ shall pine away!   2 Thes. ii. 8.
And though the heavens must Christ retain
Till he world restores again;   Acts iii. 21.
Meanwhile, let us by faith solace
Our souls, with th' wonders of his grace.

While here Christ vail'd his glory great,
As in his low and humbled state,
How did his love and tender care,
In all things for his own appear?
His soul he poured out in prayer
To God, who always him did hear;   John xi. 42.
That he would keep them from all harm,   Chap. xvii. 11.
Thro' his own name, and by his arm.
What care he took to cheer their heart,   Chapt. xiv. 1.
When he was going to depart!
Says he, it's surely good for you,
That I should to my father go;   John xvi. 7.
But I'll not leave you comfortless,   Chap. xiv. 18.
While passing thro' this wilderness;
But when from you I go away,
I'll send a comforter, who'll stay;
And with you ever shall abide,   Verse 16.
When I am gone and glorified:
He'll take of mine and shew to you,   John xvi. 14.
And open what I've spoken too.
This is the friend, whose love and care
I will commit you to while here;
Yea, I myself will come again,   Verse 22.
And then your joy it shall remain.

A
NARRATION
OF THE
WONDERS OF GRACE.

PART THE FOURTH.

OF THE WORK OF THE SPIRIT,
RESPECTING THE CHURCH IN GENERAL,
THROUGHOUT THE NEW TESTAMENT DISPENSATION,
FROM CHRIST'S ASCENSION TO HIS SECOND COMING.

When Christ our Lord ascended high
He then receiv'd immediately,
The Spirit in all his gifts and grace;
For this the Father's promise was.   Acts ii. 33.
The Spirit Christ received thus,
On purpose to bestow on us;
And at the day of pentecost
He poured down the Holy Ghost.   Ver. 1, 2, 3, 4.
In nature, God the Spirit's one
With God the Father and the Son;
And these eternal glorious Three,   1 John v. 7.
Are of an equal dignity,
For they co-equally possess
The Godhead's undivided bliss
Subsisting in one nature still,
They have but one essential will:
They're one in love and counsel too;
And one in all the works they do   John v. 19.
For thus the glorious Gospel saith,
For the obedience of faith.   Rom. xvi. 26.
These Three in One, let saints adore,
As their own God, for evermore!   Psal. lxvii. 6.
These Three in worth are not alone,
Tho' each has works which are his own:
Creation-work the Father's was;   Acts. iv. 24.
He spake, and lo, it came to pass: Gen. i. 3.
Redemption-work to Christ was given,   John x. 18.
Which to complete he came from heav'n:
And special application were
Committed to the Spirit's care!   Chap. xiv. 26.

Great was the work he had on earth,
When Son and Father sent him forth.
The Gospel of the Son of God
Was to be sounded forth abroad,   Rom. x. 18.
That those that sat in darkness might
Behold this glorious shining light.   Mat. iv. 16.
The Church of God confined was,
As then, within a small compass;
For Abraham's seed, and only they,
Enjoy'd this honour in that day.
God's law, and covenant they had,
The promises to them were made;   Rom. ix. 4, 5.
And from their loins Christ was to spring,
Whom they expected as their king.
But when he came in humble state,
Lo, they offended were hereat;
And him they did refuse to own,   John xix. 15.
Because Christ was to them unknown;
They therefore crucified the Lord,   1 Cor. ii. 8.
As an imposter they abhor'd.   John xix. 21.
But, oh! the wonder of his grace,
When Christ to heaven ascended was,
He sent the Holy Spirit down,   Acts ii. 33.
To qualify and fit his own;
To preach remission through his name,   Luke xxiv. 47.
Beginning at Jerusalem;
The great success of Gospel Grace,   John xvi. 8, 9, 10, 11.
Reserved for the Spirit was;
That so his honour might be great,
In the New Testament Church-state   Rev. iii. 6.
The Spirit is a sovereign Lord,
And as such doth his gifts afford;
Dividing to each person still   1 Cor. xii. 11.
According to his sovereign will.
Th' Apostles preach'd the gospel giv'n,
With th' Holy Ghost sent down from Heav'n;   1 Pet. i. 12.
And Peter, who deny'd his Lord,
By him was taught to preach the word;   Acts ii. 14.
The Gospel of Christ crucify'd,
Even to them that pierc'd his side.   Verse 36.
But, oh! astonishing success,

Three thousand souls were call'd by Grace;   Verse 41.
While this one sermon Peter preach'd,
The mighty Spirit their hearts had reach'd.
Then they that gladly heard his word,
In all things straightway own'd their Lord.   Acts ii. 42.
These, called Jews, the first fruits were   James i. 18.
Of that great harvest, will appear,
When all the rest are gather'd in
To Christ, and saved from all sin.   Rom. xi. 26.
But though an handful ripen'd were,
By th' Gospel-sun arising there;
The rest, that then were left behind,
Did no such influences find;   Chap. x. 16.
For lo, the body of the Jews   Acts xiii. 45.
This great salvation did refuse!
Th' Apostles by the Spirit taught,
Began to have a turn of thought,
And awfully declared to them;
That they'd turn from Jerusalem,   Verse 46.
To sinners of the Gentile race,
Who should eternal life embrace.
The Jews Church-state then broken were,
And they were scattered here and there;
Thus these were broken off by sin,   Rom xi. 20.
That Gentile sinners might come in.   Ver. 25.
The Gentile world, that then did lie,   Acts xix. 27.
In heathenish idolatry;
And Satan here did keep his seat,   Rev. ii. 13.
As in a throne of darkness great.   Eph. ii. 2.
But Jesus by his Spirit then,
Sent forth a few fishermen,
To overcome this potent One,   Luke xi. 22.
And so eject him from his throne.
The weapons of this great warfare,   2 Cor. x. 4.
Mighty, through God, the Spirit were;
And Christ, at length, did gain his end,   Verse 5.
Through outward force did not attend.
The heathen world were men of parts,
Renown'd for wisdom in all arts;   Cor. i. 22.
But by all this they knew not God   Verse 21.
And in gross darkness still abode.

The Lord, the mighty Spirit, then,
Sent forth a few unlearned men,   Acts xiii. 4.
To sound the news of Gospel-grace,   *with*
Through Christ that crucified was;   Chap. iv. 13
But when this message they did bring,
Behold, it seem'd a foolish thing,
Not worthy of the least regard,
Which therefore many did discard.   1 Cor. i. 23.
But yet the Gospel had effect,   Rom. ix. 6.
Where'er it came, to save the elect: *with* Ch. xi. 7.
These saw the wisdom of the Cross,   1 Cor. i. 24.
Which unto them God's power was.   Acts ix. 31.
Then Gospel churches planted were,   1 Cor. xii. 8, 9.
By Christ's appointment, here and there;
The Spirit, by way of miracle,
Their officers with gifts did fill;   Acts xi. 21.
And chosen ones, on every side,
Believ'd in Christ as crucified;
Submitting unto him as King,
In every instituted thing.
Yea, the Gospel so obtain'd at length,
As manag'd by the Spirit's strength,
That all the world* did own Christ's name,   *Or Roman Empire,
And make profession of the same.   which had
Thus Satan, overcome at last,   spread itself
Was down from heathenism cast;   over the
But the old Serpent soon began,   greatest part
When once the world turn'd Christian,   of the World,
To play another sort of game,   as Luke ii. 1.
And set up worship much the same;
When Antichrist began to rise,
With all his vile idolatries,   2 Thes. ii. 4.
Though in another kind of dress,
Than the old Heathens did profess;
Thus the Enemy, like a flood, came in,   Isa. lix. 19.
And thought his former ground to win;
But, lo, a standard rais'd against
Him, by the Spirit, in the saints;
While they Christ's witnesses become,
And for him suffer martyrdom!
Rome Pagan did the saints oppress;

Rome Papal caus'd them like distress.
Christ's Church, then kept in purity,
Into the wilderness did flee,   Rev. xii. 6.
Which is a place most desolate,
And doth bespeak her suff'ring state.
But, lo, a place prepared was
For her, e'en in the wilderness,
Where she should nourish'd be, and fed   Verse 14.
With Christ, the true and living bread:
For God the Spirit was with her still,   Ps. cxxxii. 14.
Her Ministers to raise, and fill   Verse 16.
With Gospel-light, life, love, and peace,
All which he blest for her increase.   Verse 15.
But when the Lord thus did her good,
Behold! the Dragon cast a flood   Rev. xii. 15.
Of Persecution-cruelty,
And thought to swallow her thereby.   Rev. xii. 16.
But, lo, the Spirit's love and care,
Did herein for the Church appear;
He made the Earth* for her engage,   * The first
And thereby did the flood assuage!   Protestant
But yet the Church did ne'er enjoy,   powers entering
A full, or long tranquility.   their protest
The Whore of Rome did still oppress   against Popery,
Her, sometimes more, and sometimes less;   thereby engaging
Just as the Lord did her permit,   in the Church's
For glorious ends, which he thought fit.   cause.
England in Popish darkness lay,
Before the Reformation day;
But 'cause our Lord had many here,   Acts xviii. 10.
His sheep, that giv'n to him were,   John x. 29.
Which he engag'd to save from sin,   Verse 16.
Salvation-tidings must come in.
The Lord the mighty Spirit then,
Did fit, and raise up chosen* men,   *Luther and
To bring the glorious Gospel in,   Calvin, &c.
Which in this land much ground did win.   the first Re-
God's chosen ones were called by Grace,   formers.
And fitted for Christ's witnesses: Acts i. 8.
But soon, alas! the Scarlet Whore,
Gain'd much of what she lost before;

And in Queen Mary's bloody reign,
Vile Popery came in again;
While cruel edicts from her throne
Commanded saints to turn or burn.
Thus Antichrist by tyranny,
Design'd Christ's Gospel to destroy,
With the professors of the same,
Whom she, vile hereticks, did name
But the Spirit strengthened them with might,   Eph. iii. 16.
To bear for Christ a witness bright;
He kept them faithful unto death,   Rev. ii. 10.
While in the fires they lost their breath;
Being fill'd with soul-transporting joy,
Which Smithfield flames could ne'er destroy.
The power of God did so attend,
That Bonner* thought there was no end   *The then
Of burning hereticks, because   Bishop of
As some went off, others arose.   London.
But this sharp time Christ made to cease,
And quickly gave the Churches peace;
And then the Gospel made progress,
Which the Spirit to the elect did bless;
For this, still like the just man's way,
Shines more and more till perfect day;   Prov. iv. 18.
And though the Enemy often would
Have come upon us like a flood,
Yet Jesus by his Grace went on,   Isa. lix. 19.
To fortify his work begun;
In Sion's out-works still to raise,
Protestant princes, who always,
As manag'd by God's mighty arm,
Did guard the Church from outward harm.
While the Spirit, by the word of Grace,   1 Pet. i. 23.
Did new create the chosen race;
For whom his special care appears,
In feeding them by overseers.   Acts xx. 28.
And though the Papists oft did plot,
Against the Church, it came to nought;
For God himself maintain'd our cause,   Psal. ix. 4.
And sav'd us from the lion's paws.   1 Sam. xvii. 37.
When the Enemy thought the day their own,

He brought King William to the crown;
That Prince, of famous memory,
Who, like the Sun, made darkness fly!
In th' latter part of Anna's reign,
How did the clouds gather again!
Then, lo, great George the First, our King,
The Lord did as our Saviour bring!
But with what spite and hellish rage,
Did the Antichristian force engage,
'Gainst him, when they as rebels rose*,   *The late
For favour shown to Sion's cause!   Rebellion in
Yea, the enemies unto this day,   1716.
Their envious plots against us lay;
But hitherto they've come to nought,
And ruin on themselves have brought;   Isa. viii. 10.
Because the Lord is on our side,   Psal. vii. 15.
He us protects, and stains their pride.   Ps. cxxiv. 2.
While Royal George the Second's care,
As a nursing-father, shines so clear;
And his illustrious bride, our Queen,
As a nursing-mother's also seen;
For whom, with the Royal progeny,
We bless the Lord, that reigns on high;
Long may they live, the nation's joy,
And terror of the enemy.   Zech. iv. 6.
Now all this work is carried on,
By th' Spirit, sent from Christ the Son;
Hence we enjoy our liberty,
To 'tend the Gospel-ministry;
Where God the Spirit manages,
On the elect, the works of Grace.
Thus the Churches have a partial rest,   Acts ix. 31.
Where Romish tyrants are supprest;
For Antichrist, the man of sin,
Hath in a long consumption been;   2 Thes. ii. 8.
Caus'd by the Spirit of Christ's own mouth,
Which doth in Gospel-light go forth.
But ere he dies, with all his might,
He'll give a struggle for his life,
And so revive again, that he
Will do much mischief instantly;

For then Christ will this beast permit,
Again to shew his rage and spite.
When Papists shall regain their ground,
And th' outward court in trodden down,   Rev. xi. 2.
This beast will raise a war against
Christ's witnesses, which are the saints;
And overcome, and kill them too,   Verse 7.
For this will be a fatal blow;
So that they shall no witness bear,
But like dead bodies will appear.   Verse 8.
Thus slain, unburied they shall lie,
In the street of Rome*, the great City,   *By which,
For three years and a half, the space,   perhaps, may
Of time that's set, nor more nor less;   be meant
Those then that dwell upon the Earth   England.
Will join together to make mirth,   Verse 10.
Because they've slain these enemies,
And think they never more will rise.
The Scarlet Whore rejoicing then,
Will say, behold, I sit a Queen,   Rev. xviii. 7.
And never shall see sorrow more,
Then, lo, her plagues come in one hour.   Verse 8.
For though these witnesses lie slain,
The Spirit of life from God again   Rev. xi. 11.
Enters into these prophets great,
And makes 'em stand upon their feet.
The witnesses a voice then hear
From Heaven, which bids them come up there: Verse 12.
Then into the Church-Heaven they
Ascend without the least delay.
And, lo, an earthquake suddenly,   Verse 13.
That part of th' City will destroy;
Then wo to the blood-thirsty Whore,
For she shall drink) not as before,
Of Sion's blood) but of her own,   Rev. xvi. 16.
By righteous judgments on her shown!   Isa. xlix. 26.
Then earthly Kings shall have the Whore,
And burn her flesh with fire therefore;   Isa. xvii. 16.
Then Sion will reward her double,   Ch. xviii. 6.
For all her Persecution-trouble,
And grievously will her torment,

For slaying of the Innocent.
Oh! this will be an heavy blow,
Before her final overthrow;
Which will most vehement enrage,
The enemies all at once to engage;
'Gainst Sion, with united strength,
Thinking to ruin her at length.
Then the river Euphrates shall
Be dried up by a miracle;   Rev. xvi. 12.
The power of the Turk likewise,
Who is the Eastern Antichrist,
That the way of Eastern Kings might be,
For them prepar'd immediately;
Who, guided by God's mighty hand,   Jer. xxxi. 9.
Together march to their own land.
Persuaded that they shall obtain,
A pleasant Canaan once again,
The ten tribes, with the other two,   Jer. l. 4, 5.
Up to the Holy Land shall go;
Perhaps with Gentile converts join'd,
Who'll serve them with a ready mind.
For this life from the dead will be,   Rom. xi. 15.
To Gentile saints, who long'd to see
The Jews' redemption brought about;
And when they stir, for joy they'll shout.
Then these aforesaid enemies,   Rev. xvi. 16.
Against them jointly will arise;   Chap. xix. 11.
And unto Armageddon brought,   to the end.
A mighty battle will be fought.
Then, lo, another scene begins,
The Spirit unto Christ resigns;
For Christ himself in person shall
Give Antichrist his final fall: 2 Thess. ii. 8.
Both the Eastern and the Western too,
From Christ shall have the fatal blow.

A
NARRATION
OF THE
WONDERS OF GRACE.

PART THE FIFTH.

OF CHRIST'S GLORIOUS APPEARING AND KINGDOM.

Our Lord will soon in clouds appear,	Mat. xxiv. 30.
And all his Royal Glory wear;	
He'll send his mighty angels then,	Verse 31.
To gather up the chosen men.	
The dead in Christ then rais'd shall be,	1 Thes. vi. 16.
And put on Immortality;	1 Cor. xv. 53.
Their bodies, they shall then put on,	
Will shine like Christ the Glory-sun;	Phil. iii. 21.
Then living saints shall changed be,	
And with the Rais'd immediately,	
Together shall ascend to meet	Thes. iv. 17.
Their King, descending to his seat.	
Then he'll remember covenant-grace,	Ezek. xvi. 60.
To Israel's long forsaken race;	Isa. lx. 15.
For they shall back again return,	
And look on him they've pierc'd, and mourn	Zech. xii. 10.
And own him for their Head and King,	Hos. i. 11.
Who doth all their salvation bring;	
For when the Spirit's poured down,	
That nation shall at once be born.	Isa. lxvi. 8.
The fountain of Christ's God-like blood	
They then shall see a sacred flood,	
Open'd to cleanse them from all sin,	Zech. xiii. 1.
Which they by faith shall then wash in.	
And when Christ comes in royalty,	
The Man of Sin he will destroy,	2 Thess. ii. 8.
And in his fury tread down those,	Isa. lxiii. 6.
Who did his glorious reign oppose.	
Then all the great ones of the earth,	Rev. vi. 15.
That hate the Lamb, shall feel his wrath;	Verse 17
Christ, like a warrior, will surprise	
His, and his people's enemies;	
Who, then as gather'd into one,	Rev. xix. 19.
By him are ruin'd and undone:	Verse 20, 21.

Christ then his Sion's cause will plead,   Isa. li. 22.
And bring her blood on Babel's head.   Verse 23.
This day of vengeance in his heart,   Isa. lxiii. 4.
Will make the enemies to smart;
For he'll rebuke them in his ire,
Which will consume like flames of fire.   Isa. lxvi. 15.
Both Turk and Pope, with all that shall
Adhere to each, at once shall fall;
And multitudes will be the slain,   Verse 16.
When Christ this victory shall obtain.
His arrows then like flaming darts,
Shall pierce into their very hearts;   Psa. xlv. 5.
Then they to rocky hills will cry
For shelter; now they fain would fly   Rev. vi. 16.
From the Lamb's wrath, but 'tis in vain,
For they in fury shall be slain.
Christ then as Lord, and King of Kings,   Chap. xix. 16.
Will reckon with them for all things,
Wherein they have set up to vie,
With him in his authority.
Christ, for his name's sake, in that day,   Zeph. iii. 8.
Will tear him as a lion's prey;   Isa. xliii. 14.
Yea love to His will make him rise,   Ezek. xxxv. 5, 6.
T'avenge them on their enemies.
Though in his patience he did bear,
Till the saints' sufferings filled were;
'Twas not because their bitter smart,
Did never touch his tender heart;   Heb. iv. 15.
For though himself in glory great,
Was far above a suffering state,   Rom. v. 9.
Yet, by his love and sympathy,
He felt his members' misery;   Acts ix. 4.
And every blow that made them cry,   Zech. ii. 8.
Did touch the apple of his eye:
For still he took it as if done   Mat. xxv. 40.
To him, because with him they're one.
And while his members were in thrall,
His joy in glory was not full:
But 'cause he's God he stays a while,
'Till Babel doth her measure fill:
And when that time is fully come,

Wo, wo then to the Whore of Rome,	Rev. xviii. 7, 8.
For there's no act of cruelty,	
That she made His to suffer by;	
But Christ will then retaliate,	Rev. xvi. 5, 6.
In vengeance-storms on her own pate.	Psa. vii. 16.
If love incens'd, and power in one,	
Can ruin her, it shall be done;	
He'll travel in his God-like strength,	Isa. lxiii. 1.
To make an end of her at length.	
If all the cries, the groans, and prayers,	
Of his dear children whom he hears,	Psa. xxxi. 15.
That in all ages have been slain,	Rev. xviii. 24.
Can ruin upon Rome obtain,	
It shall be done: for now he will	
The prayers of all his saints fulfil.	Psa. cxlv. 19.
Those that under the altar lay,	Rev. vi. 9, 10.
He bad them a while longer stay;	
Until their brethren should be kill'd,	
And the sufferings of his body fill'd.	Verse 11.
And then he'll grant the saints' request,	
Upon the Antichristian Beast.	
If God's great word, that can't be broke,	John x. 35.
Which long ago foretold this stroke,	Zeph. iii. 19.
Can bring about her overthrow,	
It must undoubtedly be so.	
God's word, Christ's love, and faithfulness,	
The prayers of saints, in their distress,	
With Rome's iniquity being full,	
Will all at once for vengeance call.	
Then like a mighty millstone, she	Rev. xviii. 21.
Shall be cast down into the sea	
Of God's fierce wrath; and then the whore	
Of Babel, shall be found no more!	
Triumphant songs the saints will sing,	Rev. xix. 1, 2, 3, 4.
For this achievement of their King;	
When he their blood avenged hath,	
On them that dwell upon the earth.	
And when our David's foes are slain,	Psa. lxxii. 7.
Like Solomon, in peace he'll reign;	
For though Christ in this awful day,	
Appears his enemies to slay;	

Yet to his own, a Saviour great,	Isa. lxiii. 1.
Who then will make their bliss complete:	
For as their bridegroom he'll appear,	Mat. xxv. 6.
To solemnize his marriage here.	Rev. xix. 7.
Christ comes to take account of those,	
Whom he as his own servants chose;	Luke xix. 15.
And every hidden, secret thing,	
To light, this awful day, he'll bring.	Eccl. xii. 14.
For we believers, small and great,	
Must stand before Christ's judgement-seat;	
There to account for what we've done,	2 Cor. v. 10.
While here we had our bodies on.	
This in the morning will begin,	
And none but saints concern'd herein,	
For in their graves, the wicked dead,	
Shall lie till the day is finished.	Rev. xx. 5.
This trial of the saints on earth,	
Is not concerning life and death;	
For actions only it respect,	
And not the persons of the elect.	1 Cor. iii. 13.
The works of saints shall then be tried,	Verse 14.
And happy they whose works abide	
The fire; for this great melting day	
Will burn up all the wood and hay!	
This day will finish all debate,	1 Cor. iv. 5.
Which to religion did relate;	
The churches then shall clearly see,	
Wherein they've kept their purity;	
And wherein they did turn aside,	
From the rule, which should have been their guide.	
The churches then shall suffer loss,	
Of all their evil works as dross.	Chap. iii. 15.
Christ's holiness will brightly shine,	Rev. ii. 18.
In his detecting every sin;	
That by his own committed was,	Verse 23.
Although they're pardon'd by free grace.	
Yea, grace will then appear most free	
And large, in all its sov'reignty,	
When we shall see all sorts of sin	Mat. xii. 31.
Forgiven to the sons of men.	
Those churches then, which least had swerv'd	

From faith and order, but observ'd	
To walk by the rule of Christ's own word,	Rev. iii. 8.
These then shall have a large reward.	1 Cor. iii. 14.
Yea, every servant of the Lord,	
Shall then receive his own reward;	Verse 8.
According as his works are found,	
His honours in that day abound.	
For Christ our gracious Lord and King,	
Will own, and crown the least good thing,	Mat. x. 42.
That each of his have done for him,	
While here they had their working-time.	John ix. 4.
The saints, as overcomers then,	Rev. iii. 21.
Of Satan, sin, and wicked men,	
Shall sit with Christ upon his throne,	
And joy to hear him say, "Well done."	Mat. xxv. 21.
Then suffering saints shall have renown,	Zeph. iii. 20.
And every scar enrich their crown;	Mat. v. 11, 12.
According to their suffering state,	
They'll have a weight of glory great.	2 Cor. iv. 17.
The saints' reward is all of grace,	
For great is their unworthiness;	Luke xvii. 10.
And when Christ gives to them a crown,	
Lo, at his feet they'll cast it down.	Rev. iv. 10.
Christ, like himself, will act herein,	
Not like the narrow sons of men;	
Whose grace, if all meet in one man,	
Is but a drop to his ocean.	Isa. xl. 15.
Christ then, according to his state,	
As King, will make his favourites great;	Esther i. 7.
And each shall marks of honour wear,	
According to his proper sphere.	
And then the Lamb's adorned bride,	1 Cor. xv. 41, 42.
Shall be exalted at his side;	
Appearing like Christ's glory-mate,	Rev. xxi. 2.
Throughout the New Jerusalem state.	Verse 11.
Amidst this paradise of rest,	
Christ, as the Tree of Life, is plac'd;	
Feasting on him we shall be fill'd,	Rev. ii. 7.
With glory-fruits, this tree will yield.	
Christ's glory-fulness then will be	
A fountain of variety;	

And from him, as our Glory-Head,   Chap. xxii. 2.
Each one shall be supplied and fed.
Drest in the glory of our Head,   Col. iii. 4.
And with immortal garments clad,   1 Cor. xv. 53.
We in the glory-kingdom here   Luke xxii. 29.
Shall reign with Christ a thousand year;   Rev. xx. 4.
For then God will fulfil his word,
To give the kingdom to our Lord;   Isa. ix. 7.
God then will openly advance,
Christ to his vast inheritance.   Psa. ii. 8.
And then the glory of our King,   Psa. lxxii. 17, 19.
Through the restored world will ring;
With which the earth shall cover'd be,   2 Pet. iii. 13.
Even as the waters fill the sea.   Hab. ii. 14.
Christ here will keep his court royal,
And in his glory presence dwell;   Rev. xxi. 3.
Then living waters, from his throne,
Clear as the chrystal streams shall run;   Chap. xxii. 1.
Of love, life, light, and lasting peace,
These streams will make a vast increase,
Which, like a river, he'll extend,   Isa. lxvi. 12.
To the seed of Abraham his friend: Chap. xli. 8.
Then songs of praise to Christ their King,
These joyful ransom'd ones will sing,   Isa. xxxiv. 10.
When they in Canaan shall possess,   Jer. xxxii. 41.
Their long expected happiness.
Elected Gentiles also will,
At Sion's breasts, milk out their fill;   Isa. lxvi. 11.
While glory, like a flowing stream,   Verse 12.
Shall be extended unto them.
The happy saved nations then,
Around the New Jerusalem,
Shall walk in holy Zion's light,   Rev. xxi. 24.
As shining in Christ's glory bright;
For there the Lamb will cast his rays,
To make the city bright always;   Verse 23.
Out-shining far the creature sun,   Isa. xxiv. 23.
And will no more on her go down.   Chap. lx. 20.
Christ then his many crowns will wear,   Rev. xix. 10.
And be adored far and near!   Psa. lxxii. 11.
Yea, his enemies shall lick the dust,   Verse 9.

And own his righteous scepter just;   Psa. xcvii. 6.
An open glory this will be,   Isa. xxiv. 23.
When thus he'll reign in majesty;
And we with bridal garments on,
Shall on his royal throne sit down.
Then Christ, with joy and ravishment,   Cant. iv. 9.
Unto himself will us present;
A glorious bride, all over bright,   Eph. v. 27.
Completely fit for his delight.
Oh! What a glory we shall be,   Isa. lxii. 3.
When raised to this high dignity;
To sit with Christ upon his throne,   Rev. iii. 21.
As heirs with the eldest Glory-Son.   Rom. viii. 17.
Nor pain, nor death, shall us surprise,
For God will wipe tears from our eyes: Rev. xxi. 4.
Those trials we pass'd through before,
With all their tears, shall be no more.
We shall be past all trouble then,
From Satan, and from wicked men;   Rom. xvi. 20.
Yea, and for ever freed from sin,   *with*
For no defilement enters in.   2 Thes. i. 7.
No grieving thought shall us molest,   Rev. xxi. 27.
When we possess this kingdom rest;   Heb. iv. 9.
The joyful triumphs of the day
Will make all sighing flee away.   Isa. xxxv. 10.
Our bridegroom then will solemnize   Isa. lxii.
His wedding-day, with glorious joys;
And while we sup with Christ our King,   Rev. xix. 9.
With free-grace shouts his court will ring;   Zech. iv. 7.
For marriage-songs will then be sung   Rev. xix. 1, 6.
In heav'n, while the new earth is hung;
On every side with peace and rest,   Isa. xi. 6, 7, 8.
As being from the curse releast.   Rev. xxii. 3.
Dear saints, rejoice, this marriage-day
Is hasting on without delay;   Heb. x. 37.
Our Lord will quickly come again,   Rev. xxii.20
And take his mighty power and reign.   Chap. xi. 17.

A

NARRATION

OF THE

WONDERS OF GRACE.

PART THE SIXTH.

OF GOG AND MAGOG;
TOGETHER WITH THE LAST JUDGMENT.

And when the kingdom state is o'er,	Rev. xx. 7.
Then Satan, loosed as before,	
Shall go and tempt, and shall deceive	Verse 8.
The nations that on Earth do live,	
Then they with him their general head,	
Shall march along as by him led,	
The camp of saints to overthrow,	Verse 9.
And the beloved City too;	
And may be think their end to gain,	
Because they're such a numerous train;	
But their design shall come to nought,	
Bu dreadful ruin on them brought.	
Christ suffers these his enemies,	
To join in this vile enterprize;	
That so his glorious justice might,	Psal. li. 4.
In their damnation, shine most bright;	
While in this bold attempt he does,	
Destroy these his malicious foes,	
By fire from Heaven; and then he'll cast	Rev. xx. 10.
Them to the lake, where torments last.	
But Christ, our shelter from the storm,	Isa. xxxii. 2.
Will keep his people safe from harm;	Chap. iv. 5.
For lo, the daughters of the King,	
With joy and gladness he will bring,	Psal. xlv. 15.
Into his Royal palace, where	
The Queen, in gold of Ophir fair,	
Is nobly plac'd at his right hand,	Psal. xlv. 9.
While wond'ring angels round her stand.	Rev. xii. 1.
Then all the elect, the entire bride,	
Shall at her royal bridegroom's side,	
Be far from danger, free from fear,	
A City named "the Lord is there;"	Ezek. xlviii. 35.
Yea, th' saints shall then be rais'd so high,	

That they with Christ, in majesty,
As awful judges shall appear,   1 Cor. vi. 2.
Of wicked men, and angels here.   Verse 3.
For Christ, as pow'rful Judge of all   Acts x. 42.
The wicked from their graves will call;
And, lo, his voice they shall obey,   John v. 29.
In this Earth-rending, awful day.
The saints, as raised from the dead,
They rise in union to their head;   Rom. viii. 11.
That so his Glory they might see,   John xvii. 24.
And fashion'd like his body be.   Phil. iii. 21.
But the wicked, they shall all come forth,
To be for ever fill'd with wrath: Dan. xii. 2.
For that's the portion of their cup,   Psal. xi. 6.
When from the dead they're raised up;
And when the last great judgment's set,
The wicked then, both small and great,
Shall at Christ's just tribunal stand,
As guilty goats, on his left hand.   Mat. xxv. 33.
And then the books shall open'd be,   Rev. xx. 12.
Whence Christ proceeds immediately,
To pass the sentence on each one,
According to the works they've done.   Verse 13.
While saints advanced to his throne,
Shall join his sentence every one;
But, oh, the terrors of that day,   Rev. vi. 16, 17.
In vain the wicked flee away!
The book of th' Law shall open'd be
In all its perfect purity;
Extending to the inward part;   Rom. vii. 14.
Condemning sin in life and heart;
By which the Judge will then proceed,
To try each thought, and word, and deed.
Then Christless-ones who have thus broke,   Mat. xxv. 41.
Must feel its soul-condemning stroke;
For nought but curses it can speak,   Gal. iii. 10.
To those who did its precepts break;   Mal. iii. 5.
And God himself will witness be,
Of all their vile iniquity.
The book of conscience, then likewise,
Will be before the sinners' eyes;   Psal. i. 20.

While he with terror reads within,
The dreadful records of his sin.
And yet another book, behold,
The awful Judge will then unfold;   Rev. xx. 12.
The sacred book of life it is,
Where all are wrote that share in bliss.
In this blest book they written are,   John iii. 36.
For life, who fled to Jesus here;   Chap. v. 24.
Here God declares by word and oath,   Heb. vi. 18.
That these deliver'd are from wrath.   Rom. viii. 1.
But here, alas! No wicked can
Put in their claim, no not a man;
For here, concerning them it's writ,
They would not unto Christ submit.   Luke xix. 14, 27.
Oh! This will be the condemnation,
That men have hated God's salvation;   John iii. 19, 20.
And all along oppos'd that Grace,
By which he sav'd the chosen race!
And yet, behold, God's great decree
Of life, shall then unfolded be;
But, lo, their names did never stand,   Rev. xiii. 8.
In the life-book of Christ the Lamb.
And then the wicked world shall know,
That God has lov'd a remnant so,
As in his word he did declare,
Although they never would give ear;
But all along did make a jest,
Of their election-interest;
Then these despisers shall behold,
And perish, as it was foretold.
Thus nought but terrors will surround,   Prov. i. 26, 27.
All those who then are Christless found;
These then have not a word to say,   Rom. iii. 19.
Against the judgments of that day.
What then remains, the sentence past,
But those condemned ones, to cast
Into the Lake of Fire, to be   Mat. xxv. 41.
Tormented to eternity?
But, oh! the bliss of raised saints,
For ever got beyond complaints!   Rev. xx. 15.
No tongue their glory can express,

As clothed with Christ's Righteousness.	Isa. xxxiii. 24.
In this the holy law's fulfill'd,	
By that obedience Christ did yield;	Rev. xii. 1.
And justice fully satisfy'd,	Rom. v. 19.
When on the Cross for us he died.	Isa. xlii. 21.
This righteousness our robe is made,	1 Pet. iii. 18.
Whose God-like glories cannot fade	Isa. lxi. 10.
This robe becomes the dignity,	Dan. ix. 24.
To which Christ's Spouse advanc'd shall be,	
When she shall see him face to face,	1 Cor. xiii. 12.
And ever live in his embrace;	1 Thes. iv. 17.
While love in all the glorious Three,	
Surrounds her to eternity.	
And when the kingdom Christ resigns,	1 Cor. xv. 24.
Has finish'd all God's great designs;	
He'll then ascend in royal state,	
Together with his Glory-Mate,	John xiv. 3.
While swift-wing'd angels on each side,	Heb. i. 14.
Attend the Bridegroom and his Bride;	
When Christ brings home his lovely Spouse,	
Into his Father's royal house;	John xiv. 2.
And there with joys, as yet unknown,	
Will her present before the throne;	Jude, ver. 24.
In that same glory, in which he	
Had view'd her from eternity;	
When God presented her to him,	John xvii. 2.
Before the earliest date of time.	
Christ, to his Father, then will say,	
"Lo, here am I, and here are they,	
Which as my children thou hast giv'n;	Heb. ii. 13.
Behold, I've brought them safe to Heav'n.	
Through changes, deaths, and dangers great	
And made their happiness complete;	
For I their Saviour did become,	Eph. v. 23.
And now have brought them safely home;	
And set them all before thy face,	Gen. xliii. 9.
Here to enjoy the God of Grace."	
Then the glory of the Trinity,	
Through Christ, as man, eternally,	
On us will cast its dazzling rays,	
To make us shining bright always.	Isa. lx. 19.

Then no more drink by sips and tastes,
But into the wide ocean cast,   Rom. ix. 23.
We shall be fill'd with boundless bliss,
Which God prepared hath for his   1 Cor. ii. 9.
This supreme glory is too great
For us to know, while in this state;
But kingdom-glory will make way,
For its amazing bright display.
This glory can no changes know,
For 'twill be one eternal flow
Of love, life, light, and joy to the full,   Psal. xvi. 11.
While God will be our all in all.   Cor. xv. 28.
Oh! bliss indeed to see God's face,
And feast on the riches of his Grace
Which are in Christ laid up, to be   Eph. ii. 7.
Unfolded to eternity!   Rom. viii. 24.
Hope then shall to fruition come,
And faith, as in its perfect bloom,
Shall into vision changed be,
When we Jehovah's glory see.   1 Cor. xiii. 12.
But love, unto eternity,
Will join our souls to One in Three;   Verse 8.
When we shall see, and shall adore,
Our God in Christ, for evermore.
Lord, keep us in his wilderness,   Ps. cxix. 117.
Until this glory we possess;
Of which we're now apparent heirs,   Rom. viii. 17.
Though in a land of pits and snares.   Jer. ii. 6.
Let's live, our God, in thy heart-love
Fix'd on us in our Head above,   Eph. i. 4.
When set up from eternity,   Prov. viii. 23.
Before old Time began to be.
Let love our drooping spirits cheer,   Cant. ii. 5.
While in this wilderness we are;
Till we are swallow'd up in thee,
In boundless vast eternity.
And turn our backs on sin and time,
When we shall in love's ocean swim
While God, the glorious Three in One,   Ezek. xlvii. 5.
Will be our sea of bliss unknown!
Now he that testifies these things,

Who is the Lord, and King of Kings,   Rev. xvii. 14.
Says, I come quickly; make no stay,   Ch. xxii. 20.
Even so, Lord Jesus, come away.
Now to our God in Christ always,   Eph. iii. 21.
Let saints ascribe blessing and praise,
Throughout all ages, without end,
And let all creatures say, Amen.

A POEM

ON THE SPECIAL
WORK OF THE SPIRIT

IN THE

HEARTS OF THE ELECT.

WHEN God, the mighty Spirit, doth begin	
To save us influentially from sin,	
He comes, as sent from th' Father and the Son,	John xv. 26.
To do the work design'd e're time begun.	2 Thes. ii. 13.
The Spirit keeps election in his eye,	2 Tim. ii. 19.
And knows exactly for whom Christ did die;	
And what the counsels were in Heav'n above,	1 Cor. ii. 10, 11.
When he engag'd in offices of love.	
And thus he seeks, and finds the chosen sheep,	
The Father gave the Shepherd Christ to keep;	John x. 29.
And though among the fallen world they be,	Eph. ii. 3.
He comes resolv'd that there they shall not die	Ezek. xxxiv. 16.
But, oh! what posture doth he find them in,	
All over-spread with guilt, and filth of sin;	
No soundness from the head to foot is found,	Isa. i. 6.
Nothing but sores and putrifying wounds.	
Haters of God, rebellious enemies,	Rom. viii. 7.
That 'gainst his way of saving sinners rise;	Phil. iii. 18.
Led captive by the Devil, at his will,	2 Tim. ii. 26.
And every lust, they're servants to fulfil.	Titus iii. 3.
And will the Lord, the Holy Spirit, dwell	1 Cor. iii. 16.
Within such hearts that are as vile as Hell?	
How is it, Lord, what take up thine abode,	
In such a heart that's loathsome unto God?	Job xv. 16.
Take us aside awhile, and let us see	Mark vii. 33.
Th' amazing depths of this love-mystery!	
For sure, this is a time of love indeed,	Ezek. xvi. 8.
Wherein the glorious Three are all agreed,	
That love should like a mighty deluge pass,	Rom. v. 20.
O'er mounts of sin, oppos'd to reigning grace.	
Lord, we adore the greatness of thy love,	Eph. ii. 4.
Which neither time, nor sin itself could move!	
The Father lov'd, and gave by settlement,	Titus i. 2.
A vast inheritance, and don't repent,	Rom. xi. 29.
And therefore sends the Holy Spirit down,	Gal. iv. 6.

To fit the heirs of glory for their crown.	Col. i. 12.
The Father lov'd, and therefore gave his Son,	John iii. 16
To save th' Elect that were by sin undone;	Hos. xiii. 9.
And now redemption-work is finished,	Heb. ix. 12
He sends the Spirit forth from Christ our Head.	John xiv. 26.
The Son he lov'd, and freely gave his life,	Eph. v. 25.
That he might sanctify his Bride and Wife;	Verse 26.
And therefore sends the Spirit, to work all grace	John xvi. 7.
In the virtue of his blood and righteousness.	
The Spirit he lov'd, and thence engaged in	Rom. xv. 30.
Those offices, in which he saves from sin,	
And therefore comes at the appointed time,	
To do the work he's taken upon him.	
He undertook the whole of application,	John xvi. 13,14,15.
And ought to have the glory of salvation.	
His love to us is equally as great,	
As th' Son's, and Father's, bears as early date.	
Salvation to the praise of glorious grace,	Eph. i. 6.
In depths of wisdom, so contrived was,	Verse 8.
That Father, Son, and Spirit, all might have	
An equal glory from the soul they save.	John v. 23.
Election is a glorious scene of grace,	
In which are saved all the chosen race.	2 Tim. i. 9.
Redemption is a new amazing scene,	
In which, as fall'n, they're saved o'er again	Mat. i. 21.
And special application, to our view	
Presents a scene bright as the other two;	
In which th' Elect are sav'd from all their sins,	1 Cor. vi. 11.
And on this foot their happiness begins	
Salvation in the whole, the Father's is,	
As he contriv'd and settled all our bliss.	Eph. i. 3.
Salvation in the whole, belongs to Christ,	
Had he not died we should have glory miss'd.	John xi. 50.
Salvation in the whole, 's the Spirit's due,	
For in his work we saved are anew;	Titus iii. 5.
By his almighty power, and quickening grace,	Eph. i. 19.
And without this we could not see God's face.	John iii. 3.
Thus we salvation owe to all the Three,	
As in this work they jointly do agree;	John v. 19.
So that whatever part we look upon,	
We may discern the love of Three in One:	

And yet each person, in his proper place,
Peculiarly has shewn his special grace;   2 Cor. xiii. 14.
And thus the Spirit, in his work doth shew
His own great love, when open'd to our view.
For, though the Father settled all our bliss,
And so provided holiness for his,   Eph. i. 4.
When he ordain'd our full conformity   Rom. viii. 29.
To Christ, the glorious pattern in his eye;
Yet still his love lies like a hidden mine,
Until the Spirit breaks up this design.   1 Cor. ii. 12.
But when the time is come, down flies the Dove,
Upon the wings of everlasting love;   Jer. xxxi. 3.
To form Christ's image in the hearts of those   Gal. iv. 19.
The Father from eternity had chose;
In which new creature he forms every limb,
By Christ, and all the grace that is in him.   John i. 16.
Hence we a likeness bear in every part,
To all the graces that are in Christ's heart;
For thus the Spirit works in new creation,   Eph. ii. 10.
On all that are appointed to salvation.   1 Thess. v. 9.
Christ's image doth in brightness far surpass
That nature-image, in which Adam was
At first created by his Maker's hand,   1 Cor. xv. 46, 47.
When he the head of all mankind did stand.
Yea, though the first man's soul was upright made,
And so a perfect moral-goodness had,
As being created in the nature-part
Of Christ's own image, stampt upon his heart,   Gen. i. 27.
So far as then did suit his present state,
And all his seed to whom he did relate.
The law of God was written in his heart,   Mat. xxii. 37.
His soul conform'd thereto in every part.
He every way was suited to behold
The God of Nature, in this lower world.
And so to love, enjoy, and take his rest
In God, as such, of whom he was possest.
Thus all mankind, in him were upright made,   Eccles. vii. 29.
For 'twas a common image that he had;
Exactly suited to a nature-state,
And th' non-elect did only so relate.
This image Adam did possess for his,

Contain'd in it the heights of nature-bliss: Ps. viii. 5, 6.
But when he fell, he lost the same by sin,
And brought an universal Deluge in
Of miseries and death, on all his seed,   Rom, v. 12.
From which the non-elect are never freed
Because they never did relation bear   John x. 26.
To Christ, by Grace; in him they have no share.
But for the elect there was provision made,   2 Tim. i. 9.
And laid in Christ, their great transcendent Head;
The Father lov'd them, as he lov'd Christ-man,   John xvii. 23.
Into relations high, e're time began,
And thence predestinated them to bear
Christ's own bright image, in their proper sphere;   Rom viii. 29.
In all its nature, grace, and glory-parts,
To be by th' Spirit formed in their hearts.
And though old Adam had a rectitude,
Which is, for substance, said to be renewed
When God the Spirit new creates our hearts,   Col. iii. 10.
Yet 'tis not *Adam's* image he imparts;
Those Nature-beauties which in Adam lay,
We have from Christ in a transcendent way.
Beauties of nature, grace, and glory too,   Chap. i. 19
All meet in Christ, and thence to us they flow.   John i. 16.
Christ's image a transcendent glory has,
Out-shining perfect Adam's lovely face,
When in his most exalted heights of bliss,
Which he in Eden did possess for his;
For yet, he was but of an earthly make,   I Cor. xv. 47
And could not then of heav'nly things partake.
He was not suited to behold God's face
In Christ, as he's reveal'd the God of Grace.
No, 'twas a blessing in reserve above,   Eph. i. 3.
Among the treasures of eternal love;
And thence it doth descend to th' chosen race,
From Christ the heavenly Man, the head of grace.
Such as the earthy man, the earthy were,   I Cor. xv. 48.
Such as the heavenly Man, the heavenly are.
The glory settled is of such a nature,
No man can see't, except he's a new creature.   John iii. 3.
'Tis new creation fits the soul for heaven,
And suits its organs to the glory giv'n.

The pure in heart God's blessed face shall see,   Mat. v. 8.
In th' heights of glory, to eternity.
Then sure, the Spirit's love's amazing great,
In that he fits us for this blessed state;
For when he takes possession of the heart,
He new creates the soul in every part.   Eph. ii. 10.
    But, oh! what opposition doth he find,
Against his work, in th' sinner's heart and mind;
'Tis well for us he is the God of Might,   Isa. xl. 28.
And both his grace and power infinite:
He finds the understanding dark as night,   Eph. iv. 18.
The will rebellious, doth against him fight;   John v. 40.
The conscious senseless, evil and unclean,   Titus i. 15.
Th' affections earthly, and so lead the van.   Chap. iii. 3.
This is the case the soul of man lies in,
When God the Spirit doth his work begin.
But, lo! he speaks, and doth command the light,   2 Cor. iv. 6.
And straightway sets the understanding right;   Eph. v. 8.
Subdues the stubborn will, and brings it low'r,   John xxi. 29.
And sweetly draws it in this day of pow'r;   Psal. cx. 3.
Quickens the conscience, turns the affections too,   Heb. x. 22.
And makes 'em in another channel flow.   Phil. iii. 20.
Thus th' Spirit produceth faith, and every grace,   Gal. v. 22, 23.
Which he draws out, each in their proper place.
And what faith in the judgment sees as best,
Faith in the will doth cleave to as its rest;   Heb. xi. 13.
And then th' affections keep an order, still
Commanded by the judgment and the will;
For the whole soul touch'd with magnetic love,
Attracted is, and set on things above.   Col. iii. 2.
But, as in the old creation, every thing
In darkness lay, before the light did spring;
So in the new, black darkness fills the heart,   Gen. i. 2.
Till glorious light irradiates ev'ry part.
When th' Spirit first convinceth of all sin,   John xvi. 8.
What darkness doth the sinner find within?
And though the soul when first by sin opprest,
Takes its old course to find out ease and rest;
By th' works of its own hands it seeks for peace,   Rom. x. 3.
Yet now it finds those springs of comfort cease.   Isa. xlii. 15.
For, lo! its open'd eye is made to see

God's law, in all its inward purity; — Rom. vii. 14.
That he has broke the same in thought and word,
And therefore guilty stands before the Lord.
But, oh! th' amazing depths the soul doth see,
Couch'd in the mystery of iniquity;
While God the Spirit opens Adam's sin,
And shews the soul it guilty was therein; — Chap. v. 12.
And that from thence, as from a fountain head,
All manner of pollution has o'erspread
The soul of man, from whence doth still arise
All sinful acts, with vile enormities: — Mat. xv. 19.
As freely as the stream from th' fountain flows,
So sinful man doth sin in all he does!
And if the soul from grosser acts of sin,
Hath, by the pow'r of God, restrained been, — Gen. xx. 6.
Yet, when to him is shewn his plague of heart, — 1 Kings viii. 38.
He sees the sin that lurks in ev'ry part;
And thus the man's upon an equal ground,
With th' vilest sinner that on Earth is found.
Now, says the soul, I see all sins do meet, — Ezek. viii. 10.
In my vile heart, as in their proper seat;
Sure, I'm chief of sinners, none like me, — 1 Tim. i. 15.
Thus plung'd into the depths of misery;
An hater of the Lord, am I by nature, — Rom. i. 30.
An unbelieving, hell-deserving creature; — John iii. 18.
That in strict justice might have thither been
Sent from the womb, e'er I the light had seen.
In sin was I conceiv'd, in sin brought forth, — Psal. li. 5.
And nothing else have done since on the Earth — Psal. liii. 3.
How great's my debt, increasing ev'ry day, — Luke vii. 41.
And yet, alas! I've not a mite to pay! — Verse 42.
Oh! what a wonder 'tis I am not sent,
Into the place of endless punishment! — Mat. xxv. 46.
For ever banish'd from God's blessed face,
Fixt in his wrath, beyond the hopes of grace! — Luke xvi. 26.
I left the Lord; he justly might leave me,
And seal me up to endless misery.
Oh! what a distance am I at by sin, — Eph. ii. 17.
And not one step can I take back again.
My righteousness, my tears, my very prayer, — Prov. xxviii. 9.
Before a holy God, most fitly are. — Isa. lxiv. 6.

Had I no other sin but what's in them,
The least of these would surely me condemn;   James ii. 10.
I cannot answer for one sinful thought,   Job ix. 3.
Much less for all the folly I have wrought.
And then, behold! the soul is as it were,
Summon'd, and brought before God's righteous bar,
In th' Conscience; where the Judge with angry looks,
Proceeds to read what's written in the books:
Whence former sins, that were forgotten quite,
Wrote in God's knowledge, now appear in sight.   Psal. 1. 21.
And now the soul doth hear a lecture read,
Out of the Law, that strikes it through with dread;   Rom. vii. 9.
While conscience bears its witness to each crime
Charg'd by the Judge, it knows the place and time.
And now the mouth is stopt before the Lord,
The man stands guilty, cannot say a word,   Rom. iii. 19.
Why the dread sentence should not on him pass,   Mat. xxv. 41.
Since all the curses he deserved has.
And now all hopes of life, by th' law, doth cease   Rom. iii. 20.
He sees, if sav'd it must be sovereign grace;
And having heard, that others, such as he,
Have had a pardon from God's mercy free.   1 Tim. i. 16.
Now this is all the plea the sinner hath,
Lord, I confess, I have deserv'd thy wrath;
And if this moment I'm sent down to Hell,
Thou would'st be holy, just, and righteous still.   Psal. cxlv. 17.
But, Lord, thou canst save such an one as I,   Mat. viii. 2.
And 'twill thy mercy greatly magnify;
But if thou should'st my great request deny,
Lord, at thy feet submissive still I lie.
It may be, thou'lt compassion have on me,   Jonah iii. 9.
And save me from the depths of misery.
And thus the soul in hope's kept from despair,
Although those hopes are slain again by fear;
For now the soul is plung'd into a pit,   Psal. lxxxviii. 6.
And by no means it can get out of it;
For as a man that's sunk in mire and clay,
That strives with all his might to get away,
The more he struggles he sinks deeper in,
So 'tis with the soul, in guilt and filth of   Psal. lxix. 2. sin.
But, oh! the horrid noise the soul doth hear,

While in this pit, which makes it quake for fear!
It hears the thunder that in Sinai was,   Heb. xii. 21.
And feels the lightning flashing in its face;
While every curse that pierceth through its heart
Is like a thunder-bolt, or flaming dart.
God's awful voice on Sinai curseth still,   Gal. iii. 10.
The soul shall die, that once hath broke my will.
And, oh! the hideous noise of Satan's roar,
Who, like a lion, seeketh to devour   1 Pet. v. 8.
Says he, come, sinful soul, thou art my prey,
Forsook of God, thou dost belong to me.
Thou'rt such a wretch, that now all hope is past,
Do what thou wilt thou shalt be damn'd at last.
And, oh! the terrors of a guilty heart,   Psal. xl. 12.
Which, like an army, march through ev'ry part;
Headed by unbelief, proclaiming war,
Against the soul that's guilty, at God's bar.
And thus the soul's encompass'd every way,
With terrors, like an army in array;   Job. vi. 4.
And apt to think, while in this horrid pit,
It can't escape, but perish must in it.
But then the Spirit, who in love begun
This work at first, doth farther carry't on.
And having shewn the soul its misery,
He now proceeds to shew the remedy;   John xvi. 14.
Christ as a Saviour, fully suited to
The soul's distress in every kind of wo.
      Is the soul guilty? Now it's made to see
Christ bore the wrath of God for such as he;   1 Pet. iii. 18.
And that Salvation from the wrath to come,   1 Thes. i. 10.
Is, by the blood of Christ, obtain'd for some.
Is the soul filthy? Now it's made to view,
There's cleansing in the blood of Jesus too.   1 John i. 7.
Is the soul naked? Doth it want a dress?
The Spirit shews Christ's perfect righteousness.   Rom. v. 19.
And doth its nature-darkness come in sight?
The Spirit then shews Christ's prophetic light.   Mat. xi. 27.
And doth it groan under the loathsomeness,
That all its parts and powers doth possess?
The Spirit then shews Christ, e'en as he is,
The fountain of all holiness, to his.   1 Cor. i. 30.

And doth it in a sense of distance lie?
The Spirit says, Christ's blood can bring thee nigh.   Eph. ii. 13.
And dost thou feel thy self a lifeless clod?
There's life in Christ, to make thee live to God   John v. 21.
And doth the soul see its own weakness too,
And that it nothing that is good can do?
Nor in the least wise save itself from sin,
Or get out of the depths it's plunged in?
The Spirit then reveals the strength that is   Isa. xlv. 24.
Laid up in Christ, for the supply of his;
And that this Saviour is a mighty one,   Ps. lxxxix. 19.
Completely fit to be relied upon.
Then tells the soul, his great salvation's free,   Isa. lv. 1.
Prepar'd for such that worst of sinners be.   1 Tim. i. 15.
But, oh! how glad the soul is of this news,   Acts ii. 41.
New light and life flow from objective views.   Psa. xxxiv. 5.
And while th' Spirit reveals Christ in each part,
By mighty power he strongly draws the heart,   John vi. 44.
To cleave to Christ, whom now the soul doth see,
An all-sufficient Saviour to be.   Matt. viii. 2.
    Now, saith the soul, I long for Christ indeed,
He is a Saviour, just such as I need;
As Prophet, Priest, and King, he glorious is,
Oh! could I say he's mine, and I am his.   Cant. v. 10.
Lord, give me Christ, or else my soul must die,   1 John v. 12.
None but this Jesus can me satisfy.
I seek not for the pleasures of this world,   Psal. iv. 6, 7.
Its empty honours, nor yet bags of gold;
These trifling toys can't satisfy my mind,
Nor can I rest, till I this Jesus find.   Psal. lxxiii. 25.
Lord, give me Christ, whatever thou denies,
Then I can freely bear all miseries
Thine are expos'd to, in this present time,   Rom. viii. 18.
If once my soul possession had of him.
Oh! happy they, that are in such a case,
Who have an interest in the God of Grace;   Psal. cxliv. 15.
But, as for me, I fear I'm none of his,
And therefore shall of endless glory miss.
Yet, who can tell? I'll wait at th' mercy-seat,   Isa. viii. 17.
And if I die, I'll die at Jesus' feet.   Esth. iv. 16.
I'll cast myself upon him, who can tell?

It may be he will save my soul from hell.
But, if he should not, yet I can but die,   2 Kings, vii. 4.
Which, though I fear, yet at his feet I'll lie.
'Twixt hope and fear, this is the soul's desire,
But yet, alas! its feet stick fast in mire.
But when th' Spirit has brought the soul thus far,
Now comes the time for his love to appear.
    Then, lo! he brings the promises of grace,   John xiv. 26.
Which do exactly suit the sinner's case;   Prov. xxv. 11.
By which he gives the soul a sweet relief,
But, oh! how soon pull'd back by unbelief.
Ten thousand doubts and fears from every part,
Arise within the trembling sinner's heart;
Each proves a weight that sinks him in the pit,
So that he thinks thence he shall never get.   Psal. lxix. 15.
And if the Spirit only did propose
The promis'd grace, and left the heart to close
Therewith, in its own pow'r, and so get out,
Alas! the work would ne'er be brought about.
But, oh! the Spirit's grace, he still goes on,
And takes the cords of love, and lets them down   Hos. xi. 4.
Into those depths, wherein the sinner's cast,
And straightway to his heart he binds them fast;
And then he draws, by his Almighty power,
Out of that pit which would the soul devour;
Then sets it on a rock that cannot move,   Psa. xl. 2.
And all this work is done by cords of love.
The Spirit says, this grace is all for thee,
Persuades the heart, and then the man's set free;   Heb. xi. 13.
And feels a mighty rock that's underneath,
That bears him up from sinking into death.
This rock is Christ, the great Foundation Stone,   1 Cor. iii. 11.
Which all the saved-ones are built upon.
And now the soul believes the promise-word,   John iv. 50.
And wholly gives itself up to the Lord,   2 Cor. viii. 5.
To be for ever sav'd in God's own way,
And kept in Jesus' hands till the great day.   2 Tim. i. 12.
But, oh! the glorious light that now appears,
Makes darkness flee, and drives out guilty fears.
And now the soul's like one caught up to heav'n,   2 Cor. xii. 2.
And stands amaz'd to see what God has giv'n;

While pard'ning grace, and peace on every side,   Jer. xxxi. 34.
Flow through the soul, and cause a mighty tide   Isa. lxvi. 12.
Of glorious joy, that overflows the banks,   1 Pet. i. 8.
And soon breaks out in streams of praise and thanks.

    Oh! bless the Lord with me, the soul doth cry,   Psal. xxxiv. 3.
For I shall praise him to eternity.   Psal. cxlv. 2.
I once condemned at God's bar did lie,
And thought he would his justice magnify.
In my eternal ruin; oh! but he
Has glorified his grace in saving me.   Eph. ii. 5.
I, that just now, fill'd with the guilt of sin,
Lay at hell's mouth, just ready to drop in,
Am now drawn from those depths of misery;
I, that was once far off, am now made nigh   Verse 13.
I feel th' embraces of God's bosom-love,
A taste of what I shall enjoy above.
How is it, Lord, that I should saved be?   John xiv. 22.
What! pass by thousands, and lay hold on me!   Rom. ix. 21.
'Tis not because I better was than they,   Chap. iii. 9.
No, my salvation comes another way;
'Twas sovereign grace sav'd me, and that alone;
Lord, take the glory, let grace wear the crown.   Psal. cxv. 1.
And thus a new song's put into the mouth,   Psal xl. 3.
When once the soul to liberty's brought forth.
Set on the rock, amazing prospects hence,
Transport the soul beyond the joys of sense:
One while it views the Father's wondrous grace,   1 John iii. 1.
Sees itself safely lie in his embrace;
Another while it spies Christ on the tree,   1 Pet. ii. 24.
Then, says the Spirit, behold, he died for thee;
See how the Father bruis'd him for thy sin,
And by his stripes thy healing doth come in.   Isa. liii. 5.
O'ercome with love, then, lo! the soul doth cry,
What! did my dearest Jesus for me die?   Gal. ii. 20.
Did all my sins together on him meet?   Isa. liii. 6.
Were these the nails that pierc'd his hands and feet?
Then straightway from the joys of pard'ning grace
A flood of godly sorrow flows apace;
Now't looks on him it pierc'd, and mourns indeed,   Zech. xii. 10.
Hates every sin that made its Saviour bleed;
And thus breaks forth, Lord! what a wretch I've been?

How have I wounded thee by ev'ry sin?
And, did'st thou give thy precious life for me?   Mat. xx. 28.
O'ercome with love I give myself to thee.
Oh! keep me safe from sin in thine embrace,   Ps. cxix. 117.
And make me live to th' glory of thy grace.
Again, the soul as in an extasy,
Astonish'd at the Father's love doth cry,   Ezek. xvi. 63.
What, is my God for ever pacify'd?
And, doth this peace flow thro' Christ's wounded side?   Col. i. 20.
Lord, I'm asham'd, confounded, and no more
Can make excuses, as I did before.
Now I confess I'm vile, lie down in shame,   Jer. iii. 25.
Even while I glory in Jehovah's name.   Ex. xxxiv. 5, 6.
Lord, I'm beneath thy love, even as a creature,   Job vii. 17.
Much more as filthy by my sinful nature.   Ch. xv. 16.
And, hast thou loved me ere time begun,   Jer. xxxi. 3.
And grac'd me in thy well-beloved Son?   Eph. i. 6.
What, didst thou take my sins, and on Christ lay,   Isa. liii. 6.
And pardon me when I had nought to pay?   Luke vii. 42.
What, did my hateful sins ne'er change thy mind,   Job xxiii. 13.
Oh! my heart melts, that I should be unkind.
Lord, since my sins can make no change in thee,   Mal. iii. 6.
Let thy great love transforming be to me.   2 Cor. iii. 18.
And now the soul's enlarg'd, when grace doth draw   Ps. cxix. 32.
To run in God's commands, and love his law;   Verse 97.
Christ having dy'd, to free it from that thrall
The curse-part of the law hath brought on all;   Gal. iii. 13.
By which it is to the law of Moses dead,
And being married to its risen head,
In pleasant fruit to God it doth abound,   Rom. vii. 4.
Beyond what can in moralists be found.
Not do and live, the new-born soul doth sway
But having life it freely doth obey.   2 Cor. v. 15.
Not without law to God in any thing,
But under the law to Christ, Mount Sion's King.   1 Cor. ix. 21.
Thus faith and love, repentance, godly fear,   Eph. v. 9.
Joy, hope, and patience, fruits of the Spirit, are   Gal. v. 22.
By him produc'd, and drawn forth ev'ry way,   Rom. v. 3, 4.
While in this world the new-born soul doth stay.   Verse 5.
    And thus the Spirit works in all the elect,   Titus i. 4.
By which he makes them saints as the effect;   Rom. i. 7.

But yet his work admits of great degrees
In every part, just as the Spirit please;   1 Cor. xii. 11.
And hence doth flow all that variety,
Which in the saints' experience we see:
Perhaps there's scarcely two that can be brought,
That have in every thing alike been wrought;
And yet the work's the same in all for kind,
Heart answers heart, as face doth face, we find: Pro. xxvii. 19.
All that have pass'd under this work of grace
Convinced are of sin, and righteousness;   Joh. xvi. 9, 10.
From wrath to come, to Christ's they're made to fly,   Heb. vi. 18.
And being sav'd, the Lord they glorify;   Luke i. 74, 75.
For now the soul begins to live to him,   2 Cor. v. 15.
Who gave himself to save it from all sin;   Titus ii, 14,
For though at first, faith deals with Christ as Priest,
To be from guilt of sin and wrath releast;
Yet priestly grace submits it to Christ-King,
And makes it love his laws in every thing.
And thus the soul is rais'd from death and sin,
Fill'd with new life, and feels sweet peace within;   Eph. ii. 1.
And apt to think, that now all storms are past,
And that its present, joyful frames will last.   Psal. xxx. 7.
    But when the Sun's withdrawn the soul doth mourn,
For clouds and darkness back again return;
And though its feet on Christ the Rock are plac'd,   Psal. xl. 2.
Alas! 'tis weak, and can't as yet stand fast.
When stormy tempests from all parts arise,
New scenes of trouble fill it with surprise;
For though th' new creature's form'd in ev'ry part,   2 Cor. v. 17.
Yet still the old man dwelleth in the heart;   Rom. vii. 20.
And these contrary to each other are,   Gal. v. 17
Which make the new-born soul a seat of war.   Cant. vi. 13.
Unthought of foes straightway appear in sight,
And the new-born babe unskilful is in fight.   Heb. v. 13.
It wonders why the Canaanites remain,
And's apt to think it shall by them be slain.
Oh! says the soul, I fear the work's not right,
Because I am in such a dismal plight;
I find such dreadful thoughts that work within,   Mat. xv. 19.
Which make me fear I'm in a state of sin:
Sure, what I feel can ne'er consist with grace,

I fear my comfort but delusion was.   2 Thes. ii. 11.
Then Satan he strikes in; 'tis true, says he,
Thou'rt right in this, thy comfort could not be
From God; for none of his do ever find
Such blasphemies, as fill thy heart and mind.
Give up thy hope, for 'tis a vanity
To think all's well when God's thy enemy;
Thou'rt not elect, and but a temporary,
That have but common faith, and so miscarry.   Mat. xiii. 22.
Nay, he sometimes proceeds to say, thou'rt lost,
In that thou'st sinn'd against the Holy Ghost;   Mat. xii. 32.
But, oh! what deep distress is caus'd by this,
They that have felt it best know what it is.
And, 'tis a wonder of the Spirit's grace,
That he don't leave the soul in such a case,
But, by some word or other, doth impart
Suitable comfort, speaking to the heart.   Hos. ii. 14.
      'Tis he that opens all that mystery
Of sin and grace, that in its heart doth lie;   Rom. vii. 21, 23.
And tells the soul it should not doubt its state
Because it finds corruptions strong and great.
There is, saith he, the new man and the old,
Both dwell in saints; they can't do what they would;   Gal. v. 17.
These as two fountains, have in thee a place,
The one's the spring of sin, the other grace;
Old Adam's image is the spring of sin.
And in thy flesh there dwelleth no good thing.   Rom. vii. 18.
Christ's image is the spring of ev'ry grace,
And nothing flows from thence but holiness.   Verse 25.
'Tis true, these fountains mix when in the stream,
So that no thought, nor word, nor way is clean;   1 Kin. viii. 46.
The purest acts of grace, while saints are here,   Isa. lxiv. 6.
Are mixt with sin, the streams are never clear;
Yet, if the muddy'd streams are trac'd with skill,
They're found to flow from diff'rent fountains still.
The flesh and spirit, these two enemies,
Like armies fierce, against each other rise;   Cant. vi. 13.
Satan, the Prince of Darkness, with his train,
Musters sin's force, which puts thy soul to pain;   2 Cor. xii. 7.
But Christ, on th' other hand maintains the fight,   Psal. cxliv. 1.
Strengthens thy grace, and puts thy sin to flight.

Then fear not, though thou hast but little strength,	Isa. xli. 10.
For Christ, and grace, shall overcome at length;	Mat. xii. 20.
Thy Captain hath a glorious conquest made,	Col. ii. 15.
O'er all thy foes, already, in thy stead.	
Christ gave thine enemies their mortal blow,	
And in his strength thou shalt o'ercome them too;	Rom. viii. 37.
Be valiant then until thy foes are slain,	
For 'tis to learn thee war, that they remain;	Judg. iii. 1, 2.
Set up thy banners in King Jesus' name,	Psal. xx. 5.
Put on thy armour, holy war proclaim;	Eph. vi. 1.
With courage then fight all that do oppose,	2 Pet. v. 9.
And well thou may'st, for thine are vanquish'd foes.	
When thus th' Sp'rit has taught the soul, at length	
Its hope revives, afresh it gathers strength;	
And then concludes, if I do what I hate,	Rom. vii. 16.
It's no more I, but sin, that's an inmate.	Verse 17.
Then faith triumphs, gives thanks to God in Christ,	Verse 25.
In and through whom comes all its victories.	1 Cor. xv. 57.
This grace of faith, which the Spirit doth produce,	1 Cor. 12. 9.
By the same Spirit's put to various use;	
Faith, as the new man's eye, an organ fit,	
To see the things of God in gospel light.	1 Cor. ii. 14.
Faith, as the new man's hand, doth Christ embrace,	John i. 12.
With all that's given by the Father's grace.	
Faith, as the new man's foot, to Christ doth go,	Chap. vi. 35.
And through him, unto God the Father too.	Heb. vii. 25.
Faith eyes the evidence of things not seen,	Chap. xi. 1.
Faith's hand embraceth what the eye takes in;	Verse 13.
And also fights the battles of the Lord,	Verse 34.
Taking its weapons from God's faithful word.	Eph. vi. 17.
Faith's foot doth follow Christ where'er he goes,	2 Cor. v. 7.
And tramples on whatever doth oppose.	Rev. xiv. 4.
Faith's eye at first is weak, and though there's sight,	Rom. xiv. 1.
Yet can't look stedfastly on objects bright,	
'Till visive Spirits flow from Christ the Head,	Eph. i. 17.
By which the new man's eye is strengthened.	Verse 18.
Faith's hand, at first, is weak, and trembles so,	
That it can't hold what free grace doth bestow;	
And though it takes up Christ, its proper shield,	Eph vi. 16.
Yet still it's weak, and him can scarcely wield;	
Till vital spirits from Christ do make it strong,	Rom. iv. 20.

To clasp about God's great salvation. Verse 21.
Faith's foot, at first, is weak, with trembling pace
It goes to Christ, for all salvation grace,
'Till life and strength from Christ confirms it more;
Then, like the nimble hind, it can trip o'er 2 Sam. xxii. 34.
The mounts of opposition in its way,
And run to Christ with freedom ev'ry day:
For after God the Spirit has reveal'd,
Christ to the soul, and it believes, 'tis seal'd. Eph. i. 13.
This special privilege some saints possess,
Which is the greatest on this side Heaven's bliss.
    Three witnesses on earth, we read there are,
The spirit, water, blood, that witness bear, 1 John v. 8.
Unto God's great salvation in the whole,
And the special int'rest of the new-born soul.
The blood, Christ's own obedience on the cross,
Bears witness, that Salvation's wrought for us. Heb. ix. 12.
The blood, as sprinkled in the conscience, doth
Bear witness, that we saved are from wrath. Chap. xii. 24.
But, though this is a testimony bright,
It only is receiv'd in God's own light;
The soul can't see Christ's death was for that end,
To save his own, if the Spirit don't attend;
Nor can it say, a dying Saviour's mine, Gal. ii. 20.
Unless the Lord the Spirit please to shine.
The water, grace, and sanctity within,
Bear witness, that the soul is sav'd from sin. 1 John iii. 14.
This likewise is a witness of great strength,
Which the new-born soul gives credit to at length.
But if the Spirit on his work don't shine,
Alas! the soul can't see it, nor take it in.
Thus the blood and water, when the Spirit shines Ps. xxxvi. 9.
Do jointly testify of pardon'd sins.
And 'tis the witness that these two do bear,
The new-born soul doth listen first to hear;
For though the Spirit by a whispering voice,
Speaks to the heart, and makes it to rejoice; Hos. ii. 14.
Yet the soul can't rest in what from him doth hear,
Unless the blood and water witness bear;
From these, at times, it's fully satisfy'd,
Whence heav'nly joy flows like a mighty tide; 1 Pet. i. 8.

But if the Spirit once withdraw his light,
Straightway the soul is all as dark as night.   Isa. l. 10.
And thus some saints go on for days and years,
One while in hopes, another while in fears;
One while the Spirit shines, the soul doth hear
The witness, that the blood of Christ doth bear.   Eph. i. 7.
Anon he doth withdraw his glorious rays,
Then doubts prevail, the soul begins, and says,
I fear 'twas not for me Christ shed his blood,
The peace I had from thence was never good;
Again the Spirit shines, makes grace appear,
And then the water doth its witness bear;
From whence the soul concludes its right to Heav'n,   1 Pet. i. 3, 4.
Because it finds there's a new nature giv'n.
And as it sees inherent grace to bud,
It listens to the witness of Christ's blood;
Goes on rejoicing in received grace,   Ezek. xvi. 15.
And's apt to set it up in Jesus' place.   Verse 17.
But then the Spirit withdraws his influence
And makes it die unto a life of sense;
Then raises it to live by faith upon,
The God of all salvation in his son.   Hab. iii. 17, 18.
And now the Spirit himself doth witness bear,   Rom. viii. 16.
Of what from the other two the soul did hear;
Proclaims God's love aloud in ev'ry part,
And makes such strong impressions on the heart;
Which casts out bondage-fear, and slavery,   1 John iv. 18.
And makes the soul stand fast in liberty;   Gal. v. 1.
He opens what before was greatly hid,
And shews the soul what God the Father did,
E'er time began, how he hath lov'd and blest,   Eph. i. 3, 4.
That remnant, which he then did chuse in Christ;   Rom. xi. 5.
And gave to be the Mediator's Wife,
Whose names were written in the book of life;   Luke x. 20.
And then the Spirit himself doth witness bear
Unto the soul, and says, thy interest's here.
Much like as Nathan, in another case,   2 Sam. xii. 7.
Thou art the man, that stand'st in all this grace   Rom. v. 2.
And that he may unto the soul impart,
The knowledge of God's love, he speaks his heart.
     Behold! says he, oh, soul! I've loved thee,

My love's as ancient as eternity;	Jer. xxxi. 3.
My love was free, a sov'reign act of grace,	Exod. xxxiii. 19.
With which I did thee in my Son embrace.	
I pass'd by thousands, that before me lay,	Rom. ix. 21.
And chose thee out of the same lump of clay;	Verse 11.
Not for thy goodness that I did foresee,	
For in no wise thou better wast than they.	Chap. iii. 9.
My love to Jacob was immensely great,	Mal. i. 2.
When his brother Esau I did reprobate;	Verse 3
My sov'reign grace did set thee then apart,	
For mine own self, and then I fixt my heart	Psal. iv. 3.
Upon thee, and provide all that bliss,	
Which thou shalt to eternity possess.	
Yea, I provision made for that great end,	
To bring thee through the ways and means design'd.	1 Pet. i. 2.
All this I gave thee by a special grant,	2 Tim. i. 9.
When with thy Head I made the covenant.	Ps. lxxxix. 3.
And though by sin thou'st plung'd thyself into	
The depths of guilt and filth, distress and woe;	Hos. xiii. 9.
Which brings eternal ruin upon all	Eph. v. 6.
That I pass'd by, and left in Adam's fall;	Eccles. iv. 10.
Yet I was at no loss to carry on	
My great designs of grace, in Christ my Son.	
Thy heinous sin did make no change in me,	Hos. iii. 1.
Because my love is from eternity.	Jer. xxxi. 3.
And what 'twas from eternity that's past,	
Through time, and to eternity 'twill last;	Ps. xxxiii. 11.
Although by sin thou had'st the passage stopp'd,	
Which through my Son again I've open'd up;	Isa. xii. 18.
And though thou often changest in thy frame,	
I never change, my heart is still the same.	Mal. iii. 6.
Thou'rt ever safe, enclosed in my arms,	
And none shall pluck thee thence, or do thee harm.	John x. 29.
Thus doth the Lord the Spirit's witness prove,	
Unto the soul, the Father's grace and love.	
And then, behold, he takes the grace of Christ,	Chap. xvi. 14.
And this presents before its open'd eyes.	
The Spirit speaks the language of Christ's heart,	
When he the knowledge thereof doth impart;	
And says, I have thee loved from eternity,	
Even as my God and Father, loved me.	John xv. 9.

Thee, as my Father's gift, I did embrace,	Chap. xvii. 9, 10.
My heart clave to thee in the greatest grace	
I joy'd in thee, and thou wast very dear	Eph. v. 25.
To me, in all relations thou didst bear.	Prov. viii. 31.
And the glory which my Father gave to me,	
In my great love, I then did give to thee;	John xvii. 22.
Although I well foreknew, that thou would'st prove	
Rebellious and ungrateful, slight my love;	Isa. xlviii. 8.
Run deep in debt, and sell thyself for nought,	Chap. lii. 3.
And so deserve the woes that sin hath brought;	
Which would have thy eternal ruin been,	
If I had not engag'd to bear thy sin.	
But, oh! behold, the workings of my heart,	Hos. xi. 8.
My bowels mov'd, with thee I could not part;	
Though treach'rously thou went'st astray from me,	Jer. iii. 20.
My faithful heart was still the same to thee:	Heb. xiii. 8.
My love broke forth, thy surety I became,	Gen. xliii. 9.
Engag'd to pay thy debt, and bear thy blame;	
Though I knew well a vast expence 'twould be,	John xviii. 4.
To save thee from eternal misery,	
Yet, I resolv'd for thee to bear all pain,	Isa. l. 6.
Conquer thy foes, and set thee free again;	Hos. xiii. 14.
This I went through, the bitter work is done,	John xix. 30.
And now for thee I ascend my Father's throne.	Heb. ix. 24.
For glory has not chang'd the least my heart,	Chap. xiii. 8.
Still I'm resolv'd, with thee I'll never part.	
There's none shall separate thee from my love,	Rom. viii. 35.
And I'll take care to set thee safe above.	
And this the Spirit himself doth testify,	Verse 16, 17.
Which straightway fills the heart with glorious joy;	1 Pet. i. 8.
For now he gives the soul to read its name,	
Recorded in the life-book of the Lamb.	Rev. xxi. 27.
Yea, the Spirit seals whate'er for us is done,	
Bestow'd, or wrought, by the Father and the Son.	
And now the soul doth satisfaction take,	
From the Spirit's witness, for his witness sake;	1 John ii. 27
For though these things in part it heard before,	
From the witness that the blood and water bore;	
Yet still it went a way that's round about,	
To find its title, and search interest out.	Mal. i. 2.

It us'd to listen first to grace within,

And see if that kept down indwelling sin;
And if the water did its witness bear,
Through that it went the blood of Christ to hear.
But if the water did not witness bright,
The witness of the blood, the soul did slight,
Saying, what's this to me, if I can't see
Such and such measures of true sanctity?
And while the soul takes up its comfort hence,
Alas! it often wants its evidence,   Lam. iii. 28.
And's like a ship toss'd in tempestuous seas,   Mat. xiv. 24.
That's driven where the wind and water please.   James i. 6.
Corruption-waves the wind of strong temptation,
So toss the soul, it questions its salvation;   Acts xxvii. 20
Because, as yet, it has not learn'd the skill,
To cast its anchor fast within the vail;   Heb. vi. 19.
Yet, through the pilot's care, shall land at rest,   Chap. iv. 9.
Although in storms it often is distrest.
     But sealed saints are taught a higher way,
To take their comfort from what God doth say;   Num. xxiii. 19.
And they first hear the Spirit's evidence,
And take their satisfaction up from hence;
They know the Spirit is Truth, and cannot lie,   1 John ii, 27.
And these can rest in his veracity.
They hear what th' Spirit saith, and know 'tis he,   Rev. ii. 7.
By the same light, that they their int'rest see.
In faith of int'rest then they go to hear,
The witness that the blood of Christ doth bear;
Credit the same, and are confirmed more
In the faith of what they rested in before.
Then next proceed to the water evidence,
Believe the same, and grow more strong from hence
But if inherent grace is not all bright,
Yet the Spirit's evidence is still in sight.
These souls, indeed, thirst after holiness,   Phil. iii. 10, 11.
With rich increases of all sorts of grace
But if they want the Spirit's influence,
And all within looks very dark to sense,
Yet still in faith they're in a steady frame,   Heb. iv. 3.
Because the Spirit's witness is the same:
These, like the nimble hind, skip o'er a slough,   Psal. xviii. 33.
That feeble saints are apt to plunge into;

Trip o'er the mountains, take their walks above,
On the high places of eternal love;
While weakling-saints still in the valley stay,   Hab. iii. 19.
And scarce can creep o'er mole-hills in their way;
Yet safe in state as one the other is,   Rom. xiv. 4.
Although their comfort differs in degrees;
And both are equally the Spirit's care,   Zech. xii. 8.
Each for their proper place he doth prepare.
And as he gives degrees of inward strength,
Degrees of trials draws it out at length;
Each grace shall have its proper exercise,
Which hard tho' 'tis to flesh, the saints should prize,   James i. 2.
Because by these the Spirit makes us bright,   Isa. i. 25.
And fits us for the inheritance in light;   Col. i. 12.
Yea, for that very place for us design'd,
Made ours by lot, where we at last shall stand.   Dan. xii. 13.
But, oh! what various trials saints go through,   Ps. xxxiv. 19.
While in this weary wilderness below.
       How oft doth Satan set his gins and snares,   Jer. ii. 6.
T'entrap, and fill them with perplexing cares?
Some e'er aware are caught in Satan's gin,
And plunged deep, perhaps, in heinous sin;   2 Tim. ii. 26.
By which the lion would the lambs devour,
But that they're sav'd by sov'reign grace and power   1 Pet. v. 8.
He draws them out, sets them on ground that's good,
And makes fresh application of Christ's blood;
Leads to that fountain open set for sin,
Helps them to wash, and then their robes are clean.   Zech. xiii. 1.
Again, what snares he sets, when as thief,   Rev. vii. 14.
He robes our joy, and feeds our unbelief?   Eph. vi. 11.
What endless mazes, labyrinths of woe,
Some of the saints, on this account, go through?
Others are frighted with the lion's yell,
Hear little but the cursed noise of hell;
While blasphemies, the devil's fiery darts,   Eph. vi. 16.
Are thrown with hellish rage into their hearts;
Which, powder-like, combustible with sin,
Are apt to catch the sparks which he strikes in;
Which fills their souls with such amazing fear,
They're apt to sink e'en into deep despair;   1 Sam. xxvii. 1.
And think, when wounded, and half slain with dread,

The killing darts still from themselves proceed.
Indeed, some saints that long have been in fight,
Have learn'd more skill, and judge of things aright;
These see their enemy when in the field,   2 Cor. ii. 11.
Have learn'd the art of war, and use their shield;   Ps. xviii. 34.
So that when Satan strikes at any part,
They hold up Christ, and so they quench his dart.   Eph. vi. 16.
Though archers shoot, their hands are all along,   Gen. xlix. 23.
By th' hands of Jacob's mighty God made strong;   Verse 24.
But while the engagement lasts, e'en these do find,
It's work enough, when all is done, to stand.   Eph. vi. 13.
But when the Spirit gives them victory,
They give a shout, the Devil's forc'd to fly.   James iv. 7.
By all these ways the lion would devour,
But that the saints are kept by mighty power.   1 Pet. i. 5.
He reads the proclamation made from Heav'n,
All sin, and blasphemy shall be forgiven;   Mat. xii. 31.
Then makes fresh application to the soul,
And thus the Spirit makes the wounded whole
    Again, what conflicts have the saints within,
Caus'd by the law of grace, and that of sin?   Rom. vii. 21. &c.
So that through fear, at times, they're apt to say,
With David (try'd) I perish shall one day.   1 Sam. xxvii. 1.
But God the Spirit's still on grace's side,
He, as a Fountain, makes its streams abide;   John vii. 38.
Still passing o'er corruptions in their way,
Till sin's no more, and grace in glory's sea.   Chap. iv. 14.
    Yea, the saints are often in their spirits hurl'd,
Either by smiles or frowns of this vain world;
It's flatt'ring smiles do often tempt their love,
But then the Spirit takes their souls above;
Gives them to view unseen, eternal things,   2 Cor. iv. 18.
Which sudden death of worldly pleasure brings.
On the other hand, its frowns strike thro' their hearts,
A thousand fears, which pierce like killing darts.
But here again, the Spirit gives victory,
Shews them the world's a vanquish'd enemy;   John xvi. 33.
That Christ has conquer'd for them, in their room,
Which they themselves, by faith, shall overcome.   1 John v. 4.
Again, the Lord himself in providence,
Doth try his own by bitter things to sense;   Gen. xxii. 1, 2.

What various changes are upon the saints,	Job xi. 17.
Within, without, which fill them with complaints;	
Perhaps one heavy trial's scarcely o'er,	
Another comes, more pinching than before;	Chap. i. 16, 17, 18.
But yet the Spirit makes all things work for good,	
In virtue of the Mediator's blood;	Rom. viii. 28.
By these he purifies us from our tin,	
Brightens our grace, purges out our sin:	Isa. i. 25.
And every tried grace, e'er long, shall be	
Found unto honour, and great dignity.	1 Pet. i. 7.
Yea, the Spirit will maintain the work of grace,	Phil. i. 6.
Till every saint is fitted for his place;	
Each member in Christ's body mystical,	
Distinctly's wrought, to make its glory full;	2 Cor. v. 5.
And as each member has its proper place,	1 Cor. xii. 18.
Each variously in beautify'd with grace;	
Which, when they're fitly plac'd, Christ's body full,	Eph. iv. 13.
Will cast a perfect glory on the whole.	
The variety, and harmony of parts,	
Thro, unity, will cast resplendent darts;	
Each diff'ring glory will reflect its light	
Upon the rest, and make them shine more bright.	
Then the Spirit's work most gloriously will shine,	
And well become an agent that's divine.	
His work shall then to open view be brought,	
Which all along in secret he had wrought.	Ps. cxxxix. 15.
The Saints, the Angels, Son, and Father too,	
Shall with the highest satisfaction view	
This curious piece, enrich'd with so much art,	
While heaven'ly transports ravish every heart!	
Thus glorious shall the bride of Christ be made,	
A meet companion for her glorious head;	
All inward glory, clothed with wrought gold,	Psal. xiv. 13.
The heavn'ly bridegroom will his bride behold.	
Break forth, and say, thou'st ravish'd me, my dove,	Cant. iv. 9.
Then take her in the embraces of his love,	
And fix her in her proper glory-sphere,	
Next to himself, to shine in's kingdom here.	Mat. xiii. 43.
Then the Saints shall reign with Christ a thousand years,	Rev. xx. 4.
Each in their shining orb, like marshall'd stars.	Dan. xii. 3.
And when he has judg'd the world, and has resign'd	

The kingdom to the Father, comes the end   1 Cor. xv. 24.
Then God himself in highest glory shall,
Unto eternity, be All in All   Verse 28.
And then we shall adore the Three in One,   Rev. vii. 12.
For all that each of them for us have done.
Now then let's praise the Father and the Son,
Who jointly sent the Holy Spirit down.
And let's adore the Spirit's boundless love,
Who, by his work, fits us to dwell above.
Let's shout salvation unto One in Three!   Verse 10.
From this time forth, and to eternity.

FINIS

H Y M N S

COMPOSED ON

SEVERAL SUBJECTS:

Speaking to yourselves in Psalms and Hymns, and Spiritual Songs,
and making melody in your hearts to the Lord. —Eph. v. 19.

HYMN I.

The Mystery of the Trinity revealed in Christ.

The glories of Jehovah shine	Heb. i. 3.
In his own Son, who is Divine,	Rom. ix. 5.
Well he could tell the Father's name,	John i. 18.
Because his nature is the same.	Chap. x. 30.

The Father, Son, and Spirit be	
One God most High, yet One in Three;	1 John v. 7.
The Godhead's glory jointly share,	John v. 23.
Because that they co-equal are.	Phil. ii. 6.

This is a mystery too bright,	
To be beheld by nature's light;	
From men of reason 'tis conceal'd,	1 Cor. ii. 14.
Though in the gospel it's reveal'd.	

They set their reason up to pry,	Rom. i. 22.
Into this sacred mystery;	
But it, alas! is blinded quite	
By looking on this dazzling light.	

It's not an organ fit to see,	1 Cor. i. 21.
The glory of this mystery;	
Jehovah this to babes reveals,	Mat. xi. 25.
And from the prudent it conceals.	

The eye that sees 'tis gospel-faith,	Heb. xi. 1.
Discerning what the Scripture saith;	
O blessed 'tis to be a babe,	Mat. xviii. 3.
Taught by the Spirit to cry Abb.	Rom. viii. 15.

O guide us, least we go astray,	Jer. iii. 4.
And lead us still in Christ the way;	Ps. cxxxix. 24.
Then shall we to thy bosom run,	Psa. xliii. 4.
And see thee in thine only Son,	John xiv. 9.

Where thou reveal'st thy glorious face,   2 Cor. iv. 6.
And all thy wond'rous acts of grace;   Eph. i. 3, 4, 5.
Here we shall live, and thee adore,   John xvii. 3.
When sin and time shall be no more.

HYMN II.

The Mystery of Grace in Christ's Person.

Of all God's wonders Christ's supreme,   Isa. ix. 6.
Immanuel is his glorious name;   Mat. i. 23.
Two natures in his person be,   Rom. ix. 5.
Divine, humane; O mystery!   1 Tim. iii. 20.

Of all contrivements this was high,
The project of eternity;   1 Cor. ii. 7.
When God ordain'd his only Son,   1 Pet. i. 20.
To be with human-nature, One!

That he might a fit medium be,   1 Tim. ii. 5.
In whom the great, eternal Three,
The Godhead's glory might display,   2 Cor. iv. 6.
With a most bright, resplendent ray.

Here righteousness and peace do meet;   Psl. lxxxv. 10.
Mercy and truth each other greet;
All attributes love's glory wear,   1 John iv. 8.
As they, in Christ, for us appear.

Bright beams of love, thro' Christ, do shine
On Saints, as in a direct line;   Eph. i. 6.
Here we are warm'd, and kept alive.
His quick'ning rays do us revive.   Mal. iv. 2.

The glorious gospel is the glass,
Where we behold with open face,   2 Cor. iii. 18.
The glory of the Diety,
That shines in Christ transparently.   2 Cor. iv. 6.

And while the prospects we enjoy,
Our souls do shine exceedingly;
We, by the Spirit, changed are,
Into an image similar.   2 Cor. iii. 18.

HYMN III.

The Glory of the Gospel above the Law.

The ministry of Moses' law
Was glorious indeed;   2 Cor. iii. 7.
But what was all old Israel saw,
To that which does exceed   Verse 9.

If legal glory was so bright,   Verse 10.
That yet was to decay;
How great must be the gospel-light,   Verse 11.
That is to last alway?

That dispensation was but night,   Cant. ii. 17.
Moon-light, indeed, they had;   Ps. cxix 105.
But Christ, the sun of glory bright,   Ps. lxxxiv. 11.
Our gospel-day hath made.

No wonder that the moon and stars   Heb. viii. 13.
Are vanish'd out of sight;
Since Christ, the glory-sun appears   Chap. ix. 11.
With his out-shining light.

The law had figures, types and shades,   Verse 9.
Of glorious things to come;   Chap. x. 1.
Which in the gospel are display'd   Col. ii. 17.
And follow in their room.

The faith of saints who then did live
Long'd for the break of day,   Psal. xiv. 7.
When Christ, the gospel-sun, should drive
Their mystic shades away.   Cant. iv. 6.

This is the day our Lord hath made,   Ps. cxviii. 24.
In which our souls rejoice;

And in his light we are made glad,	Psal. iv. 6, 7.
To hear the joyful voice.	

How blest are they that know the same!	Ps. lxxxix. 15.
They shall walk all the day,	
Exalted in his glorious name,	Verse 16
Enlightened with his ray.	Ps. xviii. 28.

High praises to our glorious Lord,	Isa. xxxiii. 21.
The sun of righteousness;	Mal. iv. 2.
Whose healing wings to us afford	
Such life and happiness.	Psal. xxx. 5.

HYMN IV.

The Love of the Father.

The greatness of the Father's love,	Eph. ii. 4.
To us he did commend,	Rom. v. 8.
When he the Saviour from above,	
Into the world did send.	1 John iv. 9.

His own beloved Son he gave,	John iii. 16.
That in his bosom lay;	Chap. i. 18.
that his heart-love might passage have	Isa. xli. 18.
To flow to us alway.	Psal. cv. 41.

His justice did the Shepherd smite,	Zech. xiii. 7.
As standing in our place;	3 Cor. v. 21.
That on the little ones he might,	
Now turn his hand of grace.	

The Father's love's a boundless sea,	Ep. iii. 17, 18.
Whence all our blessings flow;	Chap. i. 3, 4.
Its depths unfathomable be,	Job. xi. 7.
Beyond what we can know!	

His love's eternal, infinite,	Jer. xxxi. 3.
Unchanging, full and free;	Mal. iii. 6.
In this he rests with great delight,	Zeph. iii. 17.
And joys in such as we.	

With loving-kindness draws us, Lord,	Hos. xi. 4.
To live to thee always;	2 Cor. v. 14, 15.
New strength to us, this will afford,	Cant. i. 4.
To give thy name the praise.	Psal. cxv. 1.

HYMN V.

The Love of Christ.

How did our Lord his love commend,	1 John iii. 16.
In laying down his life;	Heb. ix. 26.
Of sin to make a perfect end,	Eph. v. 25.
For us his bride and wife!	

Christ knew before what he must bear,	John xviii. 4.
To save us from the curse;	Gal. iii. 13.
Yet he in love resolved were	Hos. xiii. 14.
To give himself for us.	Titus ii. 14.

Sorrows from men, and rage from hell	Luke xxiii. 35.
Wrath from his Father too,	Mark xv. 34.
In one great storm upon him fell,	
And made the waters flow.	

Into his soul these waters came,	Mat. xxvi. 38.
When he was made our sin;	2 Cor. v. 21.
But ne'er could quench that ardent flame	
Of love, he had within!	Cant. viii. 6, 7.

Into these waters he did go,	Joh. xviii. 11.
Though there no standing were;	Psal. lxix. 2.
They prest the human nature so,	John xix. 28.
He gave his life up there.	Luk. xxiii. 46.

The swelling floods could never drown	Cant. viii. 7.
Our Lord Redeemer's love;	
His heart was fixt upon his own,	John xiii. 1.
And nothing could it move.	Heb. xiii. 8.

Into what depths did Christ descend,	Eph. iv. 9.
To raise us to his throne?	Rev. iii. 21.

He gives us life, that ne'er shall end,   John x. 28.
By laying down his own!   Verse 15.

In love he dy'd, in love he rose,   Eph. v. 25.
And did to God ascend;   John xx. 17.
In love he ever pleads our cause,   Heb. vii. 25.
As advocate and friend.   1 John ii. 1.

Our Lord, e'er long, will take us home,   John xiv. 3.
To live in his embrace;   1 Thes. iv. 17.
We, in his bosom, shall have room.
He'll tell us all his grace.   John xiii. 7.

We can but lisp love's story now,   1 Cor. xiii. 11.
We see but little here;   Verse 12.
Its heights and depths we cannot know   Eph. iii. 19.
Till we with Jesus are   2 Cor. v. 8.

HYMN VI

The Love of the Spirit.

The Lord the Spirit his love commends,   John xi. 16.
By making his abode   Gal. iv. 6.
In us, as he from Christ descends,   Rom. viii. 17.
To fill the heirs of God.

He is as sovereign in his love,   Rom. xv. 30.
As Son and Father be;
And when on his elect he moves,
He is an agent free.   1 Cor. xii. 11.

His love did bear an ancient date,
Even from eternity;   Psal. xxv. 6.
To us it is immensely great,
And cannot changed be.   Mal. iii. 6.

It's well for us he is Jehove;   2 Cor. iii. 17.
And all his thoughts endure;   Psal. xxxiii. 11.
His office-work flows from his love,   Jer. xxxi. 3.
And therefore is secure.

Sent from the Father and the Son,	John xiv. 26.
Their mind he doth fulfill;	Chap. xvi. 13.
But yet in all he carries on	
His own design and will.	
Of opposition we are full,	Rom. vii. 18.
We quench and grieve him too;	1 Thes. v. 19.
But yet his love comes over all,	Eph. iv. 30.
In one eternal flow.	
We are his habitation still,	Eph. ii. 22.
With us he will endure;	John xiv. 16.
Oh! may his holy presence kill	Rom. viii. 13.
Our sin, and make us pure.	1 John iii. 3.

HYMN VII.

Eternal Life in the Father's Gift.

The life of God's elect's secure,	Col. iii. 3.
Bound up with Christ our head;	1 Sam. xxv. 29.
In that great covenant most sure,	Ps. lxxxix. 28.
The Father with him made.	Verse 3.
To us eternal life he gave,	1 John v. 11.
By promise and by oath;	Heb. vi. 17.
That we might consolation have,	Verse 13.
And be secur'd by both.	
God ne'er repents his gifts of grace,	Rom. xi. 29.
Jehovah cannot lie;	Num. xxiii. 19.
This gives to us, a sinful race,	Mal. iii. 6.
Such vast security!	Hos. xi. 9.
He blest us, in our head above,	Eph. i. 3.
With life that shall endure;	Psal. xxi. 4.
In him we ever stand in love,	Eph. i. 6.
In him our title's sure.	Rom. viii. 17.
No motives God from us did take,	Chap. ix. 11.
His gift of life was free;	

| In that great promise he did make, | Titus i. 2. |
| There no conditions be. | Ezek. xi. 20. |

It is of grace, and therefore sure,	Rom. iv. 16.
Though we unworthy be;	Gen. xxxii. 10.
The thoughts of God's own heart endure	
To all eternity.	Psal. xxxiii. 1.

Oh! shed thy boundless love abroad,	Rom. v. 5.
That we may thee adore;	
Since we are blest by our own God,	Psal. lxvii. 6.
With life, for evermore.	Psal. cxxxiii. 3.

HYMN VIII.

The Beauty of Christ's Spouse, from Cant. vi. 10.

As morning light the saints look forth,	
In purity and holiness;	1 John iii. 3.
In Gospel faith, and order both,	Col. ii. 5.
Jesus, the lord, they do profess.	1 Cor. viii. 6.

Clouds may obstruct the morning light,	Hos. xiii. 3.
But yet the day doth still go on,	Prov. iv. 18.
Unto a clear meridian bright,	
And darkness flees before the sun.	Cant. iv. 6.

Christ is our Sun, and he will rise,	Mal. iv. 2.
To make our glory-day complete;	Isa. lx. 1, 2,
No clouds now fill the Church's skies,	
But his bright beams will dissipate.	Chap. lxii. 4.

Our beauty now is like the moon,	
That shineth with a borrow'd light;	
Increasing, waning, changing soon,	1 Cor. xv. 41.
And full of spots, though she is bright.	

Our fairness, by created grace,	Phil. iii. 12.
Now wrought in us, is incomplete;	1 Thes. iii. 10.
Changes and spots do fill our face,	Job x. 17.
Tho' God's own work hath beauty great.	Psal. xlv. 13.

But we, as Christ the Sun, are clear,	
Completely, like our glorious head;	1 John iv. 17.
As we in him to God appear,	Col. ii. 10.
Our beauty is most perfect made.	Ezek. xvi. 14.

But, O! when shall the Lamb's dear bride,	
That now is cloath'd with Christ the sun:	Rev. xii. 1.
Be openly placed at his side,	Psal. xlv. 9.
And put her royal garments on,	Isa. lii. 1.

When God shall out of Zion shine,	Psal. l. 2.
A perfect beauty she shall be;	
No clouds will then her lustre stain,	Isa. lxii. 1, 2.
Angels will be amaz'd to see.	

The glory that the bride will wear;	Rev. xxi. 9-11.
When in Christ's throne she shall sit down.	Chap. iii. 21.
And with him in the kingdom share,	Chap. xx. 4.
While God shall be her glory-crown!	Isa. xxviii. 5.

HYMN IX.

The Saints' happiness after Death.

Saints at their death do go to rest,	Dan. xii. 13.
In the bosom of their Father's love;	
Their happy spirits fully blest,	Rev. xiv. 13.
To worship with the Church above.	

All toilsome labour then doth cease,	
No sin, nor sorrow, can come there;	1 Pet. i. 4.
They enter into perfect peace,	Isa. lvii. 2.
And see God's face in vision clear.	1 Cor. xiii. 12.

God is to them a sea of bliss,	Isa. lx. 19.
That never can exhausted be;	
In Christ he is the life of his,	John xvii. 3.
In glory, to eternity.	

At God's right hand fullness of joy,	Psal. xvi. 11.
In richest plenty overflows;	

Where saints do feast, and never cloy,	
Because their living pleasure grows.	Rev. vii. 17.
The perfect spirits of the just,	Heb. xii. 23.
At home with Christ, are happy made;	2 Cor. v. 8.
There waiting till their sleeping dust	
Is rais'd in glory from the dead.	1 Cor. xv. 43.
No more to sorrow, sin, or die;	Rev. xxi. 4.
For raised saints with Christ must reign	Chap. xx. 4.
In glory, and in majesty,	
When he from heav'n shall come again.	1 Thes. iv. 16.
And when that dispensation's o'er,	
With Christ our Lord we shall ascend	
To glory, ready long before,	Mat. xxv. 34.
Too great to know a change or end!	Verse 46.

HYMN X.

The Work of the Spirit.

The babes in Christ, how safe they are	Isa. xlii. 3.
Their life and growth's secure,	John xi. 26.
By virtue of the Spirit's care,	
Who doth with us endure.	John xiv. 16.
He takes us by the arms, and so	
He gently leads us on,	Hos. xi. 3.
Till he has taught our souls to go	
By faith, to Christ alone.	John vi. 45.
While we are weak we go by sense,	John xx. 29.
And he doth condescend	
To give us some supports from thence	John xx. 27.
As a most tender friend.	
Till he doth give us strength and skill,	Gal. ii. 20.
By naked faith to go	2 Cor. v. 7.
To th' fullness that in Christ doth dwell,	Col. i. 19.
For grace and glory too.	

This Holy Spirit makes us so,	2 Thes. ii. 13.
He'll form us like our head;	Rom. viii. 29.
It is his office so to do,	
Till we are perfect made.	1 Cor. xv. 49.

He is that power that works in us,	Eph. iii. 20.
That's able to subdue	Phil. iii. 21.
Whatever doth his grace oppose	Psal. cxxxviii. 8.
And still his work pursue;	

Till he in glory finisheth	Phil. i. 6.
The work of sanctity;	
In triumph over sin and death	1 Cor. xv. 57.
By his own energy.	Rom. viii. 11.

HYMN XI.

The same.

The Spirit forms our souls anew;	Eph. ii. 10.
By him we're born again:	John iii. 5.
He nurseth and he feeds us too,	Isa. lxvi. 13.
And with us doth remain.	John xiv. 16.

And though we often him do grieve,	Eph. iv. 30.
His love comes over all;	
And sweetly he doth us relieve,	Psal. li. 12.
When we have got a fall.	Ps. xxxvii. 24.

He ripens us for glory bright,	
And fits us for our place,	Dan. xii. 13.
Among the saints that dwell in light,	Col. i. 12.
And see God, face to face.	1 Cor. xiii. 12.

And when his work is finished,	
How glorious shall we be!	Psal. xlv. 1.
Exactly like our pattern-head,	1 John iii. 2.
In full conformity.	Rom. viii. 29.

HYMN XII.

Sin and Grace.

The saints, at times, do look within,
And are discouraged,   Rom. vii. 24.
By reason of indwelling sin,   Verse 17.
That's through their nature spread.   Verse 18.

For as the great Apostle saith,
So every Saint doth find,
A law, he in his members hath,   Verse 23.
That wars against his mind.

Nay, warring only is not all,
Sin oft-times wins the field;
And by its force so powerful,
The captive soul doth yield.

But yet in Saints there's a new mind,   Rom. viii. 25.
That doth all evil hate;   Verse 15.
In what the old doth pleasure find,
The new abominate.   Psal. xcvii. 10.

The Saints' imperfect state on earth
Doth oft-times make them weep;   Rom. xii. 15.
And soon they'd lose their joy of faith,   Phil. i. 25.
If power did not keep.   1 Pet. i. 5.

Old *Adam's* image we have borne,
It's through our nature spread;   2 Cor. xv. 48.
By virtue of our union
To him our earthly head.

But this shall be demolished;
Christ's image we shall bear;
And as he is our heavenly head,   Verse 49.
His glory we shall wear.   Col. iii. 4.

In Christ's bright image we shall shine,
In perfect purity;   Eph. v. 26.

And none of the old *Adam's* stain
Shall in our nature be.   Verse 27.

When we shall see Christ as he is,
We shall be like him made;   1 John iii. 2.
In soul and body like to his,   Phil. iii. 21.
Who is our glory-head.

The nearness of our union   John xv. 5.
To Christ doth this secure;   Chap. xiv. 19.
And all the bliss, laid up for his,   1 Pet. i. 4.
That ever shall endure.

HYMN XIII.

Faith on Christ as a representing Head.

The Saints that are made strong in love,   1 John iv. 18.
By faith, do live on Christ above;   Gal. ii. 20.
In all that he to them is made,   1 Cor. i. 30.
As their compleat and glorious head.   Eph. v. 23.

They view him on his Father's throne,   Rev. iii. 21.
As conqueror, for them sat down;   Heb. ix. 24.
Who finish'd sin, and made an end   Verse 26.
Of all that did the same attend.   Gal. iii. 13.

This gives us boldness while we're here,   1 John iv. 17.
And will do so when Christ appears;
For as he is, even so are we,
Though in this lower world we be

Encompass'd round with enemies,   Psal. xxv. 19.
Which often do our souls surprise.   Lam. i. 16.
But Christ them all has overcome,   John xvi. 33.
With glorious triumph, in our room.   Col. ii. 15.

Indwelling sin attends us here,   Rom. vii. 17.
But we in Christ, our head, are clear;   Cant. vi. 10.
As he is holy, so are we,   Rom. xi. 16.
Presented in his purity.   Col. i. 22.

And as in him, to God, we now
Are perfect made, and conqu'rors too,   Col. ii. 10.
So surely shall we e'er long have
All that our longing souls can crave.   Psal. cxlv. 19.

E'en personal victory, compleat,   Rom. xvi. 20.
O'er all our foes, both small and great;   Isa. liv. 17.
O'er sin and Satan, death and grave,   1 Cor. xv. 57.
Each one of Christ's shall conquest have.

HYMN XIV

The revealing Work of the Spirit

Christ is a mystery that's high,   1 Tim. iii. 16.
Far out of nature's sight!   Mat. xvi. 17.
But Saints his glory do espy   John i. 14.
In God the Spirit's light.   Eph. i. 17.

Christ's person, and his offices,   Isa. ix. 6.
We in this light behold;   John xvi. 14.
And all the riches of his grace,   Eph. iii. 8.
That never can be told.

The Spirit reveals Christ's sacrifice   Heb. x. 15.
Infinitely compleat;   Chap. ix. 12.
And he presents unto faith's eye,
Christ as our mercy-seat.   Chap. iv. 16.

He shews us how the Father laid
Our sins on Christ our Lord;   Isa. liii. 6.
And therefore him an offering made,   Verse 10.
By justice' dreadful sword.   Zech. xiii. 7.

And in his light we do behold,   Psal. xxxvi. 9.
Our sins are cast away,   Is. xxxviii. 17.
And buried in the depths of blood,
As in a boundless sea.   Mic. vii. 19.

He gives us prospects while we're here,
Of Christ's bright righteousness;   Isa. lxi. 10.

And doth enable us to wear,   Gal. iii. 27.
By faith, this glorious dress.   Ex. xxviii. 2.

Of Christ he also gives us views,
As made our holiness;   1 Cor. i. 30
With int'rest in his fullness too,   John i. 14.
Our needy souls to bless.   Phil. iv. 19.

Let's praise the Father, and the Son,   Psal. cxlvii. 1.
And bless the sacred Dove,   Mat. iii. 16.
For all that he for us hath done,
In application-love.   Rom. xv. 30.

HYMN XV.

Another.

What reason have the saints to prize   Psal. li. 11.
The blessed Spirit of grace;   Zech. xii. 10.
Who strengthens, and anoints our eyes   Rev. iii. 18.
To see our Father's face!   2 Cor. iii. 18.

The mystery of God's unknown,   Col. ii. 2.
To men of worldly skill;   2 Cor. i. 21.
The spirit hath this glory shown,   Mat. xi. 25.
To whom Jehovah will.   Verse 26.

And as God's nature, so his acts
Of counsel, and of love;   1 Cor. ii. 11.
The Spirit only shews those tracks,   Verse 10.
Where special grace did move.   Eph. i. 3.

'Tis he reveals our father's heart,   Rom. v. 5.
And gives our souls to know,   1 Cor. ii. 12.
What God to us freely imparts,   Rom. viii. 32.
Is love's eternal flow.   Jer. xxxi. 3.

O that our souls might praise and love,
The blessed One in Three,   John v. 7.
For each of their respective works   Ps. xxxvii. 39.
That in salvation be!

HYMN XVI.

The Spirit as Comforter and Earnest.

The Lord the Spirit gives us rest,	Heb. iv. 3.
And Gospel-liberty,	2 Cor. iii. 17.
Because we in our Lord are blest,	Eph. i. 3.
And by the Son made free.	John viii. 36.

He casteth out our bondage-frames,	Rom. viii. 15.
And gives us to behold,	
How God did write our several names,	Phil. iv. 3.
In the book of life of old.	Rev. xiii. 8.

Nor sin, nor time, can e'er deface,	Eccles. iii. 14.
The bright records above;	Luke x. 20.
In counsel fix'd, e'er time took place,	Heb. vi. 17.
Wrote by eternal love.	Jer. xxxi. 3.

He, as the Lord our Comforter,	John xiv. 16.
His blessed witness bears;	Rom. viii. 16.
And tells us, that with Christ we are	
Made children, and joint-heirs.	Verse 17.

The Spirit, he the earnest is	
Of what we shall enjoy,	2 Cor. i. 22.
When God shall be to each of his,	1 Pet. i. 4.
Their all immediately.	1 Cor. xv. 28.

He is that stream of life and love,	
Which doth our souls refresh;	Psal. xlvi. 4.
That flows from the river-head above,	Psal. xxxvi. 8.
Through the Channel of Christ's flesh.	Isa. xxxii. 2.

O may this living water flow,	Isa. xliv. 3.
To made us fruitful ground;	Verse 4. 5.
'Twill make our new obedience grow,	Gal. v. 25.
And every grace abound.	2 Cor. viii. 7.

HYMN XVII.

The Acts of Divine Love.

WELL may our souls, amazed say,	
What hath our Father done,	Nu. xxiii. 23.
For such as we, vile dust and clay,	Job iv. 19.
In his beloved Son!	Mat. iii. 17.
He lov'd, he chose, he blest us too,	Eph. i. 3, 4.
According to his heart;	2 Sam. vii. 21.
In Christ he fix'd our union so,	1 Cor. i. 30.
That nothing can us part.	Rom. viii. 35.
Jehovah's love, to Christ and we,	
That is for kind but one,	John xvii. 23.
Ordain'd our full conformity	Rom. viii. 29.
To him, the first-born Son.	Heb. i. 6.
Our grace relations flowing hence,	
On his dependent were;	John xx. 17.
He hath in all pre-eminence,	Col. i. 18.
And is the supreme Heir.	Heb. i. 2.
God lov'd the head and members with	
An infinite delight;	Zeph. iii. 17.
And all that he to Christ did give,	John xvii. 2.
In him were view'd most bright.	Eph. i. 6.
This love ordain'd the heights of bliss,	Chap. i. 3.
Before the world began;	Titus i. 2.
And made them sure to Christ and his,	Ps. lxxxix. 28.
Ev'n every chosen man.	
Not Adam's fall, the least, could mar	Ps. xxxiii. 11.
Love's project, laid so deep;	Eph. i. 9.
God's wrath divine, Christ was to bear,	Zech xiii. 7.
To save his own lost sheep!	Mat. xviii. 11.
And safely bring them home again,	Ez. xxxiv. 12.
Through all those various ways,	I Pet. i. 2.
Infinite wisdom did ordain,	Eph. i. 8.

Electing love to praise;	Verse 6.

And when love's myst'ry is unfold,	Eph. ii. 7.
In all its glory-deeps;	Rom. xi. 33.
In which it was contriv'd of old,	Eph. iii. 9.
The chosen ones to keep,	Jude, verse 1.

Oh! what a scene of wonders bright,	
Will open to our view;	1 Cor. xiii. 12.
We shall be ravish'd with delight,	
and feast on pleasures new!	Ps. xxxvi. 8.

HYMN XVIII.

The Blessedness of dwelling in God's Love.

How blessed are the saints, that dwell	
In God, as he is love!	1 John iv. 8.
They taste those pleasures sweet, which fill	Ps. xvi. 11.
The perfect saints above.	Heb. xii. 22.

Dwelling in love doth perfect ours,	
By its sweet influence;	1 John iv. 17.
The new-born soul, with all its powers,	
Enkindled is from hence	Verse 19.

This fire of love our souls doth melt,	
And forms its image too,	2 Cor. iii. 18.
In us, who have its power felt,	Chap. v. 14.
While God, as love, we know.	

This love casts out tormenting fear,	1 John iv. 18.
And sweetly gives us rest,	Heb. iv. 3.
In its own bosom, while we're here,	
Till we are fully blest.	

With perfect sight of this great love,	1 Cor. xiii. 12.
And perfect likeness too;	
Which can't be till we dwell above,	2 Cor. v. 1.
As saints with Jesus do.	Verse 8.

HYMN XIX.

Glorying in Tribulation.

In tribulation saints rejoice,	2 Cor. vii. 4.
Yea, glory in it too;	Rom. v. 3.
Because it patience sets on work,	
As they by faith do know.	
And patience doth experience work;	Verse 4.
Saints learn in such a frame;	Ps. cxix. 71.
It's good for them to kiss the rod,	
And listen to the same.	Mic. vi. 9.
And fresh experience hope doth work,	
By which we wait on God,	Isa. viii. 17.
Who sanctifies, and saves his own,	Heb. xii. 10.
From every scourging rod.	Ps. xxxiv. 19.
And hope it maketh not ashamed;	Rom. v. 5.
In God we make our boast,	Ps. xxxiv. 2.
Because his love is shed abroad,	
Ev'n by the Holy Ghost.	
Which God hath sent into our hearts,	Gal. iv. 6.
To manifest his grace;	1 Cor. ii. 12.
In every scene of Providence,	Isa. iii. 10.
That opens in its place.	Eccles. iii. 1.
The Spirit, as a flood of love,	Isa. xliv. 3.
The thirsty soul doth fill;	
Which in submission unto God,	1 Sam. iii. 18.
Doth make it fruitful still.	Col. i. 10.
This soul doth see each Providence	Rom. viii. 28.
Is but one constant flow	Ps. xxiii. 6.
Of boundless love, in wisdom great,	Eph. i. 8.
Its heights and depths to show.	Chap. iii. 18.
If tribulation looketh in,	
Love's at the bottom still;	Heb. xii. 6.

That manageth, and governs all,
God's providential will.   Rom. viii. 28.

This makes us glory in distress,   2 Cor. xii. 9, 10.
And worketh every grace,
Which shall, when Jesus comes, be found   James, i. 3.
To glory, honour, praise.   1 Pet. i. 7.

HYMN XX.

The Saints' Resurrection secured
in Union to a risen Jesus.

If we believe that Jesus died,   1 Thes. iv. 14.
To satisfy for sin,   Heb. ix. 26.
To save us from deserved curse,   Gal. iii. 13.
And take away death's sting;   1 Cor. xv. 55.

No reason, then, have saints to fear,   Heb. ii. 15.
What stingless death can do
It's but a quiet sleep in him   1 Thes. iv. 14.
We are united to.

Our mould'ring dust, while in the grave,
In union doth remain   Isa. xxvi. 19.
To Christ, who as our living head,   John xiv. 19.
Will raise it up again.   John vi. 39.

If we believe that Jesus rose,   1 Thes. iv. 14.
Discharg'd from every sin,   Isa. l. 8.
And broke the bands of death and grave,
That once did hold him in.   Acts ii. 24.

We have no need to mourn, as those   1 Thes. iv. 13.
Who sorrow without hope;
Since Christ the glorious first-fruits was,   1 Cor. xv. 20.
Of all the after-crop.   Verse 23.

If death or grave could him have held,
We all had perished;   1 Cor. xv. 18.

| But Christ judicially was rais'd, | Isa. liii. 8. |
| By the Father, from the dead. | Acts iv. 10. |

Our rising is secur'd in his;	2 Cor. iv. 14.
And when he comes again,	Heb. ix. 28.
In glory bright, we shall be brought	1 Thes. iii. 13.
With him, to sit and reign.	Rev. xx. 4.

HYMN XXI.

The Cause of Fainting under the Rod.

The saints, at times, are apt to faint,	Jer. viii. 18.
When try'd by Providence;	Psal. lxvi. 10.
How bitter is our sad complaint,	Job xxiii. 2.
When we do judge by sense!	

Alas! our nature is so weak,	Psal. ciii. 14.
And so defil'd by sin,	Job xv. 16.
We oft-times think our hearts will break,	
When trouble looketh in.	Job xvi. 14.

But all this comes for want of faith,	Psal. xxvii. 13.
In constant exercise,	Deut. xxxiii. 25.
On what Jehovah's promise saith,	
Of new and full supplies.	Phil. iv. 19.

Did we believe that we should see,	
New cov'nant-goodness still,	Psal. xxiii. 6.
To follow us where e'er we be,	
Our souls with joy 'twould fill.	Psal. cvii. 9.

Did we believe our eyes should see,	
New wonders of free grace,	Psal. cvii. 24.
Afresh display'd to such as we,	Verse 28.
In every trying case.	2 Cor. xii. 9.

With what an holy cheerfulness,	2 Cor. vi. 10.
And triumph, should we go	Rom. viii. 37.
Through every sorrow and distress,	Rom. viii. 35.
We meet with here below.	2 Cor. xii. 10.

Lord, bear our fainting spirits up,   Isa. xl. 29.
With cordials from above;   John vi. 63.
And let us freely drink the cup   Mat. xxvi. 42.
That's sweetened with thy love!   Rev. iii. 19.

'Tis but a while, and we shall see   1 Cor. xiii. 12.
How great thy goodness is,   Psal. xxxi. 19.
When we shall be at home with thee,   2 Cor. v. 8.
Complete in joy and bliss.   Heb. xii. 23.

HYMN XXII.

God the Saint's Portion.

Oh! what a privilege it is,
In Jesus to be blest;   Eph. i. 3.
Saints that can see it for themselves   Lam. iii. 24.
Do enter into rest.   Heb. iv. 3.

With favour we are satisfy'd,   Deut. xxxiii. 23.
And full with blessing so,
Our souls can crave no more than what   1 Cor. ii. 12.
Our Father did bestow.   Sam. xxiii. 5.

In the eternal covenant,
The charter of our bliss,
Where we, with Christ, are made joint heirs,
Of all Jehovah is!   Rom. viii. 17.

Jehovah freely gave himself,   Jer. xxx. 22.
As our eternal all;
A portion which we could not spend,   Ps. lxxiii. 26.
Though bankrupts in the fall!   Hos. xiii. 9.

Here's all our happiness compris'd,   Ps. xxxiii. 12.
As in a total sum;
And hence, as from the fountain-head,   Deut. xxxiii. 29.
The streams of blessing come.

Christ is the treasury of all   Col. i. 19.
the Father's boundless grace;

| And from his fulness saints receive, | John i. 16. |
| According to their place. | 1 Cor. xii. 12. |

Jehovah so did give himself,	
To ev'ry of his heirs,	Rom. viii. 7.
That each have all in him, while each	Ps. cxix. 57.
His lot of glory share.	Dan. xii. 13.

Lord, since thou'rt ours for evermore,	Ps. xlviii. 14.
Fill us with praises high	Ps. cxlix. 6.
And let us feast on God in Christ,	Ps. xxxvi. 8.
E'en to eternity!	Ps. xvi. 11.

HYMN XXIII.

The Saints' Holiness in the Root Christ

Christ is the root of holiness;	John xv. 1.
In him the branches be	Verse 2.
Completely so, for both do make	
But one most holy tree.	Rom. xi. 16.

Each branch that in relation stands	
To Christ, the holy root,	
In his perfections are beheld,	Col. i. 22.
For in him is our fruit.	Hos. xiv. 8.

What joy of faith doth hence arise,	Phil. i. 25.
That we are now in him;	1 John iv. 17.
Completely holy to our God,	
Without a spot of sin!	Cant. iv. 7.

Great cause have we to joy in Christ,	Phil. iii. 3.
In whom we're now beheld;	Col. ii. 10.
And from whom we, e'er long, shall be,	
With his perfections fill'd.	1 John iii. 2.

We, in ourselves, are filthy still;	Isa. lxiv. 6.
We long to be set free,	Rom. vii. 24.
From sin, yea from indwelling sin,	
And like our Lord to be.	Phil. iii. 10, 11.

Our holy Jesus is to us
Our root of influence;   John xv. 5.
The highest pitch of sanctity
We shall derive from hence.   1 Cor. xv. 49.

Our holiness is here secur'd,   John xiv. 19.
In union faith may rest;   Heb. iv. 3.
'Tis but awhile, and with the same
We shall be fully bless'd.   Col. iii. 4.

HYMN XXIV.

Christ's Kingdom of Rewards.

When Christ the second time appears   Heb. i. 28.
In glory, with his saints to reign,   Rev. xi. 17.
How great will he his triumph, where
He once was crucified and slain!   Isa. xxiv. 23.

Christ veil'd his glory here on earth,   Phil ii. 6, 7.
And freely gave himself for us,   Titus ii. 14.
To die a cursed, shameful death,   Phil. ii. 8.
To save his own from wrath and curse.   Gal. iii. 13.

But without sin he'll come again,   Heb. ix. 28.
His, and his Father's glory wear;   Luke ix. 26.
And bring with him a royal train,   Mat. xxv. 31.
When he erects his kingdom here.   2 Tim. iv. 1.

The Father will exalt his throne,   Psa. lxxix. 4.
And set him on a mighty seat;   Verse 27.
With large rewards his sufferings crown,   Psa. ii. 8.
And make his glory-kingdom great.   Isa. ix. 7.

Christ then will give rewards of grace   Chap. xl. 10.
To all the saints, both small and great;   Rev. xi. 18.
And each according to their place,   1 Cor. iii. 8.
Shall have their proper glory-seat.   Mat. xix. 28.

There's nothing that they here did do
For him, or his, but shall be found   1 Cor. xv. 58.

To honour, praise, and glory, too,	1 Pet. i. 7.
When overcomers shall be crown'd.	Rev. ii. 10.

The saints themselves, and service owe,	1 Cor. vi. 20.
To him that bought them with his blood;	1 Pet. i. 19.
And by his Spirit assists them too,	Rom. viii. 26.
In all their actions that are good.	2 Cor. iii. 5.

They are unprofitable still,	
In all that they as servants do;	Luke xvii. 10.
Obedience to their Master's will	
Is but the duty which they owe.	Rom. xii. 1.

How gracious then is Christ our Lord,	
To such poor worthless worms as we;	Job xxv. 6.
Our meanest service he'll reward,	1 Cor. xv. 58.
Though it a cup of water be.	Mat. x. 42.

Dear Jesus, let thy love constrain	2 Cor. v. 14.
Our souls, to serve and follow thee;	Rev. xiv. 4.
And, O! make haste and come again,	Cant. viii. 14.
That we with thee may ever be.	1 Thes. iv. 17.

HYMN XXV.

Christ Crucified, Risen, and Ascended.

We joy to hear our Saviour's voice,	John iii. 29.
From his triumphant throne;	1 Pet. iii. 22.
He conquer'd all our enemies,	
And then on high sat down.	Heb. i. 3.

And thence to us, behold, he says,	
I'm he that once was dead;	Rev. i. 18.
I in a tomb interred lay,	Mat. xxvii. 60.
When I for you had bled.	1 Pet. i. 18, 19.

But having vanquish'd death and sin,	Heb. ix. 26.
Satan, with all his powers;	Col. ii. 15.
My father sent his angel in	Mat. xxviii. 2.
To op'n the prison doors.	Isa. liii. 8.

Thus did strict justice set me free,	Acts ii. 24.
In triumph I arose;	Rom. i. 4.
I did ascend in majesty,	Psa. lxviii. 17, 18.
And led my captive foes.	Eph. iv. 8.
My father did advance me high,	Chap. i. 20, 21.
Gave me the sealed book;	Rev. v. 7.
Where there no creature could come nigh,	
To cast thereon a look.	Verse 3.
And now I live at God's right hand,	Rev. i. 18.
In bliss for evermore;	Psa. xi. 11.
Death and the grave I now command,	Rev. i. 18.
Rule all things by my power.	Mat. xxviii. 18.
My glorious triumph and my reign,	Phil. ii. 9, 10, 11.
Was sounded when I died;	
And I e'er long will come again,	Rev. xxii. 20.
To crown my dearest bride.	Chap. ii. 10.
Our bridegroom-king, is this thy voice,	Mat. xxv. 6.
To such poor worms as we?	Isa. xli. 14.
Our hearts are cheer'd, our souls rejoice,	Cant. i. 4.
We long thy face to see.	Rev. xxii. 20.

HYMN XXVI.

God the Saints' Refuge.

God, in the Mediator, is	1 Tim. ii. 5.
An habitation sure;	Psa. lxxi. 3.
A strong defence to each of his,	Psa. lix. 9.
A rock that will endure.	Psa. xciv. 22.
Our refuge, and our hiding-place,	Deut. xxxiii. 27.
When trouble draweth nigh;	
Then to the riches of his grace	Psa. lix. 16.
The saints for succor fly.	Heb. iv. 16.
Psa. lxxxvi. 7.	
When stormy tempests beat around,	Isa. xxv. 4.

No evil can betide;   Psa. xci. 10.
That soul, that in this rock is found,   Verse 1.
In safety shall abide.   Prov. xviii. 10.

For while our God is our defence,   Psa. lix. 17.
Our bread of life is sure;
Our living waters flow from hence,   Isa. xxxiii. 16.
And therefore will endure.

O! may our souls for ever praise,   Psa. xliv. 8.
The riches of that grace,   Eph. ii. 7.
That unto us itself displays,
In Christ our hiding-place.   Isa. xxxii. 2.

HYMN XXVII.

Adam's Headship.

THE first man was, by God ordain'd,
An head to all his seed;   1 Cor. xv. 45.
And while his Eden bliss remain'd,
He perfect was indeed.   Gen. i. 31.

His happiness was very great,   Ver. 28, 29, 30.
When in the garden plac'd;
In nature-bliss he was complete,   Chap. ii. 8.
With its perfections grac'd.

Thus man, at first, was upright made,
Free from the bent of sin;   Eccl. vii. 28.
And while the crown was on his head,   Psa. viii. 5.
His God commun'd with him.

His Maker then a law did give,
Which bound him to obey;
The voice of which was, do, and live,   Gen. ii. 16.
Transgress, and thou shalt die.

A perfect stock of nature-bliss,
He then for us possess'd;   1 Cor. xv. 4.

With strength and will to stand for his.
And so have made them bless'd.

But, oh! how soon did Adam break;   Psa. xlix. 12.
His trade was quickly o'er;
Pure nature-strength did prove too weak
A match for hellish power.   Gen. iii. 6.

Poor Adam fell from heights of bliss,   Verse 18, 19.
Into the depths of woe;
By hark'ning to the tempter's voice
He did himself undo.   Hos. xiii. 9.

The law that doing, bid him live,
Now curst him bitterly;
And did its dreadful sentence give,
In dying, thou shalt die.   Gen. ii. 17.

Thus we, by sin, in Adam, lost
Our nature-happiness;
And were exposed to the worst   Lam. v. 16.
Of death, with all distress.   Rom. v. 12.

Wo to the man that's left alone,
In this distressed plight;   Eccles. iv. 10.
For whom Christ's blood did not atone,   Heb. x. 27.
For he must bear sin's weight.

Sin press'd the fallen angels down,   2 Pet. ii. 4.
To depths of misery;   Jude, ver. 6.
And canst thou stand, O sinful man,   Psal. i. 5.
When God shall deal with thee?   Ezek. xxii. 14.

O! happy souls, for whom Christ died,   John x. 15.
To be their hiding-place;   Isa. xxxii. 2.
These shelter in his wounded side,   Heb. vi. 18.
And saved are by grace.   Eph. ii. 8.

HYMN XXVIII.

Christ's Taking our Nature.

The son of God, behold!	Isa. lxv. 1.
He let the angels go;	
When of our nature he took hold,	Heb. ii. 16.
He lov'd a remnant so.	John xv. 9.
The seed of Abr'ham was	
So fix'd upon his heart,	Heb. ii. 14.
That 'cause the children had frail flesh,	
He took thereof a part.	
When in the Virgin's womb,	Luke i. 31.
The cov'nant-nature he,	
Did for his special end assume,	Heb. ii. 15.
To set the children free.	
Christ, for the chosen seed,	1 Pet. ii. 9.
Did human frailties bear;	Heb. iv. 15.
That so our natures might be freed,	1 Cor. xv. 49.
And fit for glory's sphere.	Mat. xiii. 43.
Christ, in our nature, hath	Rom. viii. 3.
Obey'd, and satisfy'd;	Phil. ii. 8.
Slain him who had the pow'r death,	
When on the cross he dy'd.	Heb. ii. 14.
And that his people might	Mat. i. 21.
From death be ransomed,	Hos. xiii. 14.
The Prince of Life gave up his right,	Acts iii. 15.
And went among the dead.	John x. 18.
Yea, to the darksome tomb,	Mat. xxvii. 60.
Christ's holy flesh he gave;	Acts ii. 27.
That he our Saviour might become,	1 Cor. xv. 57.
From the power of the grave.	Hos. xiii. 14.
But having finished	John xix. 5.
His deep humility;	Mark xv. 46.

| Then, lo! our representing Head, | Eph. v. 53. |
| Rose, and ascended high. | Chap. iv. 8. |

In Christ we raised were;	
In Christ we did ascend;	Chap. ii. 6.
In Christ we sit together there,	
While angels do attend.	Heb. i. 14.

And thus our nature is,
In Christ, advanced high;
Which doth secure the heights of bliss
Our persons shall enjoy.

HYMN XXIX.

Another.

Let saints adore the love of Christ,	2 Cor. viii. 9.
Who did our nature take,	Heb. ii. 14.
And so did join, to his divine,	Rom. ix. 5.
That both one person make.	

It was not Adam's seed, as such	Heb. ii. 16.
The Son of God put on;	John i. 14.
This union high did ne'er bring nigh,	
Those that were left alone.	Eccles. iv. 10.

Although some common benefits	Psal. cxiv. 16.
The non-elect enjoy,	Mat. v. 45.
Since Christ did come, our flesh assume,	1 Tim. iv. 10.
And for his people die.	John x. 15.

There was no need that Christ should take	
The nature of the rest,	Rom. xi. 7.
Whose persons ne'er had right to share,	
With those in heavenlies bless'd.	Eph. i. 3.

God's children, by adopting love,	1 John iii. 1.
As heirs appointed were,	Rom. viii. 17.
With Christ, of life, for the Lamb's wife	Titus i. 2.
His glory was to share.	John xvii. 22.

And since to magnify God's love,	Rom. v. 8.
His wisdom had ordain'd,	Eph. i. 8.
That we should stand in the first man,	1 Cor. xv. 45.
And fall with all mankind.	Rom. v. 12.
Hence a necessity came in,	John xi. 50.
If Christ his Bride enjoy;	
That he come down, her flesh put on,	Luke xix. 10.
And die, to raise her high.	Eph. v. 25.
And Christ so greatly lov'd his own,	John xv. 9.
The seed of Abraham,	Gal. iii. 29.
That with delight he took his flight,	Psal. xl. 8.
And in our nature came.	Heb. x. 5.
Yea, that Christ might not be alone,	John xii. 24.
In heaven, on earth he dy'd,	
Then rose in love, and went above,	Eph. iv. 10.
In th' nature of his bride.	
In which, for her, he doth possess	Heb. vi. 20.
The heights of heav'nly bliss;	
And he'll fulfil his dying will,	John xvii. 24.
And set her where he is.	Chap. xiv. 4.

HYMN XXX.

The Misery of a Natural State.

Oh! what a filthy thing is man,	Job xv. 16.
Unclean his nature is;	Verse 14.
And to the full there's none that can,	
Express his loathsomeness.	Prov. xiii. 5.
He's shapen in iniquity,	Psal. li. 5.
Conceiv'd, and born in sin;	John ix. 34.
His father Adam's misery	
He is involved in.	Rom. v. 14.
Thus from the womb he goes astray,	Psal. lviii. 3.
By nature, speaking lies;	

Each walking in that wicked way,	Isa. liii. 6.
Most pleasing in his eyes.	
The vilest of iniquity	Job xv. 16.
He freely drinketh in;	
And thus increaseth misery,	Rom. ii. 5.
By adding sin to sin.	Deut. xxix. 19, 20.
Yea, man by nature is a slave,	
To Satan at his will;	2 Tim. ii. 26.
Whate'er that enemy would have	
He's ready to fulfil.	Eph. ii. 23.
He's law accurst, condemn'd to die,	Gal. iii. 10.
Guilty of Adam's sin;	Rom. v. 19.
Deserves to die eternally	Chap. vi. 23.
For what himself hath been.	1 Cor. vi. 11.
He neither will nor power hath,	John v. 40.
To get out of this pit;	Chap. vi. 44.
If Jesus save him not from wrath,	1 Thes. i. 10.
He perish must in it.	John viii. 24.

HYMN XXXI.

Encouragement for Sinners to come to Christ,
under the first Work of the Spirit.

You that through fear distressed are,	Sam. xxii. 2.
That feel the guilty of sin;	Ps. xxxviii. 3.
That see the depths of nature's filth,	Kings viii. 38.
And loathe the state you're in.	Ezek. xxxvi. 31.
Poor soul give ear, and Jesus hear,	Isa. lv. 3.
He speaks unto thy case;	Chap. l. 4.
He in no wise will such despise,	Psal. li. 17.
That seek to him for grace.	Heb. iv. 16.
He's promis'd not to cast thee out,	
If thou to him dost come;	John vi. 37.
Whate'er thy sin time past has been,	Mat. xii. 31.

Thoul't find there yet is room.   Luke xiv. 22.

Then come from sin, and enter in   Isa. xxvii. 13.
To Christ, thy hiding place,   Chap. xxxii. 2.
And thou shalt live, and ever give,   John xi. 25.
High praises to free grace.   Zech. iv. 7.

HYMN XXXII.

The Same.

What dost thou want, poor sin-sick soul?   Isa. i. 5.
Dost see thy misery?   Hos. v. 13.
Christ is a saviour, on him roll,   1 Tim i. 15.
And thou shalt never die.   John xi. 26.

Of pardon dost thou see a need?   Psal. li. 1.
Wouldst be from wrath set free?   1 Thes. i. 10.
Then come to Christ, who once did bleed,   1 Pet. iii. 18.
To succour such as thee.   Heb. vii. 25.

Christ's wounds will shelter thee in peace,   Eph. ii. 14.
When storms of wrath arise;   Isa. xxxii. 2.
His blood will give thy conscience ease,   1 John i. 7.
And cure thy maladies.   Isa. liii. 5.

And dost thou want a perfect dress,   Chap. lxvi. 6.
To stand in before God?   Col. i. 22.
Then come to Christ for righteousness,   Isa. xiii. 24.
He'll clothe thee with his robe.   Luke xv. 22.

Dost thou want holiness of heart,   Phil. iii. 10.
Or life? then come to him;   John vii. 37.
His Holy Spirit he'll impart,   Verse 29.
With which he's fill'd to the brim.   Chap. iii. 34.

Dost thou want strength? *that* Christ will give,   Isa. xl. 29.
Then thou shalt nimbly run;   Verse 31.
Meanwhile, to Jesus look, thoul't live,   Chap. xlv. 22.
By seeing of the Son.   John vi. 40.

HYMN XXXIII.

On Divine Mercy, in Allusion to a Building.

Mercy, that glorious attribute,	
God did design to raise,	Isa. xxx. 18.
Into a stately Edifice	Ps. lxxxix. 2.
That is to last always.	
His wisdom drew the perfect plan,	Eph. i. 8.
According to his heart,	2 Sam. vii. 21.
In all that glory he design'd	
The whole, and every part.	
The firm foundation laid in Christ,	2 Tim. ii. 19.
Ev'n from eternity,	2 Cor. v. 19.
Was God's resolving in himself	Eph. i. 9.
Mercy to magnify.	Gen. xix. 19.
And each display ordain'd to raise	Mic. vii. 18.
The glory of this frame,	Eph. i. 6.
Were as the superstructive Rooms	
Erected on the same.	Rom. ix. 18.
But, O what ways did wisdom take,	
Subserving mercy's end;	Rom. xi. 32.
'Twas hence the ruins of the fall,	Hos. xiii. 9.
In counsel, were design'd	Eph. i. 11.
To be that very plat of ground	Rom. xi. 32.
Where mercy should be rais'd,	Exod. xxxiv. 6, 7.
In all its bright magnificence,	
To be for ever prais'd.	
But yet strict justice could not bear	
To lose its rightful ground,	Ch. xxxiv. 7.
Unless a worthy price was paid,	
And satisfaction found.	
Then wisdom found the mighty One,	Ps. lxxxix. 19, 20.
Who did engage to pay,	

Whatever justice could demand,	Isa. l. 6.
At the affixed day.	Ps. xl. 7, 8.

This project pleas'd the glorious Three,	Isa. xlii. 21.
For they are One in will;	1 John v. 7.
Then to each other they engag'd	
To build up mercy still.	Ps. lxxxix. 2.

The time-works of the One in Three	
Do all conspire to raise,	Titus iii. 4, 5, 6.
This princely seat of majesty,	
That mercy may have praise.	Psal. xxx. 12.

And when the top-stone once is laid,	
The Heavens shall shout its praise,	Zech. iv. 7.
And sing the glories of this House	
To never-ending days!	Ps. lxxxix. 1.

HYMN XXXIV.

The Soul calling upon itself to return to its rest.

Return, return, my soul to God,	
For he's thy resting-place;	Ps. cxiv. 7.
In him thou shalt have safe abode,	Prv. xviii. 10.
Whatever be thy case.	Ps. xci. 4, &c.

God, from eternity, hath dealt	
In bounty rich with thee;	Psal. cxvi. 7.
He gave thee then his own great self,	Jer. xxx. 22.
By deed of gift most free.	

What bounteous riches of free grace	Eph. ii. 7.
Has God thy Father shown,	
To thee, when in a sinful case,	Ezek. xvi. 4.
Self-ruin'd, and undone!	Hos. xiii. 9.

He gave his only Son for thee,	John iii. 16.
Thy sacrifice to die;	1 Cor. v. 7.
That thou might'st be from wrath set free,	1 Thes. i. 10.
And sav'd eternally.	Isa. xlv. 17.

Yea, thou may'st take a further view,
What God's free love hath done;
He gave his Holy Spirit too,   Thes. iv. 8.
To make thee like his Son.   Rom. viii. 29.

He gives thee grace and glory too,   Ps. lxxxiv. 11.
What canst thou wish for more?
And till the Kingdom he bestow   Luke xii. 32.
He'll keep thee by his pow'r.   1 Pet. i. 5.

Then, O my soul, dwell thou at home,   Psal. xc. 1.
Thou needs not go abroad;   Isa. xxv. 4.
What, tho' distressing times should come,
Thou still may'st rest in God.   Heb. iv. 3.

HYMN XXXV.

The Incomprehensibleness of Divine Love.

How little can the saints conceive,   Job xxvi. 14.
Of love that's infinite;
In part they know, in part believe,
But yet want fuller sight.   2 Cor. v. 7.

Our eye is weak, our object bright,
Alas! such babes are we;   Heb. v. 13.
That can't yet bear love's dazzling light, 1 Cor. iii. 2.
Nor its full glory see.

Transporting glances now and then,   1 Pet. i. 8.
The eye of faith takes in;   Gal. ii. 20.
But love's too bright for mortal men,
And still remains unseen.   1 Cor. xiii. 9.

The saints, indeed, are vessels made,   Rom. ix. 23.
To hold eternal love;   Eph. iii. 18.
But yet, while here, we scanty are,
Not like the saints above.

They are enlarg'd, they are complete,   Heb. xii. 23.
They see, while we believe;   1 Cor. xiii. 12.
But love is so immensely great,   Eph. ii. 4.

No Finite can conceive!

They in the light of vision see,	
And still in raptures praise;	Rev. i. 5, 6.
But yet, unto eternity,	
There will be new displays.	Eph. ii. 7.

Because the creature finite is,	
And can't at once take in,	
The fulness of Jehovah's bliss,	Job xi. 7.
Where heirs of glory swim.	Isa. xl. 19.

Thy love, O Lord! our Souls adore,	
Its past created skill;	Eph. iii. 19.
We long to be enlarged more,	
And then to drink our fill.	Ps. xxxvi. 8.

HYMN XXXVI.

Salvation in Election, and Covenant Settlements.

SALVATION, O how sweet,	Ps. lxxxix. 15.
How joyful is the sound!	
Free reigning grace, through Jesus Christ,	Rom. v. 21.
O how it doth abound.	Verse 20.

How deeply was it laid,	Rom. xi. 33.
In God's eternal mind!	Eph. i. 9.
This way in which we it possess,	John xiv. 6.
Wisdom did early find.	

An early view God took,	Prov. viii. 23.
Of Jesus' human frame;	Rev. iii. 14.
Then fashion'd the vast creature lump	
According to the same.	Col. i. 16.

Out of this creature-lump	Rom. ix. 21.
The Father pitch'd upon	Eph. i. 4.
A remnant which his grace design'd,	Rom. xi. 5.
To give to Christ the Son.	John x. 29.

Then did the Son accept
Of this presented bride;   Chap. xvii. 6.
And in these glorious settlements
The marriage-knot was ty'd.   Hos. ii. 19.

No creature can conceive,
How rich this bride is made;   1 Cor. iii. 21.
She's jointur'd in the glory of
Her husband, Lord, and Head.   John xvii. 22.

Our Lord will reign e'er long,   Luke i. 33.
Upon King *David's* throne;   Verse 32.
And in this glory we shall share,   Mat. xix. 28.
Because with him we're One.   Eph. v. 31.

HYMN XXXVII.

The Covenant of Grace.

Jehovah made a covenant
Of grace with Christ his Son,   Ps. lxxxix. 3.
In which he made a promise-grant   Titus i. 2.
Of life, e'er time begun.

I'll be thy God, *Jehovah* said,
To the Mediator, when   Gen. xvii. 7.
He was set up as cov'nant-head   Prov. viii. 23.
Of all the chosen men.   Eph. i. 4.

Yea, and in thee a God I'll be,
To all thy children too;   Gen. xvii. 8.
Whate'er I am, on thee and them,
In Cov'nant I bestow.

All the perfections of my bliss
Shall jointly make yours full;   Isa. lx. 19.
My glorious self you shall possess,
When I'm your all in all.   1 Cor. xv. 28.

And to make known my glorious grace,   Rom. ix. 23.
Thy children I'll permit,

To fall into a wretched case,	Ezek. xvi. 5.
And most distressed plight.	
This project greatly will redound,	Eph. i. 12.
To the glory of Three-One,	1 John v. 7.
When thine shall see my grace abound,	Rom. v. 20.
O'er all that they have done.	Ezek. xvi. 6.
My Son, thou shalt my servant be,	Isa. xlix. 3.
To bring them back again,	Verse 6.
Thou shalt bear their iniquity,	Chap. liii. 11.
And I'll reward thy pain.	Verse 12.
To this Christ readily agreed,	Chap. l. 6.
Engaging then to pay,	Hos. xiii. 14.
The debts of all the chosen seed,	1 Pet. ii. 9.
That like sheep went astray.	Isa. liii. 6.
The Father then engag'd to give	
To Christ, his numerous seed;	Chap. liii. 10.
That thro' his death they all should live,	Verse 11.
This pleas'd him well indeed.	Ps. xl. 8.
A fullness of all sorts of grace,	
In cov'nant were bestow'd;	2 Tim. i. 9.
In all things it well-order'd was,	2 Sam. xxiii. 5.
For all the heirs of God.	Rom. viii. 17.
The Spirit, the spring of grace within,	John vii. 38, 39.
Was in this cov'nant giv'n;	
Who then engag'd in offices,	Isa. xliv. 3.
To bring us safe to Heav'n.	1 Pet. i. 2.
Repentance, faith, and holiness,	
Herein were treasured;	Eph. i. 3.
As gifts for all the chosen race,	2 Tim. i. 9.
And not conditions made.	Ezek. xxxvi. 25.

HYMN XXXVIII.

The Saints' Afflictions secured in Covenant.

Our God made covenant	Ps. lxxxix. 3.
With Christ, our chosen Head,	
And large provision for our want,	Psal. cxi. 5.
Was herein safely laid.	
Both grace and glory too,	Ps. lxxxiv. 11.
Herein were freely given:	2 Tim. i. 9.
And firmly settled also	Eph. i. 3.
On all the heirs of Heav'n.	James ii. 5.
Herein our gracious God,	Psal. ciii. 8.
Reserv'd a liberty,	
When to chastise us with his rod,	2 Sam. vii. 14.
And when to let's go free.	Mic. vii. 18.
As each should most conduce,	
To the glory of his grace;	Psal. ciii. 13.
And to the special saving use,	Heb. xii. 10.
Of us the chosen race.	
Our Father said to Christ,	
If thine my precepts break,	Ps. lxxxix. 31.
I'll visit their iniquities;	
Of stripes they shall partake.	Verse 32.
But yet I'll never break	
The cov'nant I have made;	Verse 34.
Nor thee, nor them, will I forsake,	Josh. i. 5.
Nor alter what I've said.	
Not as a Judge severe,	Isa. liv. 9.
But as a Father, I	Heb. xii. 7.
Will make them my chastisements bear,	
For their iniquity.	Psal. cvii. 7.
In the end to do them good,	Deut. viii. 16.
And purge away their sin,	Isa. xxvii. 9.

In the virtue of thy ransom-blood,	Zech. ix. 11.
To make their nature clean.	1 John i. 7.

HYMN XXXIX.

The Saints' Freedom from Wrath.

We, the elect of God, foreknown,	Rom. viii. 29.
E'en from eternity,	
By an eternal choice pick'd out,	Eph. i. 4.
In Jesus are made free,	Gal. v. i.
From wrath, the due desert of sin;	1 Thes. i. 10.
For Christ endur'd the storm,	Mark xv. 34.
That he might be our hiding place,	Isa. xxxii. 2.
To screen us from all harm.	Chap. xxv. 4.
The Son hath made us free indeed,	John viii. 36.
And in the Spirit's light,	Psal. xxxvi. 9.
'Tis witness'd to our conscience, that	Rom. viii. 16.
In us God takes delight:	Zeph. iii. 17.
Delight in us, as we stand in	
Our dying, rising Head;	Mat. iii. 17.
That paid our debts, and triumph'd too,	Col. ii. 15.
In all being finished.	John xix. 30.
This great salvation from God's wrath,	Heb. ii. 3.
Which the Gospel doth display,	John v. 24.
Contrived was, e'er time begun,	Eph. iii. 11.
'Tis not of yesterday.	
God's Chosen never were design'd,	
To anguish, wrath, and pain,	1 Thes. v. 9.
But to obtain salvation,	
Through Christ the Lamb, as slain.	Rev. v. 9.
The Father's love did this bestow;	2 Tim. i. 9.
The Son he wrought it out;	Rom. v. 18.
The Spirit he applies the same,	1 Cor. vi. 11.
And thus it comes about.	

Then let the Saints all glory give   Psal. cxv. 1.
To God the Three in One;   1 John v. 7.
Each person hath an equal hand
In our salvation!   Ps. xxxvii. 39.

HYMN XL.

The Glories of Christ's Righteousness.

Blest Saints, that in Christ's righteousness,   Rom. iv. 6.
Stand in *Jehovah's* sight,   Col. i. 22.
Before his glorious throne complete,   Chap. ii. 1.
Faultless, and shining bright.   Rev. xiv. 50.

Not only faultless we appear,
From all pollution free,   Cant. iv. 7.
But splendid, glorious in the eyes,   Psal. xlv. 13.
Of flaming purity.   Jude, ver. 24.

Had *Adam* stood, and we in him,
In perfect righteousness;
Which was the all the law requir'd,   Gal. iii. 12.
Our glory had been less.   1 Cor. xv. 48.

For why? Though he in *Eden* was
In this so perfect made,   Eccles. vii. 29.
At best 'twas but a creature-robe,
That subject was to fade.   Isa. lxiv. 6.

But, O the glories of Christ's robe,   Ex. xxxviii. 2.
In which his children stand,   Rom. iii. 22.
Wrought by the Man that stood in God,
The Man of his right hand.   Psal. lxxx. 17.

The Man, the Fellow of the Lord,   Zech. xiii. 7.
Jehovah did him call;
The Man that was in God made strong,   Psal. lxxx. 17.
Able to go through all.   Ps. lxxxix. 19.

That mighty work God gave to him,   John xvii. 4.
Of our salvation great;   Heb. ii. 3.

To raise us from the dismal fall,
And render us complete.

Mat. i. 21.
Col. i. 22.

Not only suff'ring of that death,
That else we should have dy'd;
But also bringing in this robe,
In which we're justified.

1 Pet. iii. 18.
Dan. ix. 24.
Acts xiii. 39.

Christ's own obedience wrought this robe,
So beauteous, so divine!
Here God's perfections cast their rays,
And in this robe we shine.

Rom. v. 19.
2 Cor. v. 21.

Rev. xii. 1.

Then let us glory in our Lord,
Who is our shining dress;
And let our faith still deal with God,
Through Christ our righteousness.

Isa. xlv. 25.

Col. ii. 6.
Isa. xlv. 24.

HYMN XLI.

The same.

The glories wrapt up in this word,
The Lord our righteousness;
The Saints below, nor Saints above,
Nor Angels can express.

Jer. xxiii. 6.

Psal. cvi. 2.

Could we by searching find out God,
Then we might quickly know,
The brightest glories of this robe,
Till then we can't do so.

Job xi. 7.

This robe is everlasting call'd;
Its glory doth abide;
Because the righteousness of God,
This covers us his Bride.

Dan. ix. 24.
Prov. viii. 18.
2 Cor. v. 21.
Isa. lxi. 10.

Our Father view'd us in this robe,
As if 'twas really done;
And in this did delight in us,
Before the world began.

2 Cor. v. 19.
Rom. iv. 17.
Zeph. iii. 17.
Jer. xxxi. 3.

Its glory was unchangeable,	Heb. xiii. 8.
E'en from eternity;	
And will the dates of time out-last,	Isa. li. 6.
How happy then are we!	Rom. iv. 6, 7.

In this we're sav'd most gloriously;	Prov. xi. 4.
Lord raise our souls above,	Col. iii. 2.
To sing the ancient wonders of	Ps. lxxvii. 11.
The settlements of love!	Eph. i. 3, 4.

This song of our salvation,	Isa. xii. 2.
To God, through Christ alone;	Rev. vii. 10.
By reigning grace, thro' righteousness,	Rom. v. 21.
We'll sing when time is done.	Ps. lxxxix. 1.

HYMN XLII.

The Saints' Duty and Privilege, to pray for Pardon of Sin,
when under fatherly Chastisements.

God, as a Father dear,	
His children doth correct,	Heb. xii. 7.
Because they're full of failings here	Jer. v. 6.
That they may them inspect.	Mic. vi. 9.

'Tis not avenging wrath,	Psal. xxi. 9.
Whence our chastisements come;	Ps. lxxxix. 32.
For that on Christ was poured forth,	Mark xv. 34.
When he stood in our room.	1 Pet. iii. 18.

But love our Father moves,	
His anger to display,	Rev. iii. 19.
That we may see he disapproves	Hab. i. 13.
Of every sinful way.	Jer. xliv. 4.

In such a case as this	
Let Saints to God draw nigh,	James iv. 8.
For he a God of pardon is,	Neh. ix. 17.
And loves to hear their cry.	Psa. xxxiv. 15.

Our Lord taught his to pray	Luke xi. 2.

To God, for pard'ning grace,	Verse 4.
To be extended day by day,	
In every sinful case.	
Our privilege is great,	Deut. iv. 7.
In that we have to do	Heb. iv. 13.
With God upon a mercy-seat,	Exo. xxv. 22.
That loves his grace to shew.	Isa. xxx. 18.
His grace is infinite;	
His bowels for us move;	Jer. xxxi. 20.
In pardon God takes great delight,	Mic. vii. 18.
Where he has fix'd his love!	Eph. ii. 3.
May this our souls engage,	Psal. lxv. 2.
T' approach our Father's throne,	Heb. iv. 16.
Since duty and our privilege,	
Are closely join'd in one.	Isa. xl. 31.

HYMN XLIII.

The Saints Vessels of Mercy, and Heirs of Glory.

Vessels of mercy are the Saints,	Rom. ix. 23.
And they shall ever be	
Fill'd with God's love, freed from complaints,	John xvii. 26.
When they Christ's glory see.	Verse 24.
Vessels of mercy shall, e'er long,	
In glory's ocean swim;	Ezek. xlvii. 5.
And they shall sing the Lamb's new song,	Rev. xv. 3.
With joy fill'd to the brim.	Isa. xxxv. 10.
The heirs of glory shall possess	James ii. 5.
Their heritage, so vast,	1 Pet. i. 4.
Prepar'd for them e'er time began,	Mat. xxv. 34.
When they in Christ were blest.	Eph. i. 3.
Their bodies shall be rais'd again,	1 Cor. iv. 14.
And have re-union	
With their immortal spirits, then	

They'll shine like Christ the Sun!   Phil. iii. 21.

Ready assistants they shall be
Unto the swift-wing'd soul,   1 Cor. xv. 44.
Through the ages of eternity,   Eph. iii. 21.
Where pleasures ever roll.   Psal. xvi. 11.

The saints shall all awake and sing,   Isa. xxvi. 19.
For Christ will give the word;   John v. 28.
Then from their dusty beds they'll spring,   Verse 29.
And mount to meet their Lord.   1 Thes. iv. 17.

When Christ in glory comes again,   Mat. xvi. 27.
He all the Saints will bring,   Zech. xiv. 5.
And set them down upon his throne,   Rev. iii. 21.
To reign with him their King.   Mat. xix. 28.

Thus *Zion* will arise and shine,   Isa. lx. 1.
And then the world shall see   John xvii. 23.
We are the fav'rites of the King,   Isa. lx. 14.
In's royal palace free!   Psal. xlv. 15.

But, oh! what notes of lofty praise,
Redeemed ones will sing;   Rev. v. 9, 10.
Glory to God, and to the Lamb,   Verse 13.
Through all the Court shall ring!

Elected Angels, round the throne,   Rev. vii. 11.
Will join the heav'nly mirth;   Verse 12.
And to our God, salvation   Verse 10.
Will echo through the earth!   Chap. v. 13.

Angels are they that wait upon   Heb. i. 14.
Our Lord, the King of Kings;   Rev. xix. 16.
We, as the bride of Christ, the Son,   Chap. xxi. 9.
Hence higher glory springs.   Verse 11.

The glory we shall have with Christ,
Throughout the kingdom-day,   Rom. viii. 17.
All rise to glory that's the high'st,   Luke xxii. 29.
In the great Eternity.   1 Cor. xv. 28.

HYMN XLIV.

Christ our Hiding Place.

Jehovah's grace an hiding place,
In Christ prepared hath,   Isa. xxxii. 2.
For all his own, whom he hath shown,
Their due desert of wrath.   Rom. iii. 19.

Poor soul, give ear, what dost thou fear?
Dost see a storm of wrath,   Gal. iii. 10
In black clouds spread, hang o'er thy head,
That threatens thee with death?   Eze. xviii. 20.

In such a case, Christ is the place
Of refuge from the storm;   Isa. xxv. 4.
If there thou flee, thou'lt surely be
Safe-guarded from all harm.   Ch. xxxiii. 16.

Christ once has borne the dreadful storm,
Of God's avenging wrath;   Mark xv. 34.
That such as thee might shelter'd be,
In him from endless death.   John v. 24.

Then haste away and make no stay,
To th' refuge city flee,   Nu. xxxv. 15.
Thy way is clear, thou need'st not fear,
For 'tis the promise free.   John vi. 37.

Oh then, poor heart! flee as thou art,
Though over-spread with sin;   Rom. iii. 12.
In Christ there's room, for all that come,   Luke xiv. 22.
Whatever they have been.   1 Tim. i. 13, 16.

The way is plain to Christ thy hope,
Do not dispute thy right;   Chap. i. 15.
The oath and word, of God the Lord,
Secure thee in thy flight.   Heb. vi. 18.

HYMN XLV.

Man's Destruction of himself,
and his Salvation of Christ.

In the first man all men began	1 Cor. xv. 47.
To sin against the Lord;	Rom. v. 12.
Breaking his laws, and for this cause	Gen. iii. 6.
Deserv'd the threat'ning word.	Deut. xxviii. 16, &c.

All kinds of death, in sentence, hath	
Pass'd on all men in one;	Rom. v. 12.
The first man left the rest in debt,	Mat. vi. 12.
As bankrupts, quite undone.	Luke vii. 42.

In this sad case, there's none, alas!	
By any means, that can	Psal. xlix. 7.
A ransom give, that they may live,	
So poor is fallen man.	Rev. iii. 17.

He can't make peace, this work must cease,	
Redemption is so great;	
If all men join'd in one combin'd,	
They could not it compleat.	Psal. xlix. 8.

For to begin, all men did sin,	
The law will nothing 'bate;	James ii. 10.
But will have all, though since the fall,	Verse 11.
Man's in an helpless state:	

It bids him do, and suffer too,	
But all his strength is gone;	Rom. v. 6.
The law is weak, since man it brake,	Chap. viii. 3.
And life can give to none.	Gal. ii. 16.

And thus God's *Israel,* when he fell,	
Destroy'd himself by sin;	Hos. xiii. 9.
But help was laid on Christ his Head,	Ps. lxxxix. 19.
And thence it doth come in.	1 Tim. i. 15.

For that free grace might here take place,	
And reign through righteousness,	Rom. v. 21.

God sent his Son, his holy One,	Gal. iv. 4.
To take on him our flesh.	Heb. ii. 16.

In which he dy'd, and satisfy'd	1 Cor. xv. 3.
God's law, and justice both;	Isa. xlii. 21.
Rose from the dead, and now doth plead,	Rom. viii. 34.
And thus saves His from wrath.	Thes. i. 10

HYMN XLVI.

Christ the Fountain of Grace.

Jehovah's grace all meets in Christ,	Col. i. 19.
As waters in their sea:	Gen. i. 10.
And hence the needy have supplies,	
Exceeding full and free.	Phil. iv. 19.

Rivers of life, of joy and peace,	
Jehovah open'd wide,	Isa. xli. 18.
When to make way for rich free grace,	
His justice pierc'd Christ's side.	Zech. xiii. 7.

Christ risen, and ascended high,	Ps. lxviii. 18.
Set on his Father's throne,	Rev. iii. 21.
A fountain is of rich supply,	Eph. iv. 10.
To all that are his Own.	John i. 16.

Come thirsty soul, come without price,	Chap. vii. 37.
Drink, for this Water's free;	Isa. lv. 1.
All stores of grace are laid in Christ,	Eph. iii. 8.
For such that needy be.	Isa. xli. 17.

If thou art weak, and canst not go,	Chap. xxxv. 3.
To drink at th' fountain-head;	
Yet God will cause the streams to flow,	Psal. xlvi. 4.
And thereby make thee glad.	

Thy God will give thee strength and skill,	Isa. xl. 31.
To go for all supply,	
To full and free salvation's well,	Chap. xii. 3.
And draw out thence with joy.	

While faith doth deal with Christ above,	Gal. ii. 20.
As full of grace for thee,	John i. 14.
There thou may'st drink thy fill of love,	Cant. v. 1.
That can't exhausted be.	Eph. iii. 8.

HYMN XLVII.

God's Love to His,
the Ground of their Submission to his Will.

When God the Spirit sheds abroad,	Rom. v. 5.
The love of Three in One,	1 John v. 7.
It makes the Saints think well of God,	Psal. cxix. 68.
And like what he has done.	Mark vii. 37.

Dear Saint, in faith, think whose thou art,	
As lov'd, and bought with blood,	Acts xxxvii. 23.
For this will influence thy heart,	1 Pet. i. 19.
To all that's truly good.	2 Cor. v. 14.

Has God lov'd thee? his love will draw;	Jer. xxxi. 3.
Has Christ laid down his life?	1 John iii. 16.
'Twill make thee love his royal law,	James ii. 8.
And serve him as his wife.	Rom. vii. 4.

God's providential will also,	Dan. iv. 35.
Manag'd by Christ thy King;	Mat. xxviii. 18.
This love will make thee bow unto,	1 Sam. iii. 18.
And all its glories sing.	Psal. cxlv. 11.

Here wisdom, goodness, power, join,	
To bring all things to pass,	Eph. i. 11.
Subservient to the great design,	
Of God's electing grace.	John xvii. 2.

And canst thou, then, find fault, O Saint,	Jonah iv. 9.
When Providences frown?	Gen. xlii. 36.
What God sees good thou canst not want,	Ps. xxxiv. 10.
Since all things are thy own.	1 Cor. iii. 22.

Then give thy Father leave to choose,	Psal. xlvii. 4.

He'll give thee what is best;	Ps. lxxxv. 12.
Could'st thou but learn, thy will to lose	Luke xxii. 42.
In His, thou'd'st be at rest.	Heb. iv. 3.

HYMN XLVIII.

Christ as Rivers of Water in a dry Place.

Hark! new-born souls, thou thirsty one,	1 Pet. ii. 2.
That walk'st in places dry;	Isa. xxxii. 2.
That seek'st for water, and there's none	Chap. xli. 17.
Thy thirst to satisfy.	

Thou seek'st for streams of pard'ning grace,	Psal. xxv. 11.
Through justisfying blood;	Rom. v. 9.
For cleansing grace, for joy and peace;	Psal. xix. 12.
O these would do thee good.	Psal. cvi. 5.

Thou seek'st *within* for streams of grace,	
To ease and comfort thee;	Jer. ii. 13.
But creatures all speak emptiness,	
Each says, it's not in me.	Job xxviii. 14.

Thou wait'st at Ordinances' pool,	John v. 3.
And cause thou findest none,	
That yet has flow'd into thy soul,	
Thou think'st thou art undone.	Isa. vi. 5.

But stay, poor heart, yet give an ear,	Chap. li. 1.
For sure thou shalt not die;	Verse 14.
Since *Israel's* God saith, he will hear,	Chap. xli. 17.
And all thy wants supply.	Verse 18.

A rich provision of all grace,	Col. i. 19.
God made in Christ, his Son,	John i. 14.
That ev'ry way doth suit the case,	1 Cor. i. 30.
Of such that are undone.	Mat. xi. 5.

God's grace, in Christ, a river is	Psal. xlvi. 4.
That lasting, full and free;	John vii. 37.

A fountain of eternal bliss,   Chap. iv. 14.
Set ope for such as thee.   Isa. lv. 1.

Then go to Christ with thy complaints,   Psal. cxlii. 2.
He'll surely hear thy cry;   Psal. cxlv. 19.
And if thou hast ten thousand wants
He'll richly them supply.   Phil. iv. 19.

HYMN XLIX.

God in Christ the Strength of his People.

Our God, in Christ his dwelling place,   Psal. lxviii. 5.
A strength is to his poor,   Isa. xxv. 4.
And needy ones, in their distress,
What can we wish for more?   Ps. lxxiii. 25.

Whate'er *Jehovah* is, or has,   Gen. xvii. 7.
He not only decreed,   2 Tim. i. 9.
But gave in th' covenant of grace,   Ps. lxxxix. 3.
To Christ, and all his seed.   Gal. iii. 16.

Now we may trust for ever in   Isa. xxvi. 4.
The Lord *Jehovah's* might;
He's strong to bear, and pardon sin,   Num. xiv. 17, 18.
Since justice has its right.   Rom. iii. 26.

He's strong to pity all his own,   Hos. xi. 8, 9.
In each distressing case;   Psal. cvii. 6.
And cov'nant-power all along   1 Pet. i. 5.
Maintains the work of Grace.   Phil. i. 6.

And since God's power keeps the Saints,   Psal. xcvii. 10.
As in a fortress strong;   Psal. cxliv. 2.
And richly doth supply our wants;   Isa. xxxiii. 16.
Let's make the Lord our song.   Chap. xii. 2.

HYMN L.

Faith, the Gift of God, the Effect of Christ's Death,
and the Work of the Spirit.

Faith is a precious grace;	
Lord, 'tis a gift of thine;	Eph. ii. 8.
Its nature's suited to converse	
With things that are divine.	Heb. xi. 1.
This gift provided was,	Jer. xxiv. 7.
Before the world was made;	2 Tim. i. 9.
And laid up for the chosen race,	
In Christ, their Cov'nant-Head.	Eph. v. 23.
Faith from Christ's fullness springs,	John i. 16.
Into the hearts of those,	Acts xv. 9.
Whom God hath blest in heav'nly things,	Eph. i. 3.
According as he chose.	Verse 4.
This faith of God's elect,	Titus i. 1.
It is a faith of price;	2 Pet. i. 1.
And flows to us as the effect,	
Of the death of Jesus Christ,	Phil i. 29.
The Spirit works this grace,	1 Cor. xii. 9.
By his almighty power,	Eph. i. 19.
In every of the chosen race,	Acts xiii. 48.
At the appointed hour.	John v. 25.
Faith lives in Christ its root,	Gal. ii. 20.
And 'cause its union lasts,	John xiv. 19.
It brings forth all its precious fruit,	Col. i. 6.
Though nipp'd with stormy blasts.	1 Pet. i. 6, 7.
And he that hath begun	Heb. xii. 2.
This work, will still maintain,	
And to perfection carry on,	Phil. i. 6.
Till Jesus comes again.	

HYMN LI.

Christ's dying Love.

Well may the Saints with wond'ring eyes,	John xiv. 22.
Behold their Saviour's dying love;	Cant. viii. 6.
It fills the Angels with surprize,	1 Pet. i. 12.
And spirits of just men above!	Heb. xii. 23.
But, O what senseless hearts have we,	Isa. i. 3.
That dwell in houses made of clay!	Job. iv. 19.
How little doth Christ's love, we see,	
From all else snatch our souls away.	Col. iii. 2.
How is it Lord? O let us see,	
How greatly thou hast lov'd thy own;	John xiii. 1.
And gather up our souls to thee,	Chap. xii. 32.
Astonish'd at thy love made known!	
What! didst thou leave thy glory great,	2 Cor. viii. 9.
And take our nature weak and frail;	Heb. ii. 14.
Obey and die, our foes defeat,	Phil. ii. 8.
Because thy love could never fail!	Cant. viii. 7.
What! give thy life for enemies;	Rom. v. 10.
Ungrateful wretches, that we were,	
Whose carnal mind in enmity,	Isa. xlviii. 8.
Doth rise against a Saviour dear.	Rom. viii. 7.
If dying for a friend doth prove,	
The greatest grace that finites bear,	John xv. 13.
Then let's adore Christ's dying love,	Rom. v. 8.
As infinite beyond compare!	Ps. lxxxix. 6.
Christ's love hath heights, and depths, and lengths,	Eph. iii. 18.
Which all our knowledge doth surpass;	Verse 19.
And we shall love him with our strength,	Mark xii. 30.
When once we see him face to face.	2 Cor. xiii. 12.
Mean while, O Lord! we'll praise thy name,	Acts ii. 47.
As we're enkindled with thy love;	1 John iv. 19

And when our sparks rise to a flame,
We'll sing in higher strains above!   Rev. vii. 10.

HYMN LII.
Another.

O Let the Saints admire,
The glories of Christ's love;   Eph. v. 25.
This is the song the heav'nly choir,
In triumph sing above.   Rev. v. 12.

Let's join with heart and voice,   Chap. i. 5, 6.
While in the church below;   Eph. v. 19.
And warble forth our heav'nly joys,   1 Pet. i. 18.
Which from Christ's love do flow.   John xv. 11.

Honour to him that came   Rev. v. 13.
From Heav'n, and laid side   John vi. 38.
His glory great, to bear our shame,   Isa. l. 6.
That he might save his Bride!

The Lord of Glory made   1 Cor. ii. 8.
Himself a servant here,   Phil. ii. 7.
Obey'd, and suffer'd in our stead,   1 Pet. iii. 18.
That we might glory share!

The Father's spotless Lamb   1 Pet. i. 19.
Was made our sin and curse;   2 Cor. v. 21.
The glorious Prince of Life became   Acts iii. 15.
A sacrifice for us!   Eph. v. 2.

The Son of God's delight,   Mat. iii. 17.
His Father's wrath endur'd;   Mark xv. 34.
That, we who had deserv'd it, might   Rom. iii. 19.
From vengeance be secur'd!   1 Thes. i. 10.

Christ made himself most poor,   Mat. viii. 20.
That we enrich'd might be,   2 Cor. viii. 9.
And live with him for evermore,   1 Thes. iv. 17.
His glory great to see!   John xvii. 24.

This matchless grace of his,
Let Saints while here adore; Rev. v. 9.
And when we see him as he is, 1 John iii. 2.
We'll praise him evermore! 1 Pet. iv. 11.

HYMN LIII.

The Love of the Father
in making Christ our Shepherd.

How wondrous is the Father's grace, 1 John iii. 1.
Which he fixt on the chosen race; Jer. xxxi. 3.
They were secur'd e'er time begun, Jude, verse 1.
When God bestow'd them on his Son. John xvii. 6.

In their full number as his sheep, Chap. x. 29.
Made him their shepherd, them to keep; Chap. x. 2.
And, then, behold, he gave at large,
The Shepherd, Christ, his special charge.

God bid him feed the lambs and sheep, Chap. xxi. 15, 16,*with*
And them from wolves and lions keep, Chap. xvii.18.
Safe in his bosom, while his arm Isa. xl.11.
Of pow'r defended them from harm. John x. 11, 12.
Then charg'd him that he should not lose
One of the sheep that he had chose; Chap. vi. 39.
But die to bring them back to him, Chap. x. 18.
White in his blood, as wash'd from sin. Rev. i. 5.

Conduct them thro' this world, their way Isa. xlix. 10.
And raise them up at the last day; John vi. 44.
Then promis'd Christ he should go thro' Isa. xlii. 4.
The work he gave him then to do: Verse 6, 7.

See of the travail of his soul, Isa. liii. 11.
Which should content him to the full;
And for his work rewarded be Verse 12.
With glory, and great dignity. Phil. ii. 9.

Christ full of love, then readily Isa. l. 6.
Did with the Father's will comply; Psal. xl. 8.

And when these sheep were stray'd by sin,	Isa. liii. 6.
That they might be brought back again,	Ezek. xxxiv. 16.
God bid the sword of justice smite	Zech. xiii. 7.
His Shepherd, Fellow, his Delight;	Prov. viii. 30.
Then rais'd Christ up from death and grave,	Acts ii. 24.
And gave him pow'r his sheep to save.	John xvii. 2.
Advanc'd him to his own right hand,	1 Pet. iii. 22.
Where Heav'n and Hell he doth command,	Rev. i. 18.
And rules the world, for the Church's good,	Eph. i. 22.
Which he hath bought with his own blood.	Acts xx. 28.
In which his special love and care,	Isa. xxvii. 3.
Doth for his called sheep appear;	1 Chron. xvi. 21, 22.
And Christ his *other* sheep will bring,	
In his own time, and fold them in.	John x. 16.
And then the Lamb shall feed them here,	Rev. vii. 17.
And lead to living fountains clear;	
Our Shepherd's office is to last	Ezek. xxxvii. 24.
Until the thousand years are past;	Rev. xx. 4.
And then Christ will with His ascend	
To glory, that shall know no end;	Mat. xxv. 46.
And all this is the Father's will,	John vi. 40.
Then let's adore, and praise him still.	Eph. i. 3.

HYMN LIV.

The Love of Christ in giving himself for his Sheep.

Those whom the Father lov'd and blest,	Eph. i. 3, 4.
E'er time began, he gave to Christ;	John xvii. 6.
And Christ embrac'd them as his own,	
Rejoicing in them as foreknown.	Prov. viii. 31.
God told him then what it would cost,	
To save his sheep when they were lost;	Jer. l. 6.
That Christ must lay aside that bliss	2 Cor. viii. 9.
And glory which he did possess.	John xvii. 5.

Go, take their nature, sin and curse,	Heb. ii. 14.
And bear his wrath upon the cross;	Mark xv. 34.
And Christ most readily did yield,	Isa. l. 6.
His Father's will should be fulfill'd.	Psal. xl. 8.
God's glory lay most near Christ's heart,	John vii. 18.
And with his sheep he could not part,	Chap. x. 28.
But down he came to seek and save	Luke xix. 10.
All those the Father to him gave.	John x. 29.
God's justice fill'd Christ's bitter cup,	Luke xxii. 42.
And for his sheep he drank it up;	John xix. 30.
Tho' sore amaz'd, when he beheld	Mark xiv. 33.
God's wrath and curse, with which 'twas fill'd.	Gal. iii. 10.
Which made him to his Father pray,	
If possible, it might pass away;	Mat. xxvi. 39.
But since God's glory, and our bliss,	
Depended on't, he drank up this.	John xviii. 11.
Christ could have 'scaped from those bands,	Mat. xxvi. 53.
That seiz'd on him with wicked hands;	Acts ii. 23.
Yet said, Whom seek ye? I am he;	Jn. xviii. 4, 5.
If I am bound, let mine go free.	Verse 8.
Then justice-messengers came in,	John xviii. 12.
To take the Lamb of God, made sin;	2 Cor. v. 21.
Christ gave himself up to the blow,	Gal. i. 4.
That so his sheep might be let go.	
For, as Christ is the shepherd good,	John x. 11.
He bought his sheep with his own blood;	Acts. xx. 28.
As shepherd great, they by his pow'r	Heb. xiii. 20.
Are sav'd from all that would devour.	Exod. xxxiv. 22.
Christ knows his sheep, they are his choice,	John x. 14.
He makes them live and hear his voice;	Verse 16.
As shepherd chief they are his care,	1 Pet. v. 4.
He feeds them by the waters clear.	Rev. vii. 17.
And he'll conduct them safely through	Ps. lxxviii. 53.

The way that yet they have to go;	Ps. cvii. 7.
And when he's gather'd all his own,	Isa. lvi. 8.
One fold, one shepherd, shall be known.	John x. 16.

Then from their eyes he'll wipe all tears,	Rev. vii. 17.
And feast them for a thousand years;	Chap. xx. 4.
And in the end of that long space	1 Cor. xv. 24.
He'll set them all before God's face;	Jude, ver. 24.

With a behold! I have lost none,	Isa. viii. 18.
Father, thy will and work be done;	John xvii. 4.
Then Christ and his in glory shall	Rom. viii. 17.
Be fill'd with God, their all in all.	1 Cor. xv. 28.

HYMN LV.

The Love of Christ in enduring the Cross, for the Joy that was set before him.

Those whom our Jesus lov'd,	
He lov'd unto the end;	John xiii. 1.
And in the highest instance, prov'd	Chap. xv. 13.
Himself a faithful friend.	Pro. xviii. 24.

Christ knew the covenant	John xviii. 4.
He had engaged in;	Isa. l. 5, 6.
And thro' his death, that God did grant,	Chap. liii. 12.
To save all his from sin.	Ch. xlix. 25.

And time ne'er chang'd his heart,	Heb. xiii. 8.
No, nor his people's sin;	Hos. iii. 1.
Still Christ resolv'd he'd never part	John x. 28.
With those God gave to him.	Verse 29.

Strong was the love of Christ,	Cant. viii. 6.
As death, and as the grave;	
Repentance was hid from his eyes,	Hos. xiii. 14.
That he his bride might save.	

Salvation to the Lamb	Rev. vii. 10.
Who in his mighty love,	Eph. v. 25.

Endur'd the Cross, despis'd the shame,	
And now is set above!	Heb. xii. 2.
The joy our Saviour ey'd,	John vii. 18.
His Father's glory was,	Mat. xviii. 11.
In the salvation of his bride	Heb. ix. 12.
Which he accomplish'd hath.	
And in the end of days,	1 Cor. xv. 24.
He'll set her without blame,	Col. i. 22.
With joy, before his Father's face;	Jude, ver. 24.
Salvation to the Lamb!	Rev. vii. 10.

HYMN LVI.

The Love of the Father in bruising his Son.

How did *Jehovah* love	John iii. 16.
Those he had made his own;	Ps. xxxiii. 12.
When he did give, that they might live,	1 John iv. 9.
His well-beloved Son!	Mark xii. 6.
God bid the sword awake,	Zech. xiii. 7.
And smite the shepherd through,	Isa. liii. 7.
That he might keep the straying sheep,	
From that soul-killing blow.	Rom. vi. 25.
For our iniquities	Isa. liii. 5.
The Father wounded him;	Verse 10.
Such was his grace, that fixed was	Eph. ii. 4.
On us, when dead in sin.	Verse 5.
And 'twas for enemies	Rom. v. 10.
Christ's soul was put to pain,	Isa. liii. 10.
That wretched we, might be set free,	Job xxxiii. 24.
The Lamb of God was slain.	Rev. v. 12.
Let's praise the Father's grace,	Col. i. 3.
Which thus he did commend;	Rom. v. 8.
And when above we'll sing his love,	Rev. vii. 10
For ever, without end!	Verse 12.

HYMN LVII.

Christ's praying for his People, on the bottom
of that mutual Interest the Father and the Son have in them.

Behold, how Christ when here on Earth,	John xvii. 1.
Did for his people pray,	
Before he died the cursed death,	Phil. ii. 8.
And went from hence away.	John xiii. 1.
Father, said he, I leave the world,	
But mine are in it still;	Chap. xvii. 11.
O keep them safe, from being hurl'd	Verse 15.
By sin, at Satan's will!	2 Tim ii. 26.
O make them holy, make them One,	John xvii. 17.
Among themselves to be;	Verse 21.
Let them grow up, when time is done,	
To perfect unity!	Eph. iv. 13.
Yea, make them one in thee and me,	John xvii. 21.
As thou and I are one;	
As in their measure, let them be	
Complete in union!	Verse 23.
To glory-union let them grow	John xvii. 22.
For this thou dost design;	Eph. i. 9, 10.
While sweet communion, as the flow,	1 John i. 3.
With love shall fill all thine.	John xvii. 26.
Father, not for the world I pray,	Verse 9.
But those thou'st given me;	
For these upon my heart they lay,	Prov. viii. 31.
E'en from eternity.	Verse 23.
I pray for these, for they are thine,	John xvii. 9.
The fav'rites of thy breast;	Psal. cvi. 4.
I ask what thou dost design,	Eph. iii. 11.
For those whom thou hast blest.	Chap. i. 3.

They're thine, and thou canst not deny
The breathings of my soul;   John xi. 42.
And thine are mine, and thus jointly, Ch. xvii. 10.
The ground of prayer is full.

They're mine by gift, thou mad'st them so, Verse 2.
My body, and my bride;   Col. i. 18.
They're mine by price, and conquest too, 1 Cor. vi. 20.
In them I'm glorify'd.   John xvii. 10.

Thou lov'st thy own, and can't deny 2 Tim. ii. 13.
Thy self, or change thy heart;   Mal. iii. 6.
And thou lov'st mine, as thou lov'st me, John xvii. 23.
Then glorify each part.

How strong this mutual int'rest is;   Eccles. iv. 12.
'Twas Christ's prevailing plea,
That brings salvation down to his,   Heb. vii. 25.
Though they unworthy be.   Gen. xxxii. 10.

In faith then let us use the same,   Ps. cxix. 94.
When we approach the throne;   Heb. iv. 16.
And magnify *Jehovah's* name,   Psal. xl. 16.
For all that grace has done!   2 Tim. i. 9.

HYMN LVIII.

Christ's Headship.

Our glorious Mediator, he   1 Tim. ii. 5.
Was set up from eternity;   Prov. viii. 23.
In God's first thought Christ was brought forth, Verse 25.
Before *Jehovah* form'd the Earth!   Verse 29.

As nature-head Christ was ordain'd,   1 Cor. xi. 3.
To the vast body of mankind;
Their nature-God, and being too,   Col. i. 16.
Doth from Christ's nature-fulness flow. Verse 19.

But to his own, the chosen race,   1 Pet. ii. 9.
Christ was ordain'd an Head of Grace; Col. i. 18.

It pleased God in him to lay	Verse 19.
The stores of grace, that can't decay.	2 Tim. i. 9.

Christ is an overflowing sea,	John vii. 37.
Whence all our wants supplied be;	Phil. iv. 19.
Christ's fullness we can never spend,	John i. 16.
His immense riches know no end!	Eph. iii. 8.

That remnant which the Father's grace,	Rom. xi. 5.
Did from eternity embrace	Jer. xxxi. 3.
Were blest, as chosen in his Son,	Eph. i. 3, 4.
With life and glory yet unknown!	Titus i. 2.

Their vast inheritance is sure,	1 Pet. i. 4.
Christ glory-fulness will endure;	Isa. lx. 19.
No tongue can tell the heights of bliss,	Chap. lxiv. 4.
That settled are on Christ and his.	Rom. viii. 17.

Triumphant songs of endless praise,	Rev. v. 13.
To our exalted Head let's raise;	Eph. i. 20, 21.
And let us pray him come again,	Rev. xxii. 20.
Here, to set up his glory-reign!	Isa. xxiv. 23.

HYMN LIX.

The Saints' Duty and Privilege to wait for God in trying Seasons.

It sometimes pleaseth God,	Pro. xxiv. 16.
To suffer His to fall;	Ps. lxxxix. 32.
Then as a Father takes his rod,	Heb. xii. 7.
And chastens them withal.	

But, O the dismal sights,	Lam. i. 12.
Which oft-times fill our eye,	
When God himself against us fights,	Isa. lxiii. 10.
As if our enemy.	Lam. ii. 4.

Then Satan he steps in,	1 Pet. v. 8.
And says, good days are past;	
Yea, unbelief doth join with him,	Job xvii. 11.

And tells us, night will last.	Chap. vii. 7.
But day-spring hastes apace;	Psal. xxx. 5.
For great *Jehovah* waits	Isa. xxx. 18.
To shew his all-sufficient grace	2 Cor. xii. 9.
To us, in midst of straits.	Gen. xxii. 14.
He God of Judgment is,	Isa. xxx. 18.
And takes the fittest time	Psal. cii. 13.
To work deliverance for his,	Ps. xxxiv. 19.
Then let us wait on him.	Isa. viii. 17.
For blessed are all they,	Isa. xxx. 18.
That wait upon the Lord;	
That in the darkest times can stay	Psa. l. 10.
Their souls upon his word.	Ps. cxxx. 5.
They shan't be put to shame,	Isa. xlix. 23.
Since God waits all along,	
To make himself a glorious name,	Ch. lxiii. 14.
In their salvation!	Psal. lxii. 1.

HYMN LX.

The Soul's Joy in God as its Portion.

God is my portion;	Lam. iii. 24.
My everlasting All;	Ps. lxxiii. 25.
How can I then want any good,	
Though all things else should fail?	Hab. iii. 17, 18.
My portion can't decay,	Mal. iii. 6.
Untouch'd it ever stands,	
A full, eternal spring of bliss,	Gen. xv. 1.
For *me,* in Jesus' hands.	Col. i. 19.
The creatures I may lose;	
Stripp'd naked I may be;	Job i. 21.
But since I cannot lose my God,	Ps. xlviii. 14.
I've full felicity.	Ps. cxvi. 5.

Were all the creatures gone,	2 Cor. vi. 1.
God would be *all* to me;	Phil. iv. 19.
He knows, and will supply my wants,	
How great so e'er they be.	

He'll never leave his own,	Heb. xiii. 5.
In the world, this stormy place;	
But having lov'd, he'll love to the end,	John xiii. 1.
Through each distressing case.	

Then let my soul sit loose,	Col. iii. 2.
To things which do decay;	1 John ii. 17.
And ever cleave to God, my Lot,	Ps. lxxiii. 26.
That fadeth not away.	1 Pet. i. 4.

HYMN LXI.

The Blessedness of Saints at home with Christ.

The Saints in light, how blest are they;	Col. i. 12.
How vast their endless bliss!	1 Cor. ii. 9.
When once by death dismiss'd from clay,	2 Cor. v. 1.
They see Christ as he is.	1 John iii. 2.

They've done with sin, that conflict's o'er,	1 Pet. i. 4.
By Hell they're not opprest;	Job iii. 17.
They're tried by Providence no more,	Isa. lxii. 4.
But fully are at rest.	Rev. xiv. 13.

It's Jesus will, that His should be	
For ever where He is,	John xvii. 24.
That they his glory great might see,	
To consummate their bliss.	

The Saints that are at home with Christ,	2 Cor. v. 8.
They hunger shall no more;	
Nor shall they pained be with thirst,	
As they have been before.	

No persecution sun-like heat,	Rev. vii. 16.
These happy ones shall smite;	

Nor any trial, small or great,
Shall once upon them light.

For shy? The Lamb upon the throne,   Verse 17.
Shall feed them constantly;
To living fountains lead each one,
To drink abundantly.

And as for tears, those former things,   Chap. xxi. 4.
God wipes them all away;
Death's the last night, then, lo, there springs
A bright, eternal day!   Isa. lx. 20.

A glorious day, while Saints remain
Above, in separate state;   Heb. xii. 23.
A day, when Jesus comes again,
In glory far more great;   Col. iii. 4.

And yet a day of rising bliss,
When time shall folded be;
God all in all to Christ and His,   1 Cor. xv. 28.
Unto eternity.   Ps. xlviii. 14.

Dear Saints, that dwell in tents of clay,   Job iv. 19.
Fear not to be releast;
But long to be with Christ always,
Since it so far is best.   Phil. i. 23.

THE END

INDEX

Aaron, 19
Abel, 50
Abraham, 15, 19, 46, 47, 50, 130, 143
Absalom, 19
Adam, 6-8, 23, 27, 19-122, 153, 154, 168, 202
Adoption, 63, 109
Advocate, 25-27
Afflictive Providence, 18, 20
Anti-Christ, 127, 134, 135, 137
Asa, 35, 41, 46, 168
Asaph, 52
Atonement, 65

Canaanites, 67, 163
Chastisements, 219
Christ, 2, 3, 5-13, 15-18, 21-28, 30-32, 34-37, 39, 40, 42-46, 49-71, 74, 79, 80-82, 84, 86, 90, 92-94, 96-99, 101, 103, 105, 106, 108, 115, 117-23, 125, 127, 129, 131-33, 135-38, 140-49, 151, 153, 154, 158, 160-65, 167, 168, 170, 172, 176, 177, 180, 183, 188, 195, 198-200, 204, 205, 214, 217, 218, 222-24, 226, 227, 229-32, 236, 237, 240
Christ's Kingdom, 2
Christ's Spouse, 183
Comforter, 191
Communion with God, 2-4, 7, 26, 40, 44-48, 50, 52, 53, 57, 69, 71-73
Conformity, 2, 18, 42, 49, 71
Conversation, Holiness 13, 20, 21-22, 28, 34, 50
Cornelius, 50
Covenant, 18, 71, 119, 138, 212, 213, 215
Creator, 116

Cross, 7, 25, 26, 50, 60, 66, 67, 127, 132, 148, 166, 234

David, 17, 19, 29, 32, 34, 44, 45, 48, 140
Death, 184
Destruction, 223
Divine love, 192, 211
Divine mercy, 209
Divine providence, 13, 16, 48, 59

Election, 3, 12, 119-23, 134, 135, 147, 151-74, 212
Eli, 19
Elijah, 17
Elizabeth, 35
Enoch, 27, 36, 50, 57
Ephraim, 67-69
Eternal life, 5, 43, 56, 182, 184
Eve, 6, 120

Fainting under the rod, 196
Faith, 6, 12-16, 20, 27-30, 32, 34, 36, 37, 39, 44, 47, 50, 54, 56, 69-73, 126, 128, 129, 155, 162, 165, 167, 172, 188, 228
Father, 179, 182, 231, 235, 236

Gentile, 131, 137, 143
Glorification, 63, 128
God's love, 193
Gospel, 178
Grace, 3, 6, 8, 10-14, 18, 23-29, 33, 35, 36, 39-44, 47-51, 53, 54, 56, 61, 63-66, 69-71, 73, 74, 99, 100, 104, 115, 117, 127, 130, 132-35, 138, 149, 151, 154-56, 159-61, 164, 166-70, 172, 177, 187, 213, 224

Heaven, 145

Hezekiah, 19

Holiness, 5, 8, 9, 18, 18, 22-24, 31, 35, 49, 54, 55, 71, 72, 92, 141, 158, 170

Holy Ghost, 2, 6, 7, 10, 12-15, 31, 40, 42, 43, 60, 70, 72, 129, 130, 164

Holy Spirit, 2, 7, 21, 27, 40, 41, 70-72, 74, 130, 151, 174, 181, 191

Hope, 34, 43, 69, 73

Incarnation, 125-28

Iniquity, 7, 11, 25, 36, 43, 44, 49, 51, 58, 91

Isaac, 19, 46, 47

Ishmael, 47

Israel, 15, 20, 25, 29, 30, 32, 33, 38, 48, 49, 55, 58, 60, 61, 68, 138

Jacob, 14, 29, 33, 41, 46, 48, 52, 58, 60, 68, 168

Jerusalem, 130, 131

Jews, 131

Job, 19, 45

John, 27, 36, 63

Joseph, 58-62, 64-68

Joshua, 29

Joy, 234

Judas, 59

Justification, 11, 63, 66, 71

King William, 135

Kingdom of rewards, 199

Kinsman-Redeemer, 10

Laban, 48

Law, 178

Light, 6, 8-10, 13, 20, 21, 28, 33, 52, 54, 57, 62, 63, 69-72

Love, 3, 6, 7, 12, 20-26, 30-32, 37-42, 44, 45, 48, 51-53, 55, 56, 58, 61, 62, 64, 67, 69, 70-74, 115, 120, 222, 123, 125-27, 129, 133, 140, 143, 147, 149, 151, 153, 154, 160, 162, 168, 169, 171, 173, 174, 179-81, 225, 229, 230, 231, 232, 234, 235

Man, 223

Manasseh, 67-69

Mediator, 8-10, 24, 30, 41, 65, 66, 115-17, 121, 173

Mercy, 3, 6, 11, 12, 14, 16-18, 20, 23, 25, 33, 43, 46, 54, 157, 220

Misery, 206

Mr. C_____ll, 107

Mr. Hunt, 84, 86

Mr. Moore, 87, 88

Mr. N_____n, 95

Mr. Sandiman, 95

Mr. Shepherd, 82

Mr. Skepp, 88

Mortality, 43

Moses, 10, 14, 20, 25, 29, 43, 55

Nathan, 167

New Jerusalem, 142, 143

Noah, 27

Paul, 23, 50, 55

Peace, 5-7, 11, 19, 22, 23, 25-27, 41, 127, 133, 143

Perseverance, 33

Peter, 51, 56, 131

Pharaoh, 59

Prayer, 15, 16, 26-28, 32-34, 45-47, 51, 128, 140, 156, 219, 236

Predestination, 18

Queen Mary, 134

Redemption, 10, 40, 125, 129

Reformation, 133
Regeneration, 12
Rejoicing, 194
Remnant, 5, 11, 51, 119, 147, 167
Repentance, 60
Rest, 210
Righteousness, 2, 9, 11, 12, 21, 26, 30, 31, 35, 41, 43, 49, 54, 56, 62, 63, 93, 148, 163, 217, 218
Rivers of water, 226
Rome, 132, 133, 136, 140
Royal George, 135

Saints, 184, 240
Saint's Afflictions, 215
Saint's Duty, 219, 238
Saint's Freedom, 216
Saint's Holiness, 198
Saint's Portion, 197
Saint's Refuge, 201
Saint's Resurrection, 195
Saint's Vessels, 220
Salvation, 12, 14, 15, 47, 53-57, 59, 68, 73, 126, 133, 138, 147, 152, 153, 159, 162, 166, 167, 170, 171, 174, 212, 223
Sanctification, 54, 63, 70, 71
Satan, 117, 127, 131, 132, 144, 145, 164, 172
Satisfaction, 5, 11, 12, 26
Security, 222
Sheep, 232
Shepherd, 231

Sin, 4-7, 10-12, 18, 21, 22, 24, 25, 27, 32, 35, 36, 41, 42, 43, 49, 55, 57, 58, 70, 73, 119, 120, 127, 131, 135, 138, 141, 142, 146, 151, 152, 155-47, 159, 162, 164, 166, 171, 172, 187, 206, 207, 219
Sinai, 158
Solomon, 68, 140
Soul, 210
Soul's Joy, 239
Submission to God, 225
Supplications, 15

Transgression(s), 5, 7, 11, 42-44, 48, 49, 51
Tribulation, 194
Trinity, 5, 8, 14, 41, 42, 125, 126, 129, 148, 176
Truth, 5, 10, 11, 14, 15, 16, 20, 28, 32, 37, 43, 44, 46, 54, 57, 59, 71, 170

Wait for God, 238
Walk with God, 3, 4, 8, 9, 10, 13, 15, 17-40, 53, 54, 56, 57
Wisdom, 5, 6, 9, 11, 12, 16, 22-25, 30, 32, 35, 36, 39, 41, 43, 49, 54, 59, 60, 61, 66, 73, 115, 116, 152
Work of the Spirit, 151-74, 185, 186, 189, 190, 207, 208, 228
Worship, 3, 13-16, 19, 28, 32, 33, 43, 45, 46
Wrath, 216

Zacharias, 35